Practical Go

Building Scalable Network and Non-Network Applications

Amit Saha

WILEY

I dedicate this book to all those who are working hard every day to find the right balance between the feeling of "Yes, I got this!" and "What am I even doing?" and continuing the battle that we call living.

About the Author

Amit Saha is a software engineer at Atlassian, located in Sydney, Australia. He has written *Doing Math with Python: Use Programming to Explore Algebra, Statistics, Calculus, and More!* (No Starch Press, 2015) and *Write Your First Program* (PHI Learning, 2013). His other writings have been published in technical magazines, conference proceedings, and research journals. He can be found online at `https://echorand.me`.

About the Technical Editor

John Arundel is a well-known Go writer, teacher, and mentor. He has been writing software for 40 years, and he thinks he's finally starting to figure out how to do it. You can find out more about John at `bitfieldconsulting.com`.

John lives in a fairytale cottage in Cornwall, England, surrounded by woods, wildlife, and a slowly deepening silence.

Acknowledgments

I want to thank the entire team at Wiley that made this book possible. First, Jim Minatel, who responded to my initial email expressing interest in publishing a book with Wiley. Jim then connected me with Devon Lewis, with whom I discussed the book proposal and who was instrumental in commissioning this book and overseeing the entire process. Next, I would like to thank Gary Schwartz, who in his capacity as project manager guided me throughout the entire project, ensuring that I was on track with my delivery of the chapters. Thank you, Judy Flynn, for your meticulousness in your role as the copyeditor. Finally, thank you, Barath Kumar Rajasekaran, for overseeing the proofreading process. Working with this team of fine folks was my version of a *Ulysses pact*.

John Arundel was kind enough to accept my request to be the technical reviewer of this book, and his insights and comments greatly helped to make the book better as well as making me a better Go programmer.

I want to thank all the community members on the Golang nuts and gRPC mailing lists who were always helpful in answering my questions and clarifying my doubts. My initial days of learning Go were mostly spent copying and pasting code from the "Go by example" project at `https://gobyexample.com`; hence I would like to acknowledge the efforts of the creator and maintainers of this project for their super-helpful resource.

Finally, I appreciate the efforts of the folks at Cooperpress who publish *Golang Weekly* (and the authors of the articles to which they linked) and *The Go Time* podcast. They helped me in learning Go and staying up to date with the latest happenings in the Go community.

— Amit Saha

Acknowledgments

Contents at a Glance

Contents

NOTE   A glossary of relevant terms is available for free download from the book's web page: https://www.wiley.com/go/practicalgo.

Introduction

Google announced the Go programming language to the public in 2009, with the version 1.0 release announced in 2012. Since its announcement to the community, and the compatibility promise of the 1.0 release, the Go language has been used to write scalable and high-impact software programs ranging from command-line applications and critical infrastructure tools to large-scale distributed systems. The Go language has made a huge contribution to the growth of a number of modern software success stories. For a number of years, my personal interest in Go has been due to its, for the lack of a better word, *boring* nature—that's what I like about it. It felt like it combined the power of the second programming language I learned, C, with the batteries-included approach of another favorite language of mine, Python. As I have written more programs using the Go language, I have learned to appreciate its focus on providing all the necessary tools and features to write production-quality software. I have often found myself thinking, "Will I be able to implement this failure-handling pattern in this application?" Then I look at the standard library package documentation, and the answer has always been a resounding "Yes!" Once you have grasped the fundamentals of Go, with almost zero effort on your part as the software developer, the result is a highly performant application out of the box.

My goal in this book is to showcase the various features of the Go language and the standard libraries (along with a few community-maintained packages) by developing various categories of applications. Once you have refreshed or learned the language fundamentals, this book will help you take the next step. I have adopted a writing style where the focus is on using various features of the language and its libraries to solve the particular problem at hand—one that you care about.

You will not find a detailed walk-through of a language feature or every feature of a certain package. You will learn *just enough* to build a command-line tool, a web application, or a gRPC application. I focus on a strictly chosen subset of the fundamental building blocks for such applications to provide a compact and actionable guide. Hence, you may find that the book doesn't cover the more higher-level use cases that you may want to learn about. That is intentional, as the implementation of those higher-level use cases is often dependent on domain-specific software packages, and hence no single book can do justice to recommending one without missing out on another. I also strive to use standard library packages as far as possible for writing the applications in the book. This is again done to ensure that the learning experience is not diluted. Nonetheless, I hope that the building blocks you learn about in the book will provide you with a solid foundation to leverage higher-level libraries to build your applications.

What Does This Book Cover?

This book teaches you concepts and demonstrates patterns to build various categories of applications using the Go programming language. We focus on command-line applications, HTTP applications, and gRPC applications.

The Getting Started chapter will help you set up your Go development environment, and it lays down some conventions for the rest of the book.

Chapter 1 and Chapter 2 discuss building command-line applications. You will learn to use the standard library packages to develop scalable and testable command-line programs.

Chapter 3 and Chapter 4 teach you how to build production-ready HTTP clients. You will learn to configure time-outs, understand connection pooling behavior, implement middleware components, and more.

Chapters 5 through 7 discuss building HTTP server applications. You will learn how to add support for streaming data, implement middleware components, share data across handler functions, and implement various techniques to improve the robustness of your applications.

Chapters 8 through 10 delve deep into building RPC applications using gRPC. You will learn about Protocol Buffers, implement various RPC communication patterns, and implement client-side and server-side interceptors to perform common application functionality.

In Chapter 11, you will learn to interact with object stores and relational database management systems from your applications.

Appendix A briefly discusses how you can add instrumentation into your applications.

Appendix B provides some guidelines around deploying your applications.

Each group of chapters is mostly independent from the other groups. So feel free to jump to the first chapter of a group; however, there may be references to a previous chapter.

Within each group, however, I recommend reading the chapters from beginning to end, as the chapters within a group build upon the previous chapter. For example, if you are keen to learn more about writing HTTP clients, I suggest reading Chapter 3 and Chapter 4 in that order.

I also encourage you to write and run the code yourself as you work through the book and to attempt the exercises as well. Writing the programs yourself in your code editor will build that Go muscle, as it certainly did for me while writing the programs in the book.

Reader Support for This Book

You can find links to the source code and resources related to the book at `https://practicalgobook.net`. The code from the book is also posted at `https://www.wiley.com/go/practicalgo`.

If you believe that you've found a mistake in this book, please bring it to our attention. At John Wiley & Sons, we understand how important it is to provide our customers with accurate content, but even with our best efforts an error may occur. To submit your possible errata, please email it to our Customer Service Team at `wileysupport@wiley.com` with the subject line "Possible Book Errata Submission."

Getting Started

To start off, we will install the necessary software needed for the rest of the book. We will also go over some of the conventions and assumptions made throughout. Finally, I will point out key language features you will use in the book and resources to refresh your knowledge about them.

Installing Go

The code listings in this book work with Go 1.16 and above. Follow the instructions at `https://go.dev/learn/` to install the latest version of the Go compiler for your operating system. It usually involves downloading and running a graphical installation process for Windows or macOS. For Linux, your distribution's package repository may contain the latest version already, which means that you can use your package manager to install the Go compiler as well.

Once you have it installed, no further configuration is necessary to run the programs that you will write throughout the book. Verify that you have everything set up correctly by running the command `go version` from your terminal program. You should see an output telling you which Go version is installed and the operating system and architecture. For example, on my MacBook Air (M1), I see the following:

```
$ go version
go version go1.16.4 darwin/arm64
```

If you can see an output like the above, you are ready to continue with the next steps.

Choosing an Editor

If you don't yet have a favorite Go editor/integrated development environment (IDE), I recommend Visual Studio Code (`https://code.visualstudio.com/download`). If you are a Vim user, I recommend the vim-go extension (`https://github.com/fatih/vim-go`).

Installing Protocol Buffer Toolchain

For some chapters in the book, you will need the Protocol Buffers (protobuf) and gRPC tools for Go installed. You will install three separate programs: the protobuf compiler, `protoc`, and the Go protobuf and gRPC plug-ins, `protoc-gen-go` and `protoc-gen-go-grpc`, respectively.

Linux and macOS

To install the compiler, run the following steps for Linux or macOS:

1. Download the latest release (3.16.0 at the time of this book's writing) file from `https://github.com/protocolbuffers/protobuf/releases`, corresponding to your operating system and architecture. Look for the files in the *Assets* section. For example, for Linux on a x86_64 system, download the file named `protoc-3.16.0-linux-x86_64.zip`. For macOS, download the file named `protoc-3.16.3-osx-x86_64.zip`.

2. Next, extract the file contents and copy them to your `$HOME/.local` directory using the `unzip` command: `$ unzip protoc-3.16.3-linux-x86_64 .zip -d $HOME/.local`.

3. Finally, add the `$HOME/.local/bin` directory to your `$PATH` environment variable: `$ export PATH="$PATH:$HOME/.local/bin"` in your shell's initialization script, such as `$HOME/.bashrc` for Bash shell and `.zshrc` for Z shell.

Once you have completed the preceding steps, open a new terminal window, and run the command `protoc --version`:

```
$ protoc --version
libprotoc 3.16.0
```

If you see output like the one above, you are ready to move on to the next step. To install the protobuf plug-in for Go, `protoc-gen-go` (release v1.26), run the following command from a terminal window:

```
$ go install google.golang.org/protobuf/cmd/protoc-gen-go@v1.26
```

To install the gRPC plug-in for Go, `protoc-gen-go-grpc` (release v1.1) tool, run the following command:

```
$ go install google.golang.org/grpc/cmd/protoc-gen-go-grpc@v1.1
```

Then add the following to your shell's initialization file (`$HOME/.bashrc or $HOME/.zshrc`):

```
$ export PATH="$PATH:$(go env GOPATH)/bin"
```

Open a new terminal window, and run the following commands:

```
$ protoc-gen-go --version
protoc-gen-go v1.26.0
$ protoc-gen-go-grpc --version
protoc-gen-go-grpc 1.1.0
```

If you see an output like above, the tools have been installed successfully.

Windows

NOTE   You will need to open a Windows PowerShell window as an administrator to run the steps.

To install the protocol buffers compiler, run the following steps:

1. Download the latest release (3.16.0 at the time of this book's writing) file from `https://github.com/protocolbuffers/protobuf/releases`, corresponding to your architecture. Look for a file named `protoc-3.16.0-win64.zip` in the *Assets* section.

2. Then create a directory where you will store the compiler. For example, in `C:\Program Files` as follows: `PS C:\> mkdir 'C:\Program Files\protoc-3.16.0'`.

3. Next, extract the downloaded `.zip` file inside that directory. Run the following command while you are inside the directory where you downloaded the `.zip` file: `PS C:\> Expand-Archive .\protoc-3.16.0-win64\ -DestinationPath 'C:\Program Files\protoc-3.16.0'`.

4. Finally, update the Path environment variable to add the above path: `PS C:\> [Environment]::SetEnvironmentVariable("Path", $env:Path + ";C:\Program Files\protoc-3.16.0\bin", "Machine")`.

Open a new PowerShell window, and run the command `protoc --version`:

```
$ protoc --version
libprotoc 3.16.0
```

If you see an output like the one above, you are ready to move on to the next step.

To install the protobuf compiler for Go, `protoc-gen-go tool` (release v1.26), run the following command from a terminal window:

```
C:\> go install google.golang.org/protobuf/cmd/protoc-gen-go@v1.26
```

To install the gRPC plug-in for Go, `protoc-gen-go-grpc` (release v1.1) tool, run the following command:

```
C:\> go install google.golang.org/grpc/cmd/protoc-gen-go-grpc@v1.1
```

Open a new Windows PowerShell Window, and run the following commands:

```
$ protoc-gen-go --version
protoc-gen-go v1.26.0
$ protoc-gen-go-grpc --version
protoc-gen-go-grpc 1.1.0
```

If you see an output like the one above, the tools have been installed successfully.

Installing Docker Desktop

For the last chapter in the book, you will need the ability to run applications in software containers. Docker Desktop (https://www.docker.com/get-started) is an application that allows us to do that. For macOS and Windows, download the installer from the above website corresponding to your operating system and architecture, and follow the instructions to complete the installation.

For Linux, the installation steps will vary depending on your distribution. See https://docs.docker.com/engine/install/#server for detailed steps for your specific distribution. I also recommend that for ease of use (not recommended for production environments), you configure your docker installation to allow non-root users to run containers without using `sudo`.

Once you have followed the installation steps for your specific operating system, run the following command to download a docker image from Docker Hub and run it to ensure that the installation has been successfully completed:

```
$ docker run hello-world
Unable to find image 'hello-world:latest' locally
latest: Pulling from library/hello-world
109db8fad215: Pull complete
Digest: sha256:0fe98d7debd9049c50b597ef1f85b7c1e8cc81f59c8d
623fcb2250e8bec85b38
Status: Downloaded newer image for hello-world:latest
```

```
Hello from Docker!
This message shows that your installation appears to be
working correctly.
. .
```

That completes our software installation for the book. Next, we will quickly cover some conventions used throughout the book.

Guide to the Book

In the following sections, you will learn various bits and pieces of information that will help you get the most out of the book. First, I discuss the choice of the module path for the code listings.

Go Modules

In this book, all applications will start by initializing a module as the first step. This will translate to running the go command, `go mod init <module path>`. Throughout the book, I have used a "placeholder" module path, which is `github.com/username/<application-name>`. Thus, in applications where we have written our module to consist of more than one package, the import path looks like this: `github.com/username/<application-name>/<package>`.

You can use these module paths if you are not planning to share these applications. If you plan to share your applications, or develop them further, you are encouraged to use your own module path, which is pointing to your own repository, likely a Git repository hosted on `https://bitbucket.org`, `https://github.com` or `https://gitlab.com`. Simply substitute `username` by your own username in the repository hosting service. It's also worth noting that the code repository for the book, `https://github.com/practicalgo/code`, contains the module path as `github.com/practicalgo/code/<chap1>/<application-name>`, in other words, an actual path that exists rather than a placeholder path.

Command Line and Terminals

You will be required to execute command-line programs throughout the book. For Linux and macOS, the default terminal program running your default shell is sufficient. For Windows, I assume that you will be using the Windows PowerShell terminal instead of the default command-line program. Most of the command-line executions are shown as executed on a Linux/macOS terminal, indicated by the $ symbol. However, you also should be able to run the same command on Windows. Wherever I have asked you to execute a command to create a directory or copy a file, I have indicated the commands for both Linux/macOS and Windows, where they are different.

Terms

I have used some terms throughout the book that may be best clarified here to avoid ambiguity and set the right expectations.

Robustness and Resiliency

Both terms, *robustness* and *resiliency*, express the ability of an application to handle unexpected scenarios. However, these terms differ in their expected behavior under these circumstances as compared to their normal behavior. A system is *robust* if it can withstand unexpected situations and continue to function to some degree. This will likely be suboptimal behavior, as compared to normal behavior. On the other hand, a system is *resilient* if it continues exhibiting its normal behavior, potentially taking a finite amount of time before being able to do so. I put forward the following examples from the book to illustrate the difference.

In Chapter 2, you will learn to enforce time-outs for command-line application functionality that is executing a user-specified program. By enforcing time-outs, we avoid the scenario where the application continues to hang indefinitely because of bad user output. Since we configure an upper bound on how long we want to allow the user-specified command to be executed, we will exit with an error when this duration expires before the command could be completed. This is not the normal behavior of the application—that we should wait for the command to complete—but this suboptimal behavior is necessary to allow the application to recover from an unexpected situation, such as the user-specified command taking longer than expected. You will find similar examples throughout, notably when sending or receiving network requests in Chapters 4, 7, 10, and 11. We will refer to these techniques as introducing robustness in our applications.

In Chapter 10, you will learn to handle transient failures in your gRPC client applications. You will write your applications in a manner in which they can tolerate temporary failures that are likely to be resolved soon. We refer to this as introducing resilient behavior in our applications. However, we also introduce an upper time limit, which we allow to resolve the potentially temporary failure. If this time limit is exceeded, we consider that the operation cannot be completed. Thus, we introduce robustness as well.

To summarize, resiliency and robustness both aim to handle unexpected situations in our applications, and this book uses these terms to refer to such techniques.

Production Readiness

I use the term *production readiness* in the book as all steps that you should think about as you develop your application but before you deploy it to any kind of a production environment. When the production environment is your own personal server where you are the only user of your application, the techniques that you will learn will likely be sufficient. If the production environment means that your application will perform critical functionality for your users, then the techniques in this book should be the absolute baseline and a starting point. Production readiness consists of a vast body of often domain-specific techniques across various dimensions—robustness and resiliency, observability, and security. This book shows you how to implement a small subset of these topics.

Reference Documentation

The code listings in the book use various standard library packages and a few third-party packages. The descriptions of the various functions and types are limited to the contextual usage. Knowing where to look when you want to find out more about a package or function is important to get the most out of the book. The key reference documentation for all standard library packages is `https://pkg.go.dev/std`. When I import a package as `net/http`, the documentation for that package will be found at the path `https://pkg.go.dev/net/http`. When I refer to a function such as `io.ReadAll()`, the function reference is the package `io`'s documentation at `https://pkg.go.dev/io`.

For third-party packages, the documentation is available by going to the address `https://pkg.go.dev/<import path>`. For example, the Go gRPC package is imported as `google.golang.grpc`. Its reference documentation is available at `https://pkg.go.dev/google.golang.org/grpc`.

Go Refresher

I recommend going through the topics in "A Tour of Go," at `https://tour.golang.org/list`, to serve as a refresher of the various features that we will be using to implement programs in the book. These include for loops, functions, methods, struct and interface types, and error values. Additionally, I want to highlight the key topics that we will use extensively, along with references to learn more about them.

Struct Type

We will be using struct types defined by the standard library and third-party packages, and we will also be defining our own. Beyond defining objects of struct types, we will be working with types that embed other types—other struct types and interfaces. The section "Embedding" in the "Effective Go" guide (`https://golang.org/doc/effective_go#embedding`) describes this concept. We will also be making use of anonymous struct types when writing tests. This is described in this talk by Andrew Gerrand, "10 things you (probably) don't know about Go": https://talks.golang.org/2012/10things.slide#1.

Interface Type

To use the various library functions and to write testable applications, we will be making extensive use of interface types. For example, we will be making extensive use of alternative types that satisfies the io.Reader and io.Writer interfaces to write tests for applications that interface with the standard input and output.

Learning to define a custom type that satisfies another interface is a key step to writing Go applications, where we plug in our functionality to work with the rest of the language. For example, to enable sharing data across HTTP handler functions, we will define our own custom type implementing the http. Handler interface.

The section on interfaces in "A Tour of Go," https://tour.golang.org/methods/9, is useful to get a refresher on the topic.

Goroutines and Channels

We will be using goroutines and channels to implement concurrent execution in our applications. I recommend going through the section on Concurrency in "A Tour of Go": https://tour.golang.org/concurrency/1. Pay special attention to the example use of select statements to wait on multiple channel communication operations.

Testing

We will be using the standard library's testing package exclusively for writing all of the tests, and we will use Go test to drive all of the test executions. We have also used the excellent support provided by libraries such as net/http/httptest to test HTTP clients and servers. Similar support is provided by gRPC libraries. In the last chapter, we will use a third-party package, https://github.com/testcontainers/testcontainers-go, to create local testing environments using Docker Desktop.

In some of the tests, especially when writing command-line applications, we have adopted the style of "Table Driven Tests," as described at https://github.com/golang/go/wiki/TableDrivenTests, when writing the tests.

Summary

In this introduction to the book, you installed the software necessary to build the various applications to be used in the rest of the book. Then I introduced some of the conventions and assumptions made throughout the remainder of the book. Finally, I described the key language features with which you will need to be familiar to make the best use of the material in the book.

Great! You are now ready to start your journey with Chapter 1, where you will be learning how to build testable command-line applications.

Writing Command-Line Applications

In this chapter, you will learn about the building blocks of writing command-line applications. You will use standard library packages to construct command-line interfaces, accept user input, and learn techniques to test your applications. Let's get started!

Your First Application

All command-line applications essentially perform the following steps:

- Accept user input
- Perform some validation
- Use the input to perform some custom task
- Present the result to the user; that is, a success or a failure

In a command-line application, an input can be specified by the user in several ways. Two common ways are as arguments when executing the program and interactively by typing it in. First you will implement a *greeter* command-line application that will ask the user to specify their name and the number of times they want to be greeted. The name will be input by the user when asked, and the number of times will be specified as an argument when executing the application. The program will then display a custom message the specified number of times. Once you have written the complete application, a sample execution will appear as follows:

```
$ ./application 6
Your name please? Press the Enter key when done.
Joe Cool
Nice to meet you Joe Cool
Nice to meet you Joe Cool
Nice to meet you Joe Cool
Nice to meet you Joe Cool
Nice to meet you Joe Cool
Nice to meet you Joe Cool
```

First, let's look at the function asking a user to input their name:

```
func getName(r io.Reader, w io.Writer) (string, error) {
        msg := "Your name please? Press the Enter key when done.\n"
        fmt.Fprintf(w, msg)

        scanner := bufio.NewScanner(r)
        scanner.Scan()
        if err := scanner.Err(); err != nil {
                return "", err
        }
        name := scanner.Text()
        if len(name) == 0 {
                return "", errors.New("You didn't enter your name")
        }
        return name, nil
}
```

The `getName()` function accepts two arguments. The first argument, `r`, is a variable whose value satisfies the `Reader` interface defined in the `io` package. An example of such a variable is `Stdin`, as defined in the `os` package. It represents the standard input for the program—usually the terminal session in which you are executing the program.

The second argument, `w`, is a variable whose value satisfies the `Writer` interface, as defined in the `io` package. An example of such a variable is the `Stdout` variable, as defined in the `os` package. It represents the standard output for the application—usually the terminal session in which you are executing the program.

You may be wondering why we do not refer to the `Stdin` and `Stdout` variables from the `os` package directly. The reason is that doing so will make our function very unfriendly when we want to write unit tests for it. We will not be able to specify a customized input to the application, nor will we be able to verify the application's output. Hence, we *inject* the writer and the reader into the function so that we have control over what the reader, `r`, and writer, `w`, values refer to.

The function starts by using the Fprintf() function from the fmt package to write a prompt to the specified writer, w. Then, a variable of Scanner type, as defined in the bufio package, is created by calling the NewScanner() function with the reader, r. This lets you scan the reader for any input data using the Scan() function. The default behavior of the Scan() function is to return once it has read the newline character. Subsequently, the Text() function returns the read data as a string. To ensure that the user didn't enter an empty string as input, the len() function is used and an error is returned if the user indeed entered an empty string as input.

The getName() function returns two values: one of type string and the other of type error. If the user's input name was read successfully, the name is returned along with a nil error. However, if there was an error, an empty string and the error is returned.

The next key function is parseArgs(). It takes as input a slice of strings and returns two values: one of type config and a second of type error:

```
type config struct {
        numTimes    int
        printUsage bool
}

func parseArgs(args []string) (config, error) {
        var numTimes int
        var err error
        c := config{}
        if len(args) != 1 {
                return c, errors.New("Invalid number of arguments")
        }

        if args[0] == "-h" || args[0] == "--help" {
                c.printUsage = true
                return c, nil
        }

        numTimes, err = strconv.Atoi(args[0])
        if err != nil {
                return c, err
        }
        c.numTimes = numTimes

        return c, nil
}
```

The parseArgs() function creates an object, c, of config type to store this data. The config structure is used for in-memory representation of data on which the application will rely for the runtime behavior. It has two fields: an integer field, numTimes, containing the number of the times the greeting is to be printed, and a bool field, printUsage, indicating whether the user has specified for the help message to be printed instead.

Command-line arguments supplied to a program are available via the Args slice defined in the os package. The first element of the slice is the name of the program itself, and the slice os.Args[1:] contains the arguments that your program may care about. This is the slice of strings with which parseArgs() is called. The function first checks to see if the number of command-line arguments is not equal to 1, and if so, it returns an empty config object and an error using the following snippet:

```
if len(args) != 1 {
        return c, errors.New("Invalid number of arguments")
}
```

If only one argument is specified, and it is -h or -help, the printUsage field is specified to true and the object, c, and a nil error are returned using the following snippet:

```
if args[0] == "-h" || args[0] == "-help" {
                c.printUsage = true
                return c, nil
}
```

Finally, the argument specified is assumed to be the number of times to print the greeting, and the Atoi() function from the strconv package is used to convert the argument—a string—to its integer equivalent:

```
numTimes, err = strconv.Atoi(args[0])
if err != nil {
        return c, err
}
```

If the Atoi() function returns a non-nil error value, it is returned; else numTimes is set to the converted integer:

```
c.numTimes = numTimes
```

So far, we have seen how you can read the input from the user and read command-line arguments. The next step is to ensure that the input is logically valid; in other words, whether or not it makes sense for the application. For example, if the user specified 0 for the number of times to print the greeting, it is a logically incorrect value. The validateArgs() function performs this validation:

```
func validateArgs(c config) error {
            if !(c.numTimes > 0) {
                    return errors.New("Must specify a number greater than 0")
            }
            return nil
}
```

If the value of the `numTimes` field is not greater than 0, an error is returned by the `validateArgs()` function.

After processing and validating the command-line arguments, the application invokes the `runCmd()` function to perform the relevant action based on the value in the `config` object, c:

```go
func runCmd(r io.Reader, w io.Writer, c config) error {
        if c.printUsage {
                printUsage(w)
                return nil
        }

        name, err := getName(r, w)
        if err != nil {
                return err
        }
        greetUser(c, name, w)
        return nil
}
```

If the field `printUsage` is set to `true` (`-help` or `-h` specified by the user), the `printUsage()` function is called and a `nil` error is returned. Otherwise, the `getName()` function is called to ask the user to input their name.

If `getName()` returned a non-nil error, it is returned. Else, the `greetUser()` function is called. The `greetUser()` function displays a greeting to the user based on the configuration supplied:

```go
func greetUser(c config, name string, w io.Writer {
        msg := fmt.Sprintf("Nice to meet you %s\n", name)
        for i := 0; i < c.numTimes; i++ {
                fmt.Fprintf(w, msg)
        }
}
```

The complete greeter application is shown in Listing 1.1.

Listing 1.1: A greeter application

```go
// chap1/manual-parse/main.go
package main

import (
        "bufio"
        "errors"
        "fmt"
        "io"
        "os"
        "strconv"
)
```

```go
type config struct {
        numTimes    int
        printUsage  bool
}

var usageString = fmt.Sprintf(`Usage: %s <integer> [-h|--help]

A greeter application which prints the name you entered <integer> number
of times.
`, os.Args[0])

func printUsage(w io.Writer) {
        fmt.Fprintf(w, usageString)
}

func validateArgs(c config) error {
        if !(c.numTimes > 0) {
                return errors.New("Must specify a number greater than 0")
        }
        return nil
}

// TODO - Insert definition of parseArgs() as earlier
// TODO - Insert definition of getName() as earlier
// TODO - Insert definition of greetUser() as earlier
// TODO - Insert definition of runCmd() as earlier

func main() {
        c, err := parseArgs(os.Args[1:])
        if err != nil {
                fmt.Fprintln(os.Stdout, err)
                printUsage(os.Stdout)
                os.Exit(1)
        }
        err = validateArgs(c)
        if err != nil {
                fmt.Fprintln(os.Stdout, err)
                printUsage(os.Stdout)
                os.Exit(1)
        }

        err = runCmd(os.Stdin, os.Stdout, c)
        if err != nil {
                fmt.Fprintln(os.Stdout, err)
                os.Exit(1)
        }
}
```

The main() function first calls the parseArgs() function with the slice of the command-line arguments, starting from the second argument. We get back two values from the function: c, a config object, and err, an error value. If a non-nil error is returned, the following steps are performed:

1. Print the error.

2. Print a usage message by calling the printUsage() function, passing in os.Stdout as the writer.

3. Terminate the program execution with exit code 1 by calling the Exit() function from the os package.

If the arguments have been parsed correctly, the validateArgs() function is called with the config object, c, that is returned by parseArgs().

Finally, if the validateArgs() function returned a nil error value, the runCmd() function is called, passing it a reader, os.Stdin; a writer, os.Stdout; and the config object, c.

Create a new directory, chap1/manual-parse/, and initialize a module inside it:

```
$ mkdir -p chap1/manual-parse
$ cd chap1/manual-parse
$ go mod init github.com/username/manual-parse
```

Next, save Listing 1.1 to a file called main.go, and build it:

```
$ go build -o application
```

Run the command without specifying any arguments. You will see an error and the following usage message:

```
$ ./application
Invalid number of arguments
Usage: ./application <integer> [-h|--help]

A greeter application which prints the name you entered <integer> number
of times.
```

In addition, you will also see that the exit code of the program is 1.

```
$ echo $?
1
```

If you are using PowerShell on Windows, you can use echo $LastExitCode to see the exit code.

This is another notable behavior of command-line applications that you should look to preserve. Any non-successful execution should result in a non-zero exit code upon termination using the Exit() function defined in the os package.

Specifying -h or -help will print a usage message:

```
$ ./application -help
Usage: ./application <integer> [-h|-help]

A greeter application which prints the name you entered <integer> number
of times.
```

Finally, let's see what a successful execution of the program looks like:

```
$ ./application 5
Your name please? Press the Enter key when done.
Joe Cool
Nice to meet you Joe Cool
Nice to meet you Joe Cool
Nice to meet you Joe Cool
Nice to meet you Joe Cool
Nice to meet you Joe Cool
```

You have manually tested that your application behaves as expected under three different input scenarios:

1. No command-line argument specified.

2. -h or -help is specified as a command-line argument.

3. A greeting is displayed to the user a specified number of times.

Manual testing is error prone and cumbersome, however. Next, you will learn to write automated tests for your application.

Writing Unit Tests

The standard library's testing package contains everything you need to write tests to verify the behavior of your application.

Let's consider the parseArgs() function first. It is defined as follows:

```
func parseArgs(args []string) (config, error)          {}
```

It has one input: a slice of strings representing the command-line arguments specified to the program during invocation. The return values are a value of type config and a value of type error.

The testConfig structure will be used to encapsulate a specific test case: a slice of strings representing the input command-line arguments in the args field, expected error value returned in the err field, and the expected config value returned in the embedded config struct field:

```
type testConfig struct {
        args []string
```

```
        err   error
        config
}
```

An example test case is

```
{
        args:    []string{"-h"},
        err:     nil,
        config:  config{printUsage: true, numTimes: 0},
},
```

This test case verifies the behavior when -h is specified as the command-line argument when executing the application.

We add a few more test cases and initialize a slice of test cases as follows:

```
tests := []testConfig{
        {
                args:    []string{"-h"},
                err:     nil,
                config:  config{printUsage: true, numTimes: 0},
        },
        {
                args:    []string{"10"},
                err:     nil,
                config:  config{printUsage: false, numTimes: 10},
        },
        {
                args:    []string{"abc"},
                err:     errors.New("strconv.Atoi: parsing \"abc\": invalid
syntax"),
                config:  config{printUsage: false, numTimes: 0},
        },
        {
                args:    []string{"1", "foo"},
                err:     errors.New("Invalid number of arguments"),
                config:  config{printUsage: false, numTimes: 0},
        },
}
```

Once we have defined the slice of test configurations above, we will iterate over them, invoke the parseArgs() function with the value in args, and check whether the returned values, c and err, match the expected values of type config and error, respectively. The complete test will appear as shown in Listing 1.2.

Listing 1.2: Test for the parseArgs() function

```
// chap1/manual-parse/parse_args_test.go
package main
```

```
import (
        "errors"
        "testing"
)

func TestParseArgs(t *testing.T) {
        // TODO Insert definition tests[] array as earlier

        for _, tc := range tests {
                c, err := parseArgs(tc.args)
                if tc.result.err != nil && err.Error() != tc.result.err.Error() {
                        t.Fatalf("Expected error to be: %v, got: %v\n",
tc.result.err, err)
                }
                if tc.result.err == nil && err != nil {
                        t.Errorf("Expected nil error, got: %v\n", err)
                }
                if c.printUsage != tc.result.printUsage {
                        t.Errorf("Expected printUsage to be: %v, got: %v\n",
tc.result.printUsage, c.printUsage)
                }
                if c.numTimes != tc.result.numTimes {
                        t.Errorf("Expected numTimes to be: %v, got: %v\n",
tc.result.numTimes, c.numTimes)
                }
        }
}
```

In the same directory as you saved Listing 1.1, save Listing 1.2 into a file called `parse_flags_test.go`. Now run the test using the `go test` command:

```
$ go test -v
=== RUN   TestParseArgs
--- PASS: TestParseArgs (0.00s)
PASS
ok          github.com/practicalgo/code/chap1/manual-parse          0.093
```

Passing in the `-v` flag when running `go test` also displays the test functions that are being run and the result.

Next, consider the `validateArgs()` function defined as `func validateArgs(c config) error`. Based on the function specification, we will once again define a slice of test cases. However, instead of defining a named `struct` type, we will use an *anonymous* `struct` type instead as follows:

```
tests := []struct {
                c   config
                err error
```

```
        }{
        {
                c:    config{},
                err: errors.New("Must specify a number greater than
0"),
        },
        {

                c:    config{numTimes: -1},
                err: errors.New("Must specify a number greater than
0"),
        },
        {

                c:    config{numTimes: 10},
                err: nil,
        },
}
```

Each test case consists of two fields: an input object, `c`, of type `config`, and the expected `error` value, `err`. The test function is shown in Listing 1.3.

Listing 1.3: Test for the `validateArgs()` function

```go
// chap1/manual-parse/validate_args_test.go
package main

import (
        "errors"
        "testing"
)

func TestValidateArgs(t *testing.T) {
        // TODO Insert definition tests[] slice as above
        for _, tc := range tests {
                err := validateArgs(tc.c)
                if tc.err != nil && err.Error() != tc.err.Error() {
                        t.Errorf("Expected error to be: %v, got: %v\n",
tc.err, err)
                }
                if tc.err == nil && err != nil {
                        t.Errorf("Expected nil error, got: %v\n", err)
                }
        }
}
```

In the same subdirectory as Listing 1.2, save Listing 1.3 to a file called `validate_args_test.go`. Now run the tests using the `go test` command. It will now run both the `TestParseFlags` and `TestValidateArgs` tests.

Finally, you will write a unit test for the `runCmd()` function. This function has the signature `runCmd(r io.Reader, w io.Writer, c config)`. We will define a set of test cases as follows:

```
tests := []struct {
            c              config
            input          string
            output string
            err            error
    }{
        {
            c:                  config{printUsage: true},
            output: usageString,
        },
        {
            c:                  config{numTimes: 5},
            input:              "",
            output: strings.Repeat("Your name please? Press the
Enter key when done.\n", 1),
            err:                errors.New("You didn't enter your
name"),
        },
        {
            c:                  config{numTimes: 5},
            input:              "Bill Bryson",
            output: "Your name please? Press the Enter key when
done.\n" + strings.Repeat("Nice to meet you Bill Bryson\n", 5),
        },
    }
```

The field `c` is a `config` object representing the incoming configuration, `input` is the test input received by the program from the user interactively, `output` is the expected output, and `err` represents any error that is expected based on the test input and configuration.

When you write a test for a program where you have to mimic an input from the user, this is how you can create a `io.Reader` from a string:

```
r := strings.NewReader(tc.input)
```

Thus, when the `getName()` function is called with `io.Reader` `r` as created above, calling `scanner.Text()` will return the string in `tc.input`.

To mimic the standard output, we create an empty `Buffer` object that implements the `Writer` interface using `new(bytes.Buffer)`. We can then obtain the message that was written to this `Buffer` using the `byteBuf.String()` method. The complete test is shown in Listing 1.4.

Listing 1.4: Test for the `runCmd()` function

```go
// chap1/manual-parse/run_cmd_test.go
package main

import (
        "bytes"
        "errors"
        "strings"
        "testing"
)

func TestRunCmd(t *testing.T) {

        // TODO Insert definition tests[] array as earlier
        byteBuf := new(bytes.Buffer)
        for _, tc := range tests {
                rd := strings.NewReader(tc.input)
                err := runCmd(rd, byteBuf, tc.c)
                if err != nil && tc.err == nil {
                        t.Fatalf("Expected nil error, got: %v\n", err)
                }
                if tc.err != nil && err.Error() != tc.err.Error() {
                        t.Fatalf("Expected error: %v, Got error:
%v\n", tc.err.Error(), err.Error())
                }
                gotMsg := byteBuf.String()
                if gotMsg != tc.output {
                        t.Errorf("Expected stdout message to be: %v, Got:
%v\n", tc.output, gotMsg)
                }

                byteBuf.Reset()
        }
}
```

We call the `byteBuf.Reset()` method so that the buffer is emptied before executing the next test case. Save Listing 1.4 into the same directory as Listings 1.1, 1.2, and 1.3. Name the file `run_cmd_test.go` and run all of the tests:

```
$ go test -v
=== RUN    TestParseArgs
--- PASS: TestParseArgs (0.00s)
=== RUN    TestRunCmd
--- PASS: TestRunCmd (0.00s)
PASS
ok        github.com/practicalgo/code/chap1/manual-parse        0.529s
```

You may be curious to find out what the test coverage looks like and visually see which parts of your code are not tested. To do so, run the following command first to create a coverage profile:

```
$ go test -coverprofile cover.out
PASS
coverage: 71.7% of statements
ok          github.com/practicalgo/code/chap1/manual-parse          0.084s
```

The above output tells us that our tests cover 71.7 percent of the code in main .go. To see which parts of the code are covered, run the following:

```
$ go tool cover -html=cover.out
```

This will open your default browser application and show the coverage of your code in an HTML file. Notably, you will see that the main() function is reported as uncovered since we didn't write a test for it. This leads nicely to Exercise 1.1.

EXERCISE 1.1: TESTING THE MAIN() FUNCTION   In this exercise, you will write a test for the main() function. However, unlike with other functions, you will need to test the exit status for different input arguments. To do so, your test should do the following:

1. Build the application. You will find using the special TestMain() function useful here.

2. Execute the application with different command-line arguments using the os.Exec() function. This will allow you to verify both the standard output and the exit code.

Congratulations! You have written your first command-line application. You parsed the os.Args slice to allow the user to provide input to the application. You learned how to make use of the io.Reader and io.Writer interfaces to write code that is unit testable.

Next, we will see how the standard library's flag package automatically takes care of the command-line argument parsing, validation of the type of data, and more.

Using the Flag Package

Before we dive into the flag package, let's refresh our memory of what a typical command-line application's user interface looks like. Let's consider a command-line application called application. Typically, it will have an interface similar to the following:

```
application [-h] [-n <value>] -silent <arg1> <arg2>
```

The user interface has the following components:

-h is a Boolean option usually specified to print a help text.

-n <value> expects the user to specify a value for the option, n. The application's logic determines the expected data type for the value.

-silent is another Boolean option. Specifying it sets the value to `true`.

arg1 and **arg2** are referred to as positional arguments. A *positional argument's* data type and interpretation is completely determined by the application.

The `flag` package implements types and methods to write command-line applications with standard behavior as above. When you specify the `-h` option while executing the application, all of the other arguments, if specified, will be ignored and a help message will be printed.

An application will have a mix of *required* and *optional* options.

It is also worth noting here that any positional argument must be specified *after* you have specified all of the *required* options. The `flag` package stops parsing the arguments once it encounters a positional argument, - or --.

Table 1.1 summarizes the package's parsing behavior for a sample of command-line arguments.

Table 1.1: Parsing of command-line arguments via flag

COMMAND-LINE ARGUMENTS	FLAG PARSING BEHAVIOR
-h	A help message is displayed.
-n 1 hello -h	A help message is displayed.
-n 1 Hello	Value of the flag n is set to 1 and Hello is available as a positional argument to the application.
-n 1 - Hello	Value of the flag n is set to 1 and everything else is ignored
Hello -n 1	-n 1 is ignored.

Let's see an example by rewriting the greeter application so that the number of times the user's name is printed is specified by the option -n. After the rewrite, the user interface will be as follows:

```
$ ./application -n 2
Your name please? Press the Enter key when done.
Joe Cool
Nice to meet you Joe Cool
Nice to meet you Joe Cool
```

Comparing the above to Listing 1.1, the key change is in how the `parseArgs()` function is written:

```go
func parseArgs(w io.Writer, args []string) (config, error) {
        c := config{}
        fs := flag.NewFlagSet("greeter", flag.ContinueOnError)
        fs.SetOutput(w)
        fs.IntVar(&c.numTimes, "n", 0, "Number of times to greet")
        err := fs.Parse(args)
        if err != nil {
                return c, err
        }
        if fs.NArg() != 0 {
                return c, errors.New("Positional arguments specified")
        }
        return c, nil
}
```

The function takes two parameters: a variable, `w`, whose value satisfies the `io.Writer` interface, and an array of strings representing the arguments to parse. It returns a `config` object and an `error` value. To parse the arguments, a new `FlagSet` object is created as follows:

```go
fs := flag.NewFlagSet("greeter", flag.ContinueOnError)
```

The `NewFlagSet()` function defined in the `flag` package is used to create a `FlagSet` object. Think of it as an abstraction used to handle the arguments a command-line application can accept. The first argument to the `NewFlagSet()` function is the name of the command that will be shown in help messages. The second argument configures what happens when an error is encountered while parsing the command-line arguments; that is, when the `fs.Parse()` function is called. When the `ContinueOnError` option is specified, the execution of the program will continue, even if a non-`nil` error is returned by the `Parse()` function. This is useful when you want to perform your own processing if there is a parsing error. Other possible values are `ExitOnError`, which halts the execution of the program, and `PanicOnError`, which invokes the `panic()` function. The difference between `ExitOnError` and `PanicOnError` is that you can make use of the `recover()` function in the latter case to perform any cleanup actions before the program terminates.

The `SetOutput()` method specifies the writer that will be used by the initialized `FlagSet` object for writing any diagnostic or output messages. By default, it is set to the standard error, `os.Stderr`. Setting it to the specified writer, `w`, allows us write unit tests to verify the behavior.

Next, we define the first option:

```go
fs.IntVar(&c.numTimes, "n", 0, "Number of times to greet")
```

The `IntVar()` method is used to create an option whose value is expected to be of type `int`. The first parameter of the method is the address of the variable in which the integer specified is stored. The second parameter of the method is the name of the option itself, `n`. The third parameter is the default value for the option, and the last parameter is a string that describes the purpose of the parameter to the program's user. It automatically gets displayed in the help text for the program. Similar methods are defined for other data types—`float`, `string`, and `bool`. You can also define a flag option for a custom type.

Next, we call the `Parse()` function, passing the `args[]` slice:

```
err := fs.Parse(args)
if err != nil {
        return c, err
}
```

This is the function that reads the elements of the slice and examines them against the flag options defined.

During the examination, it will attempt to fill in the values indicated in the specified variables, and if there is an error, it will either return an error to the calling function or terminate the execution, depending on the second argument specified to `NewFlagSet()` function. If a non-nil error is returned, the `parseArgs()` function returns the empty `config` object and the error value.

If a `nil` error is returned, we check to see if there was any positional argument specified, and if so, we return the object, `c`, and an error value:

```
if fs.NArg() != 0 {
        return c, errors.New("Positional arguments specified")
}
```

Since the greeter program doesn't expect any positional arguments to be specified, it checks for that and displays an error if one or more arguments are specified. The `NArg()` method returns the number of positional arguments after the options have been parsed.

The complete program is shown in Listing 1.5.

Listing 1.5: Greeter using `flag`

```go
// chap1/flag-parse/main.go
package main

import (
        "bufio"
        "errors"
        "flag"
        "fmt"
        "io"
        "os"
)
```

```go
type config struct {
        numTimes int
}

// TODO Insert definition of getName() as Listing 1.1
// TODO Insert definition of greetUser() as Listing 1.1
// TODO Insert definition of runCmd() as Listing 1.1
// TODO Insert definition of validateArgs as Listing 1.1
func parseArgs(w io.Writer, args []string) (config, error) {
        c := config{}
        fs := flag.NewFlagSet("greeter", flag.ContinueOnError)
        fs.SetOutput(w)
        fs.IntVar(&c.numTimes, "n", 0, "Number of times to greet")
        err := fs.Parse(args)
        if err != nil {
                return c, err
        }
        if fs.NArg() != 0 {
                return c, errors.New("Positional arguments specified")
        }
        return c, nil
}
func main() {
        c, err := parseArgs(os.Stderr, os.Args[1:])
        if err != nil {
                fmt.Fprintln(os.Stdout, err)
                os.Exit(1)
        }
        err = validateArgs(c)
        if err != nil {
                fmt.Fprintln(os.Stdout, err)
                os.Exit(1)
        }
        err = runCmd(os.Stdin, os.Stdout, c)
        if err != nil {
                fmt.Fprintln(os.Stdout, err)
                os.Exit(1)
        }
}
```

The `config` struct type is modified so that it doesn't have the `printUsage` field since the `parseArgs()` function now automatically handles the `-h` or `-help` argument. Create a new directory, `chap1/flag-parse/`, and initialize a module inside it:

```
$ mkdir -p chap1/flag-parse
$ cd chap1/flag-parse
$ go mod init github.com/username/flag-parse
```

Next, save Listing 1.5 to a file called `main.go` and build it:

```
$ go build -o application
```

Run the command without specifying any arguments. You will see the following error message:

```
$ ./application
Must specify a number greater than 0
```

Now run the command specifying the `-h` option:

```
$ ./application -h
Usage of greeter:
  -n int
          Number of times to greet
flag: help requested
```

The flag parsing logic recognized the `-h` option and displayed a default usage message consisting of the name that was specified when calling the `NewFlagSet()` function and the options along with their name, type, and description. The last line of the above output is seen here because when we haven't explicitly defined an `-h` option, the `Parse()` function returns an error, which is displayed as part of the error handling logic in `main()`. In the next section, you will see how we can improve this behavior.

Next, let's invoke the program specifying a non-integral value for the `-n` option:

```
$ ./application -n abc
invalid value "abc" for flag -n: parse error
Usage of greeter:
  -n int
          Number of times to greet
invalid value "abc" for flag -n: parse error
```

Note how we automatically get the type validation error since we tried specifying a non-integral value. In addition, note here again that we get the error twice. We will fix this later in the chapter.

Finally, let's run the program with a valid value for the `-n` option:

```
$ ./application -n 4
Your name please? Press the Enter key when done.
John Doe
Nice to meet you John Doe
Nice to meet you John Doe
Nice to meet you John Doe
Nice to meet you John Doe
```

Testing the Parsing Logic

The primary change in our greeter program, as compared to the first version, is in how we are parsing the command-line arguments using the `flag` package. You will notice that you have already written the greeter program, specifically the `parseArgs()` function, in a unit testing friendly fashion:

1. A new `FlagSet` object is created in the function.

2. Using the `Output()` method of the `FlagSet` object, you made sure that any messages from the `FlagSet` methods were written to the specified `io.Writer` object, `w`.

3. The arguments to parse were being passed as a parameter, `args`.

The function is well encapsulated and avoids using any global state. A test for the function is shown in Listing 1.6.

Listing 1.6: Test for the `parseArgs()` function

```go
//chap1/flag-parse/parse_args_test.go
package main
import (
    "bytes"
    "errors"
    "testing"
)

func TestParseArgs(t *testing.T) {
    tests := []struct {
        args     []string
        err      error
        numTimes int
    }{
        {
            args:     []string{"-h"},
            err:      errors.New("flag: help requested"),
            numTimes: 0,
        },
        {
            args:     []string{"-n", "10"},
            err:      nil,
            numTimes: 10,
        },
        {
            args:     []string{"-n", "abc"},
            err:      errors.New("invalid value \"abc\" for flag -n:
parse error"),
            numTimes: 0,
        },
```

```
                 {
                         args:      []string{"-n", "1", "foo"},
                         err:       errors.New("Positional arguments specified"),
                         numTimes: 1,
                 },
         }
         byteBuf := new(bytes.Buffer)
         for _, tc := range tests {
                 c, err := parseArgs(byteBuf, tc.args)
                 if tc.result.err == nil && err != nil {
                         t.Errorf("Expected nil error, got: %v\n", err)
                 }
                 if tc.result.err != nil && err.Error() != tc.result.err.Error()
{
                         t.Errorf("Expected error to be: %v, got: %v\n",
tc.result.err, err)
                 }

                 if c.numTimes != tc.result.numTimes {
                         t.Errorf("Expected numTimes to be: %v, got: %v\n",
tc.result.numTimes, c.numTimes)
                 }
                 byteBuf.Reset()
         }
}
```

Save Listing 1.6 into the directory in which you saved Listing 1.5. Name the file parse_args_test.go.

The unit test for the runCmd() function remains the same as that seen in Listing 1.4, except for the absence of the first test, which was used to test the behavior of runCmd() when printUsage was set to true. The test cases we want to test are as follows:

```
tests := []struct {
                 c          config
                 input      string
                 output string
                 err        error
         }{
                 {
                         c:          config{numTimes: 5},
                         input:      "",
                         output: strings.Repeat("Your name please? Press
the Enter key when done.\n", 1),
                         err:        errors.New("You didn't enter
your name"),
                 },
                 {
```

```
            c:              config{numTimes: 5},
            input:          "Bill Bryson",
            output: "Your name please? Press the Enter key
when done.\n" + strings.Repeat("Nice to meet you Bill Bryson\n", 5),
            },
    }
```

You can find the complete test in the run_cmd_test.go file in the flag-parse subdirectory of the book's code.

The test for the validateArgs() function is the same as the one used in Listing 1.3. You can find it in the validate_args_test.go file in the flag-parse subdirectory of the book's code. Now, run all of the tests:

```
$ go test -v
=== RUN    TestSetupFlagSet
--- PASS: TestSetupFlagSet (0.00s)
=== RUN    TestRunCmd
--- PASS: TestRunCmd (0.00s)
=== RUN    TestValidateArgs
--- PASS: TestValidateArgs (0.00s)
PASS
ok          github.com/practicalgo/code/chap1/flag-parse          0.610s
```

Great. Now you have rewritten the parsing logic of the greeter application to use the flag package and then updated the unit tests so that they test the new behavior. Next, you are going to work on improving the user interface of the application in a few ways. Before doing that, however, let's complete Exercise 1.2.

EXERCISE 1.2: HTML GREETER PAGE CREATOR   In this
exercise, you will update the greeter program to create an HTML page, which will
serve as the home page for the user. Add a new option, -o, to the application,
which will accept the filesystem path as a value. If the -o is specified, the greeter
program will create an HTML page at the path specified with the following contents:
<h1>Hello Jane Clancy</h1>, where Jane Clancy is the name entered. You
may choose to use the html/template package for this exercise.

Improving the User Interface

In the following sections, you are going to improve the user interface of the greeter application in three ways:

- Remove the duplicate error messages
- Customize the help usage message
- Allow the user to enter their name via a positional argument

While implementing these improvements, you will learn how to create custom error values, customize a `FlagSet` object to print a customized usage message, and access positional arguments from your application.

Removing Duplicate Error Messages

You may have noticed that errors were being displayed twice. This is caused by the following code snippet in the `main()` function:

```
c, err := parseArgs(os.Stderr, os.Args[1:])
if err != nil {
.       fmt.Println(err)
        os.Exit(1)
}
```

When the `Parse()` function call encountered an error, it was displaying that error to the output writer instance set in the `fs.SetOutput()` call. Subsequently, the returned error was also being printed in the `main()` function via the snippet above. It may seem like an easy fix not to print the error in the `main()` function. However, that will mean that *any* custom errors returned, such as when positional arguments are specified, will also not be shown. Hence, what we will do is create a custom error value and return that instead. We will only print the error if it matches that custom error, else we will skip printing it.

A custom error value can be created as follows:

```
var errPosArgSpecified = errors.New("Positional arguments specified")
```

Then, in the `parseArgs()` function, we return the following error:

```
if fs.NArg() != 0 {
.       return c, errPosArgSpecified
}
```

Then in `main()`, we update the code as follows:

```
c, err := parseArgs(os.Stderr, os.Args[1:])
if err != nil {
        if errors.Is(err, errPosArgSpecified) {
                fmt.Fprintln(os.Stdout, err)
        }
        os.Exit(1)
}
```

The `errors.Is()` function is used to check whether the error value `err` matches the error value `errPosArgSpecified`. The error is displayed only if a match is found.

Customizing Usage Message

If you compare Listing 1.5 to Listing 1.1, you will notice that there is no custom `usageString` specified. This is because the `flag` package automatically constructs one based on the `FlagSet` name and the options defined. However, what if you wanted to customize it? You can do so by setting the `Usage` attribute of the `FlagSet` object to a function as follows:

```
fs.Usage = func() {
    var usageString = `
A greeter application which prints the name you entered a specified
number of times.

Usage of %s: `
        fmt.Fprintf(w, usageString, fs.Name())
        fmt.Fprintln(w)
        fs.PrintDefaults()
}
```

Once we set the `Usage` attribute of the `FlagSet` object to a custom function, it is called whenever there is an error parsing the specified options. Note that the preceding function is defined as an anonymous function so that it can access the specified writer object, w, to display the custom usage message. Inside the function, we access the name of the `FlagSet` using the `Name()` method. Then we print a new line and call the `PrintDefaults()` method, which prints the various options that have been defined along with their type and default values. The updated `parseArgs()` function is as follows:

```
func parseArgs(w io.Writer, args []string) (config, error) {
        c := config{}
        fs := flag.NewFlagSet("greeter", flag.ContinueOnError)
        fs.SetOutput(w)
        fs.Usage = func() {
                var usageString = `
A greeter application which prints the name you entered a specified
number of times.

Usage of %s: <options> [name]`
                fmt.Fprintf(w, usageString, fs.Name())
                fmt.Fprintln(w)
                fmt.Fprintln(w, "Options: ")
                fs.PrintDefaults()
        }
        fs.IntVar(&c.numTimes, "n", 0, "Number of times to greet")
        err := fs.Parse(args)
        if err != nil {
                return c, err
        }
```

```
        if fs.NArg() > 1 {
                return c, errInvalidPosArgSpecified
        }
        if fs.NArg() == 1 {
                c.name = fs.Arg(0)
        }
        return c, nil
}
```

Next, you will implement the final improvement. The greeter program will now allow specifying the name via a positional argument as well. If one is not specified, you will ask for the name interactively.

Accept Name via a Positional Argument

First, update the config struct to have a name field of type string as follows:

```
type config struct {
        numTimes int
        name     string
}
```

Then the greetUser() function will be updated to the following:

```
func greetUser(c config, w io.Writer) {
        msg := fmt.Sprintf("Nice to meet you %s\n", c.name)
        for i := 0; i < c.numTimes; i++ {
                fmt.Fprintf(w, msg)
        }
}
```

Next, we update the custom error value as follows:

```
var errInvalidPosArgSpecified = errors.New("More than one positional
argument specified")
```

We update the parseArgs() function now to look for a positional argument and, if one is found, set the name attribute of the config object appropriately:

```
        if fs.NArg() > 1 {
                return c, errInvalidPosArgSpecified
        }
        if fs.NArg() == 1 {
                c.name = fs.Arg(0)
        }
```

The runCmd() function is updated so that it only asks the user to input the name interactively if not specified, or if an empty string was specified:

```
func runCmd(rd io.Reader, w io.Writer, c config) error {
        var err error
```

```
        if len(c.name) == 0 {
                c.name, err = getName(rd, w)
                if err != nil {
                        return err
                }
        }
        greetUser(c, w)
        return nil
}
```

The complete program with all of the preceding changes is shown in Listing 1.7.

Listing 1.7: Greeter program with user interface updates

```go
// chap1/flag-improvements/main.go
package main
import (
        "bufio"
        "errors"
        "flag"
        "fmt"
        "io"
        "os"
)

type config struct {
        numTimes int
        name     string
}

var errInvalidPosArgSpecified = errors.New("More than one positional
argument specified")

// TODO Insert definition of getName() as Listing 1.5
// TODO Insert definition of greetUser() as above
// TODO Insert updated definition of runCmd() as above
// TODO Insert definition of validateArgs as Listing 1.5
// TODO Insert definition of parseArgs() as above

func main() {
        c, err := parseArgs(os.Stderr, os.Args[1:])
        if err != nil {
                if errors.Is(err, errInvalidPosArgSpecified) {
                        fmt.Fprintln(os.Stdout, err)
                }
                os.Exit(1)
        }
        err = validateArgs(c)
        if err != nil {
                fmt.Fprintln(os.Stdout, err)
                os.Exit(1)
        }
```

```
        err = runCmd(os.Stdin, os.Stdout, c)
        if err != nil {
                fmt.Fprintln(os.Stdout, err)
                os.Exit(1)
        }
}
```

Create a new directory, chap1/flag-improvements/, and initialize a module inside it:

```
$ mkdir -p chap1/flag-improvements
$ cd chap1/flag-improvements
$ go mod init github.com/username/flag-improvements
```

Next, save Listing 1.7 as main.go. Build it as follows:

```
$ go build -o application
```

Run the built application code with -help, and you will see the custom usage message:

```
$ ./application -help

A greeter application which prints the name you entered a specified
number of times.

Usage of greeter: <options> [name]

Options:
  -n int
          Number of times to greet
```

Now let's specify a name as a positional argument:

```
$ ./application -n 1 "Jane Doe"
Nice to meet you Jane Doe
```

Next let's specify a bad input—a string as value to the -n option:

```
$ ./flag-improvements -n a "Jane Doe"
invalid value "a" for flag -n: parse error

A greeter application which prints the name you entered a specified
number of times.

Usage of greeter: <options> [name]

Options:
  -n int
          Number of times to greet
```

Two points are worth noting here:

■ The error is displayed only once now instead of being displayed twice.

■ Our custom usage is displayed instead of the default.

Try a few input combinations before moving on to updating the unit tests.

Updating the Unit Tests

We are going to finish off the chapter by updating the unit tests for the functions that we modified. Consider the `parseArgs()` function first. We will define a new anonymous `struct` for the test cases:

```
tests := []struct {
            args    []string
            config
            output string
            err     error
}{..}
```

The fields are as follows:

args: A slice of strings that contains the command-line arguments to parse.

config: An embedded field representing the expected `config` object value.

output: A string that will store the expected standard output.

err: An error value that will store the expected error.

Next, we define a slice of test cases representing the various test cases. The first one is as follows:

```
{
                    args: []string{"-h"},
                    output: `
A greeter application which prints the name you entered a specified
number of times.

Usage of greeter: <options> [name]

Options:
  -n int
        Number of times to greet
`,
                    err:    errors.New("flag: help requested"),
                    config: config{numTimes: 0},
    },
```

The preceding test cases test the behavior when the program is run with the -h argument. In other words, it prints the usage message. Then we have two test configs testing the behavior of the `parseArgs()` function for different values specified in the -n option:

```
        {
                args:    []string{"-n", "10"},
                err:     nil,
                config:  config{numTimes: 10},
        },
        {
                args:    []string{"-n", "abc"},
                err:     errors.New("invalid value \"abc\" for
flag -n: parse error"),
                config:  config{numTimes: 0},
        },
```

The final two test configs test the name specified as a positional argument:

```
        {
                args:    []string{"-n", "1", "John Doe"},
                err:     nil,
                config:  config{numTimes: 1, name: "John Doe"},
        },
        {
                args:    []string{"-n", "1", "John", "Doe"},
                err:     errors.New("More than one positional
argument specified"),
                config:  config{numTimes: 1},
        },
```

When "John Doe" is specified in quotes, it is considered valid. However, when John Doe is specified without quotes, they are interpreted as two positional arguments and hence the function returns an error. The complete test is provided in Listing 1.8.

Listing 1.8: Test for `parseArgs()` function

```go
// chap1/flag-improvements/parse_args_test.go
package main

import (
        "bufio"
        "bytes"
        "errors"
        "testing"
)
func TestParseArgs(t *testing.T) {
```

```go
        // TODO insert the test configs as per above
    tests := []struct {
            args []string
            config
            output string
            err    error
    }{..}

    byteBuf := new(bytes.Buffer)
    for _, tc := range tests {
            c, err := parseArgs(byteBuf, tc.args)
            if tc.err == nil && err != nil {
                    t.Fatalf("Expected nil error, got: %v\n", err)
            }
            if tc.err != nil && err.Error() != tc.err.Error() {
                    t.Fatalf("Expected error to be: %v, got: %v\n", tc.err,
err)
            }
            if c.numTimes != tc.numTimes {
                    t.Errorf("Expected numTimes to be: %v, got: %v\n",
tc.numTimes, c.numTimes)
            }
            gotMsg := byteBuf.String()
            if len(tc.output) != 0 && gotMsg != tc.output {
                    t.Errorf("Expected stdout message to be: %#v, Got:
%#v\n", tc.output, gotMsg)
            }
            byteBuf.Reset()
    }
}
```

Save Listing 1.8 into a new file, `parse_args_test.go`, in the same directory that you used for Listing 1.7. The test for the `validateArgs()` function is the same as Listing 1.3, and you can find it in the `validate_args_test.go` file in the `flag-improvements` subdirectory of the book's code.

The unit test for the `runCmd()` function remains the same as that of Listing 1.4, except for a new test configuration where the name is specified by the user via a positional argument. The tests slice is defined as follows:

```go
tests := []struct {
            c       config
            input   string
            output  string
            err     error
    }{
            // Tests the behavior when an empty string is
            // entered interactively as input.
            {
```

```
                        c:       config{numTimes: 5},
                        input:   "",
                        output: strings.Repeat("Your name please? Press the
Enter key when done.\n", 1),
                        err:     errors.New("You didn't enter your name"),
                },

                // Tests the behavior when a positional argument
                // is not specified and the input is asked from the user

                {
                        c:       config{numTimes: 5},
                        input:   "Bill Bryson",
                        output: "Your name please? Press the Enter key when
done.\n" + strings.Repeat("Nice to meet you Bill Bryson\n", 5),
                },
                // Tests the new behavior where the user has entered their name
                // as a positional argument
                {
                        c:       config{numTimes: 5, name: "Bill Bryson"},
                        input:   "",
                        output: strings.Repeat("Nice to meet you Bill
Bryson\n", 5),
                },

}
```

The complete test is shown in Listing 1.9.

Listing 1.9: Test for `runCmd()` function

```
// chap1/flag-improvements/run_cmd_test.go
package main

import (
        "bytes"
        "errors"
        "strings"
        "testing"
)

func TestRunCmd(t *testing.T) {

        // TODO Insert test cases from above
        tests := []struct{..}

        byteBuf := new(bytes.Buffer)
        for _, tc := range tests {
                r := strings.NewReader(tc.input)
                err := runCmd(r, byteBuf, tc.c)
                if err != nil && tc.err == nil {
```

```
                                        t.Fatalf("Expected nil error, got: %v\n", err)
                        }
                        if tc.err != nil && err.Error() != tc.err.Error() {
                                        t.Fatalf("Expected error: %v, Got error: %v\n", tc.err.
Error(), err.Error())
                        }
                        gotMsg := byteBuf.String()
                        if gotMsg != tc.output {
                                        t.Errorf("Expected stdout message to be: %v, Got:
%v\n", tc.output, gotMsg)
                        }
                        byteBuf.Reset()
            }
}
```

Save the Listing 1.9 code to a new file, run_cmd_test.go, in the same directory as Listing 1.8.

Now, run all of the tests:

```
$ go test -v
=== RUN    TestParseArgs
--- PASS: TestParseArgs (0.00s)
=== RUN    TestRunCmd
--- PASS: TestRunCmd (0.00s)
=== RUN    TestValidateArgs
--- PASS: TestValidateArgs (0.00s)
PASS
ok          github.com/practicalgo/code/chap1/flag-improvements          0.376s
```

Summary

We started off the chapter implementing a basic command-line interface by directly parsing the command-line arguments. You then saw how you can make use of the flag package to define a standard command-line interface. Instead of implementing the parsing and validating the arguments ourselves, you learned to use the package's built-in support for user-specified arguments and data type validation. All throughout the chapter, you wrote well-encapsulated functions to make unit testing straightforward.

In the next chapter, you will continue your journey into the flag package by learning to implement command-line applications with sub-commands, introducing robustness into your applications and more.

2

Advanced Command-Line Applications

In this chapter, you will learn how to use the `flag` package to implement command-line applications with sub-commands. Then, you will see how you can enforce predictable behavior in your command-line applications using contexts. Finally, you will learn how to combine contexts and handling operating system signals in your application. Let's jump in.

Implementing Sub-commands

Sub-commands are a way to split the functionality of your command-line application into logically independent commands having their own options and arguments. You have a top-level command—your application—and then you have a set of sub-commands, each having its own options and arguments. For example, the Go toolchain is distributed as a single application, `go`, which is the top-level command. As a Go developer, you will interact with its various functionalities via dedicated sub-commands such as `build`, `fmt`, and `test`.

You will recall from Chapter 1 that to create a command-line application, you first created a `FlagSet` object. For creating an application with sub-commands, you will create one `FlagSet` object per sub-command. Then, depending on which sub-command is specified, the corresponding `FlagSet` object is used to parse the remaining command-line arguments (see Figure 2.1).

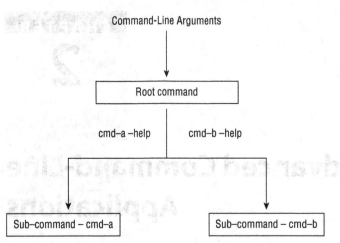

Figure 2.1: The main application looks at the command-line arguments and invokes the appropriate sub-command handler if possible.

Consider the `main()` function of an application with two sub-commands,
– `cmd-a` and `cmd-b`:

```
func main() {
        var err error
        if len(os.Args) < 2 {
                printUsage(os.Stdout)
                os.Exit(1)
        }
        switch os.Args[1] {
        case "cmd-a":
                err = handleCmdA(os.Stdout, os.Args[2:])
        case "cmd-b":
                err = handleCmdB(os.Stdout, os.Args[2:])
        default:
                printUsage(os.Stdout)
        }

        if err != nil {
                fmt.Println(err)
        }
        os.Exit(1)
}
```

The `os.Args` slice contains the command-line arguments that invoke the application. We will handle three input cases:

1. If the second argument is `cmd-a`, the `handleCmdA()` function is called.

2. If the second argument is `cmd-b`, the `handleCmdB()` function is called.

3. If the application is called without any sub-commands, or neither of those listed in case 1 or case 2 above, the `printUsage()` function is called to print a help message and exit.

The `handleCmdA()` function is implemented as follows:

```
func handleCmdA(w io.Writer, args []string) error {
        var v string
        fs := flag.NewFlagSet("cmd-a", flag.ContinueOnError)
        fs.SetOutput(w)
        fs.StringVar(&v, "verb", "argument-value", "Argument 1")
        err := fs.Parse(args)
        if err != nil {
                return err
        }
        fmt.Fprintf(w, "Executing command A")
        return nil
}
```

The above function looks very similar to the `parseArgs()` function that you had implemented earlier as part of the `greeter` application in Chapter 1. It creates a new `FlagSet` object, performs a setup of the various options, and parses the specific slice of arguments. The `handleCmdB()` function would perform its own setup for the `cmd-b` sub-command.

The `printUsage()` function is defined as follows:

```
func printUsage(w io.Writer) {
        fmt.Fprintf(w, "Usage: %s [cmd-a|cmd-b] -h\n", os.Args[0])
        handleCmdA(w, []string{"-h"})
        handleCmdB(w, []string{"-h"})
}
```

We first print a line of usage message for the application by means of the `fmt.Fprintf()` function and then invoke the individual sub-command handler functions with `-h` as the sole element in a slice of arguments. This results in those sub-commands displaying their own help messages.

The complete program is shown in Listing 2.1.

Listing 2.1: Implementing sub-commands in a command-line application

```
// chap2/sub-cmd-example/main.go
package main

import (
        "flag"
        "fmt"
        "io"
        "os"
)
```

```go
// TODO Insert handleCmdaA() implementation as earlier

func handleCmdB(w io.Writer, args []string) error {
        var v string
        fs := flag.NewFlagSet("cmd-b", flag.ContinueOnError)
        fs.SetOutput(w)
        fs.StringVar(&v, "verb", "argument-value", "Argument 1")
        err := fs.Parse(args)
        if err != nil {
                return err
        }
        fmt.Fprintf(w, "Executing command B")
        return nil
}


// TODO Insert printUsage() implementation as earlier


func main() {
        var err error
        if len(os.Args) < 2 {
                printUsage(os.Stdout)
                os.Exit(1)
        }
        switch os.Args[1] {
        case "cmd-a":
                err = handleCmdA(os.Stdout, os.Args[2:])
        case "cmd-b":
                err = handleCmdB(os.Stdout, os.Args[2:])
        default:
                printUsage(os.Stdout)
        }

        if err != nil {
                fmt.Fprintln(os.Stdout, err)
                os.Exit(1)
        }
}
```

Create a new directory `chap2/sub-cmd-example/`, and initialize a module inside it:

```
$ mkdir -p chap2/sub-cmd-example
$ cd chap2/sub-cmd-example
$ go mod init github.com/username/sub-cmd-example
```

Next, save Listing 2.1 as a file `main.go` within it. Build and run the application without any arguments:

```
$ go build -o application

$ ./application
Usage: ./application [cmd-a|cmd-b] -h
Usage of cmd-a:
  -verb string
          Argument 1 (default "argument-value")
Usage of cmd-b:
  -verb string
          Argument 1 (default "argument-value")
```

Try executing any of the sub-commands:

```
$ ./application cmd-a
Executing command A

$ ./application cmd-b
Executing command B
```

You have now seen an example of how you can implement your command-line application with sub-commands by creating multiple `FlagSet` objects. Each sub-command is constructed like a stand-alone command-line application. Thus, implementing sub-commands is a great way to separate unrelated functionalities of your application. For example, the `go build` sub-command provides all of the build-related functionality and the `go test` sub-command provides all of the testing-related functionality for a Go project.

Let's continue this exploration by discussing a strategy to make this scalable.

An Architecture for Sub-command-Driven Applications

As you develop your command-line application, it is a good idea to keep your main package lean and to create a separate package or packages for the sub-command implementations. Your main package will parse the command-line arguments and call the relevant sub-command handler function. If the arguments provided are not recognizable, a help message is displayed containing the usage message for all of the recognized sub-commands (see Figure 2.2).

Next, you lay down the foundation of a generic command-line network client, which you will build upon in later chapters. We will call this program `mync` (short for *my network client*). For now, you will ignore the implementation of the sub-commands and come back to it in later chapters when you fill in the implementation.

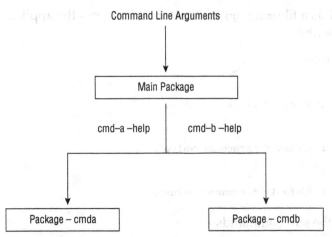

Figure 2.2: The main package implements the root command. A sub-command is implemented in its own package.

Let's look at the implementation of the main package first. Here, we will only have a single file, main.go, to start (see Listing 2.2).

Listing 2.2: Implementation of the main package

```go
// chap2/sub-cmd-arch/main.go
package main

import (
        "errors"
        "fmt"
        "github.com/username/chap2/sub-cmd-arch/cmd"
        "io"
        "os"
)

var errInvalidSubCommand = errors.New("Invalid sub-command specified")

func printUsage(w io.Writer) {
        fmt.Fprintf(w, "Usage: mync [http|grpc] -h\n")
        cmd.HandleHttp(w, []string{"-h"})
        cmd.HandleGrpc(w, []string{"-h"})
}

func handleCommand(w io.Writer, args []string) error {
        var err error

        if len(args) < 1 {
                err = errInvalidSubCommand
        } else {
                switch args[0] {
                case "http":
                        err = cmd.HandleHttp(w, args[1:])
```

```go
        case "grpc":
                err = cmd.HandleGrpc(w, args[1:])
        case "-h":
                printUsage(w)
        case "-help":
                printUsage(w)
        default:
                err = errInvalidSubCommand
        }
    }
    if errors.Is(err, cmd.ErrNoServerSpecified) || errors.Is(err,
errInvalidSubCommand) {
        fmt.Fprintln(w, err)
        printUsage(w)
    }
    return err
}

func main() {
    err := handleCommand(os.Stdout, os.Args[1:])
    if err != nil {
        os.Exit(1)
    }
}
```

At the top, we are importing the cmd package, which is a sub-package containing the implementation of the sub-commands. Since we will initialize a module for the application, we specify the absolute import path for the cmd package. The main() function calls the handleCommand() function with all of the arguments specified starting from the second argument:

```go
err := handleCommand(os.Args[1:])
```

If the handleCommand() function finds that it has received an empty slice, implying that no command-line arguments were specified, it returns a custom error value:

```go
if len(args) < 1 {
    err = errInvalidSubCommand
}
```

If command-line arguments were specified, a switch..case construct is defined to call the appropriate command handler function based on the first element of the slice, args:

1. If this element is http or grpc, the appropriate handler function is called.

2. If the first element is -h or -help, it calls the printUsage() function.

3. If it matches none of the conditions above, the printUsage() function is called and a custom error value is returned.

The `printUsage()` function prints a message first using `fmt.Fprintf` (w, "Usage: mync [http|grpc] -h\n") and then calls the sub-command implementations with the argument slice containing only `"-h"`.

Create a new directory, `chap2/sub-cmd-arch`, and initialize a module inside it:

```
$ mkdir -p chap2/sub-cmd-arch
$ cd chap2/sub-cmd-arch
$ go mod init github.com/username/chap2/sub-cmd-arch/
```

Save Listing 2.2 as `main.go` in the above directory.

Next let's look at `HandleHttp()` function, which handles the `http` sub-command (see Listing 2.3).

Listing 2.3: Implementation of the `HandleHttp()` function

```go
// chap2/sub-cmd-arch/cmd/httpCmd.go
package cmd

import (
        "flag"
        "fmt"
        "io"
)

type httpConfig struct {
        url   string
        verb string
}

func HandleHttp(w io.Writer, args []string) error {
        var v string
        fs := flag.NewFlagSet("http", flag.ContinueOnError)
        fs.SetOutput(w)
        fs.StringVar(&v, "verb", "GET", "HTTP method")

        fs.Usage = func() {
                var usageString = `
http: A HTTP client.

http: <options> server`
                fmt.Fprintf(w, usageString)

                fmt.Fprintln(w)
                fmt.Fprintln(w)
                fmt.Fprintln(w, "Options: ")
                fs.PrintDefaults()
        }

        err := fs.Parse(args)
        if err != nil {
                return err
        }
```

```
        if fs.NArg() != 1 {
                return ErrNoServerSpecified
        }

        c := httpConfig{verb: v}
        c.url = fs.Arg(0)
        fmt.Fprintln(w, "Executing http command")
        return nil
}
```

The `HandleHttp()` function creates a `FlagSet` object and configures it with an option, a custom usage, and other error handling.

Create a new subdirectory, `cmd`, inside the directory that you created earlier, and save Listing 2.3 as `httpCmd.go`.

The `HandleGrpc()` function is implemented in a similar fashion (see Listing 2.4).

Listing 2.4: Implementation of the `HandleGrpc()` function

```
// chap2/sub-cmd-arch/cmd/grpcCmd.go
package cmd

import (
        "flag"
        "fmt"
        "io"
)

type grpcConfig struct {
        server string
        method string
        body   string
}

func HandleGrpc(w io.Writer, args []string) error {
        c := grpcConfig{}
        fs := flag.NewFlagSet("grpc", flag.ContinueOnError)
        fs.SetOutput(w)
        fs.StringVar(&c.method, "method", "", "Method to call")
        fs.StringVar(&c.body, "body", "", "Body of request")
        fs.Usage = func() {
                var usageString = `
grpc: A gRPC client.

grpc: <options> server`
                fmt.Fprintf(w, usageString)
                fmt.Fprintln(w)
                fmt.Fprintln(w)
                fmt.Fprintln(w, "Options: ")
                fs.PrintDefaults()
        }
```

```
        err := fs.Parse(args)
        if err != nil {
                return err
        }
        if fs.NArg() != 1 {
                return ErrNoServerSpecified
        }
        c.server = fs.Arg(0)
        fmt.Fprintln(w, "Executing grpc command")
        return nil
}
```

Save Listing 2.4 as grpcCmd.go in the cmd subdirectory.

The custom error value, ErrNoServerSpecified, is created in a separate file in the cmd package as shown in Listing 2.5.

Listing 2.5: Custom error values

```
// chap2/sub-cmd-arch/cmd/errors.go
package cmd

import "errors"

var ErrNoServerSpecified = errors.New("You have to specify the remote server.")
```

In the cmd subdirectory, save Listing 2.5 as errors.go. You will end up with a source tree structure that looks like the following:

```
.
|____cmd
| |____grpcCmd.go
| |____httpCmd.go
| |____errors.go
|____go.mod
|____main.go
```

From the root directory of the module, build the application:

```
$ go build -o application
```

Try running the build application with different arguments, starting with -help or -h:

```
$ ./application --help
Usage: mync [http|grpc] -h

http: A HTTP client.

http: <options> server

Options:
  -verb string
```

```
                HTTP method (default "GET")

grpc: A gRPC client.

grpc: <options> server

Options:
  -body string
             Body of request
  -method string
             Method to call
```

Before we move on, let's make sure that we have unit tests for the function-ality implemented by the `main` and `cmd` packages.

Testing the Main Package

First, let's write the unit test for the `main` package. The `handleCommand()` is the key function that also calls the other functions in the package. It is declared as follows:

```
err := handleCommand(w io.Writer, args []string)
```

In the test, we will call the function with a slice of strings containing the arguments that the program may call and verify the expected behavior. Let's look at the test configurations:

```
testConfigs := []struct {
            args    []string
            output string
            err     error
}{
      // Tests the behavior when no arguments are specified to
      // the application
      {
            args:   []string{},
            err:    errInvalidSubCommand,
            output: "Invalid sub-command specified\n" + usageMessage,
      },
      // Tests the behavior when "-h" is specified as an argument
      // to the application

      {
            args:   []string{"-h"},
            err:    nil,
            output: usageMessage,
      },
      // Tests the behavior when an unrecognized sub-command is
      // to the application
```

```
        {
                args:    [] string{"foo"},
                err:     errInvalidSubCommand,
                output: "Invalid sub-command specified\n" + usageMessage,
        },
}
```

The complete test is shown in Listing 2.6.

Listing 2.6: Unit test for the `main` package

```go
// chap2/sub-cmd-arch/handle_command_test.go
package main

import (
        "bytes"
        "testing"
)

func TestHandleCommand(t *testing.T) {
        usageMessage := `Usage: mync [http|grpc] -h

http: A HTTP client.

http: <options> server

Options:
  -verb string
        HTTP method (default "GET")

grpc: A gRPC client.

grpc: <options> server

Options:
  -body string
        Body of request
  -method string
        Method to call
`

        // TODO Insert testConfigs from above

        byteBuf := new(bytes.Buffer)
        for _, tc := range testConfigs {
                err := handleCommand(byteBuf, tc.args)
                if tc.err == nil && err != nil {
                        t.Fatalf("Expected nil error, got %v", err)
                }

                if tc.err != nil && err.Error() != tc.err.Error() {
                        t.Fatalf("Expected error %v, got %v", tc.err, err)
                }
```

```
                    if len(tc.output) != 0 {
                            gotOutput := byteBuf.String()
                            if tc.output != gotOutput {
                                    t.Errorf("Expected output to be: %#v, Got:
%#v", tc.output, gotOutput)
                            }
                    }
                    byteBuf.Reset()
            }
    }
```

Save Listing 2.6 as `handle_command_test.go` in the same directory as the `main` package (see Listing 2.2).

One behavior for which we haven't written a test is the `main` package calling the correct function from the `cmd` package when a valid sub-command is specified. Exercise 2.1 gives you an opportunity to do so.

EXERCISE 2.1: TESTING SUB-COMMAND INVOCATION Update the test for the `handleCommand()` function to verify that the correct sub-command implementation is invoked when a valid sub-command is specified. You will find the approach suggested for the solution to Exercise 1.1 useful here as well.

Testing the Cmd Package

To test the `cmd` package, you will define similar test cases. Here are the test cases for the `TestHandleHttp()` function:

```
testConfigs := []struct {
        args    []string
        output  string
        err     error
}{
        // Test behavior when the http sub-command is called with no
        // positional argument specified
        {
                args: []string{},
                err:  ErrNoServerSpecified,
        },
        // Test behavior when the http sub-command is called with "-h"
        {
                args:   []string{"-h"},
                err:    errors.New("flag: help requested"),
                output: usageMessage,
        },
        // Test behavior when the http sub-command is called
        // with a positional argument specifying the server URL
```

```
        {
                    args:   []string{"http://localhost"},
                    err:    nil,
                    output: "Executing http command\n",
        },
    }
```

You can find the complete test in `chap2/sub-cmd-arch/cmd/handle_http_test.go`.

The test configurations for the `TestHandleGrpc()` function are as follows:

```
testConfigs := []struct {
                args    []string
                err     error
                output string
        }{
                // Test behavior when the grpc sub-command is called with no
                // positional argument specified

                {
                        args: []string{},
                        err:  ErrNoServerSpecified,
                },
                // Test behavior when the grpc sub-command is called with "-h"
                {
                        args:   []string{"-h"},
                        err:    errors.New("flag: help requested"),
                        output: usageMessage,
                },
                // Test behavior when the http sub-command is called
                // with a positional argument specifying the server URL
                {
                        args:   []string{"-method",
"service.host.local/method", "-body", "{}", "http://localhost"},
                        err:    nil,
                        output: "Executing grpc command\n",
                },
    }
```

You can find the complete test in `chap2/sub-cmd-arch/cmd/handle_grpc_test.go`.

The source tree for the application should now look like the following:

```
.
|____cmd
| |____grpcCmd.go
| |____handle_grpc_test.go
| |____handle_http_test.go
| |____httpCmd.go
```

```
| |___errors.go
|____handle_command_test.go
|____go.mod
|____main.go
```

From the root of the module, run all of the tests:

```
$ go test -v ./...
=== RUN   TestHandleCommand
--- PASS: TestHandleCommand (0.00s)
PASS
ok          github.com/practicalgo/code/chap2/sub-cmd-arch      0.456s
=== RUN   TestHandleGrpc
--- PASS: TestHandleGrpc (0.00s)
=== RUN   TestHandleHttp
--- PASS: TestHandleHttp (0.00s)
PASS
ok          github.com/practicalgo/code/chap2/sub-cmd-arch/cmd  0.720s
```

Great. You now have unit tests for both the packages. You have written a test to verify that the main package displays an error when an empty or invalid sub-command is specified and calls the right sub-command when a valid sub-command is specified. You have also written a test for the cmd package to verify that the sub-command implementations behave as expected.

In Exercise 2.2, you will add a validation to the http sub-command to allow only three HTTP methods: GET, POST, and HEAD.

EXERCISE 2.2: HTTP METHOD VALIDATOR   You will add validation to the http sub-command in this exercise. You will ensure that the method option only allows three values: GET (the default), POST, and HEAD.

If the method yields anything other than these values, the program should exit with a non-zero exit code and print the error "Invalid HTTP method". Write tests to verify the validation.

In this section, you learned how to write a command-line application with sub-commands. When you are writing a large command-line application, organizing the functionality into separate sub-commands improves the user experience. Next, you will learn how to implement a degree of predictability and robustness in command-line applications.

Making Your Applications Robust

A hallmark of robust applications is that a certain level of control is enforced on their runtime behavior. For example, when your program makes an HTTP request, you may want it to complete within a user-specified number of seconds, and if not, exit with an error message. When such measures are enforced, the program's behavior is more predictable to the user. The context package in the standard library allows applications to enforce such control. It defines a Context struct type and three functions—withDeadline(), withCancel(), and withTimeout()—to enforce certain runtime guarantees around your code execution. You will find various standard library packages that require a context object to be passed as the first parameter. Some examples are functions in the net, net/http, and os/exec packages. Although use of contexts is most common when you are communicating with external resources, they are certainly equally applicable to any other functionality where there may be a chance of unpredictable behavior.

User Input with Deadlines

Let's consider an example where your program asks for user input and the user has to type in the input and press the Enter key within 5 seconds else it will move on with a default name. Though a contrived example, it illustrates how you can enforce a time-out on any custom code in your application.

Let's look at the main() function first:

```
func main() {
        allowedDuration := totalDuration * time.Second

        ctx, cancel := context.WithTimeout(context.Background(),
allowedDuration)
        defer cancel()

        name, err := getNameContext(ctx)

        if err != nil && !errors.Is(err, context.DeadlineExceeded) {
                fmt.Fprintf(os.Stdout, "%v\n", err)
                os.Exit(1)
        }
        fmt.Fprintln(os.Stdout, name)
}
```

The function creates a new context using the context.WithTimeout() function. The context.WithTimeout() function accepts two arguments: the first is a *parent* Context object and the second is a time.Duration object specifying the time—in milliseconds, seconds, or minutes—after which the context will expire. Here we set the time-out to be 5 seconds:

```
allowedDuration := totalDuration * time.Second
```

Next, we create the `Context` object:

```
ctx, cancel := context.WithTimeout(context.Background(), allowedDuration)
defer cancel()
```

Since we don't have another context that will play the role of the parent context, we create a new empty context using `context.Background()`. The `WithTimeout()` function returns two values: the created context, `ctx`, and a cancellation function, `cancel`. It is necessary to call the cancellation function in a deferred statement so that it is always called just before the function returns. Then we call the `getNameContext()` function as follows:

```
name, err := getNameContext(ctx)
```

If the error returned was the expected `context.DeadlineExceeded`, we do not show it to the user and just display the name; else we show it and exit with a non-zero exit code:

```
if err != nil && !errors.Is(err, context.DeadlineExceeded) {
        fmt.Fprintf(os.Stdout, "%v\n", err)
        os.Exit(1)
}
fmt.Fprintln(os.Stdout, name)
```

Now let's look at the `getNameContext()` function:

```
func getNameContext(ctx context.Context) (string, error) {
        var err error
        name := "Default Name"
        c := make(chan error, 1)

        go func() {
                name, err = getName(os.Stdin, os.Stdout)
                c <- err
        }()

        select {
        case <-ctx.Done():
                return name, ctx.Err()
        case err := <-c:
                return name, err
        }
}
```

The overall idea of the implementation of this function is as follows:

1. Execute the `getName()` function in a goroutine.
2. Once the function returns, write the error value into a channel.
3. Create a `select..case` block to wait on a read operation on two channels:
   a. The channel that is written to by the `ctx.Done()` function
   b. The channel that is written to when the `getName()` function returns
4. Depending on which of step a or b above completes first, either the context deadline exceeded error is returned along with the default name or the values returned by the `getName()` function are returned.

The complete code is shown in Listing 2.7.

Listing 2.7: Implementing time-out for user input

```go
// chap2/user-input-timeout/main.go
package main

import (
        "bufio"
        "context"
        "errors"
        "fmt"
        "io"
        "os"
        "time"
)

var totalDuration time.Duration = 5

func getName(r io.Reader, w io.Writer) (string, error) {
        scanner := bufio.NewScanner(r)
        msg := "Your name please? Press the Enter key when done"
        fmt.Fprintln(w, msg)

        scanner.Scan()
        if err := scanner.Err(); err != nil {
                return "", err
        }
        name := scanner.Text()
        if len(name) == 0 {
                return "", errors.New("You entered an empty name")
        }
        return name, nil
}
```

```
// TODO Insert getNameContext() definition as above

// TODO Insert main() definition as above
```

Create a new directory, chap2/user-input-timeout, and initialize a module inside it:

```
$ mkdir -p chap2/user-input-timeout
$ cd chap2/user-input-timeout
$ go mod init github.com/username/user-input-timeout
```

Next, save Listing 2.7 as main.go. Build it as follows:

```
$ go build -o application
```

Run the program. If you do not input any name within 5 seconds, you will see the following:

```
$ ./application
Your name please? Press the Enter key when done
Default Name
```

However, if you input a name and press Enter within 5 seconds, you will see the name that was entered:

```
$ ./application
Your name please? Press the Enter key when done
```

John C

```
John C
```

You learned to use the WithTimeout() function to create a context that allows you to enforce a limit which is *relative* to the current time. The WithDeadline() function, on the other hand, is useful when you want to enforce a real-world deadline. For example, if you wanted to ensure that a function must be executed before June 28, 10:00 AM, you could use a context created via WithDeadline().

Next, you will learn to test such timeout behavior in your applications as part of Exercise 2.3.

EXERCISE 2.3: UNIT TESTING THE TIME-OUT EXCEEDED BEHAVIOR   Write a test to verify the time-out exceeded behavior. One straightforward way to do so is not to provide any input at all in the test so that the deadline exceeds. Of course, you should also test the "happy path," that is, where you provide an input and the deadline doesn't exceed. It is recommended to use a shorter time-out—in the order of a few 100 milliseconds to avoid time-consuming tests.

Handling User Signals

We touched upon the fact that a number of standard library functions accept a context as a parameter. Let's see how it works using the os/exec package's execCommandContext() function. One situation in which this becomes useful is when you want to enforce a maximum time of execution for these commands. Once again, this can be implemented by using a context created via the WithTimeout() function:

```
package main

import (
        "context"
        "fmt"
        "os"
        "os/exec"
        "time"
)

func main() {
        ctx, cancel := context.WithTimeout(context.Background(),
10*time.Second)
        defer cancel()
        if err := exec.CommandContext(ctx, "sleep", "20").Run(); err != nil {
                fmt.Fprintln(os.Stdout, err)
        }
        }
```

When run on Linux/MacOS, the above code snippet will yield the following error:

```
signal: killed
```

The CommandContext() function force kills an external program when the context expires. In the above code, we set up a context that will be canceled after 10 seconds. We then used the context to execute a command "sleep", "20", which will sleep for 20 seconds. Hence the command is killed. Thus, in a scenario where you want your application to execute external commands but want to have a guaranteed behavior that the commands must finish execution in a certain amount of time, you can achieve it using the technique above.

Next let's look at introducing another point of control in the program—the user. User signals are a way for the user to interrupt the normal workflow of a program. Two common user signals on Linux and MacOS are SIGINT when the Ctrl+C key combination is pressed and SIGTERM when the kill command is executed. We want to allow the user to be able to cancel this external program at any point of time if the time-out hasn't already expired using either the SIGINT or SIGTERM signal.

Here are the steps involved in doing this:

1. Create a context using the WithTimeout() function.

2. Set up a signal handler that will create a handler for the SIGINT and SIGTERM signal. When one of the signals is received, the signal handling code will manually call the cancellation function returned in step 1.

3. Execute the external program using the CommandContext() function using the context created in step 1.

Step 1 is implemented in a function, createContextWithTimeout():

```
func createContextWithTimeout(d time.Duration) (context.Context,
context.CancelFunc) {
        ctx, cancel := context.WithTimeout(context.Background(), d)
        return ctx, cancel
}
```

The WithTimeout() function from the context package is called to create a context that is canceled when a specified unit of time, d, expires. The first parameter is an empty non-nil context created via a call to the context.Background() function. The context, ctx, and the cancellation function, cancel, are returned. We do not call the cancellation function here since we need the context to be around for the lifetime of the program.

Step 2 is implemented in the setupSignalHandler() function:

```
func setupSignalHandler(w io.Writer, cancelFunc context.CancelFunc) {
        c := make(chan os.Signal, 1)
        signal.Notify(c, syscall.SIGINT, syscall.SIGTERM)
        go func() {
                s := <-c
                fmt.Fprintf(w, "Got signal:%v\n", s)
                cancelFunc()
        }()
}
```

This function constructs a way to handle the SIGINT and SIGTERM signals. A channel of capacity 1 is created with the type Signal (defined in the os package). Then we call the Notify() function from the signal package essentially to set up a listening channel for the syscall.SIGINT and syscall.SIGTERM signals. We set up a goroutine to wait for this signal. When we get one, we call the cancelFunc() function, which is the context cancellation function corresponding to the ctx created above. When we call this function, the implementation of os. execCommandContext() recognizes this and eventually force kills the command.

Of course, if no SIGINT or SIGTERM signal is received, the command is allowed to execute normally according to the defined context, ctx.

Step 3 is implemented by the following function:

```
func executeCommand(ctx context.Context, command string, arg string) error {
    return exec.CommandContext(ctx, command, arg).Run()
}
```

The complete program is shown in Listing 2.8.

Listing 2.8: Handling user signals

```
// chap2/user-signal/main.go
package main

import (
        "context"
        "fmt"
        "io"
        "os"
        "os/exec"
        "os/signal"
        "time"
)

// TODO Insert definition of createContextWithTimeout() as above
// TODO Insert definition of setupSignalHandler() as above
// TODO Insert definition of executeCommand as above


func main() {
        if len(os.Args) != 3 {
                fmt.Fprintf(os.Stdout, "Usage: %s <command> <argument>\n",
os.Args[0])
                os.Exit(1)
        }
        command := os.Args[1]
        arg := os.Args[2]

        // Implement Step 1
        cmdTimeout := 30 * time.Second
        ctx, cancel := createContextWithTimeout(cmdTimeout)
        defer cancel()

        // Implement Step 2
        setupSignalHandler(os.Stdout, cancel)
```

```
        // Implement Step 3
        err := executeCommand(ctx, command, arg)
        if err != nil {
                fmt.Fprintln(os.Stdout, err)
                os.Exit(1)
        }
}
```

The `main()` function starts by checking to see if the expected number of arguments have been specified. Here we implement a basic user interface and expect the application to be executed as `./application sleep 60` where `sleep` is the command to be executed and `60` is the argument to the command. Then we store the command to be executed and the argument to it in two string variables: – `command` and `arg`. The `createContextWithTimeout()` function is then called with a duration object specifying a 30-second time-out. The function returns a context, `ctx`, and a context cancellation function, `cancel`. In the next statement, we call the function in a deferred call.

We then call the `setupSignalHandler()` function, passing it two parameters: – `os.Stdout` and the context's cancellation function, `cancel`.

Finally, we call the `executeCommand()` function with the context object created, `ctx`; the command to execute, `command`; and the argument to the command, `arg`. If there is an error returned, it is printed.

Create a new directory, `chap2/user-signal`, and initialize a module inside it:

```
$ mkdir -p chap2/user-signal
$ cd chap2/user-signal
$ go mod init github.com/username/user-signal
```

Next, save Listing 2.8 as a new file, `main.go`, and build it:

```
$ go build -o application
```

Considering that the time-out is set to 30 seconds, let's try executing the `sleep` command with a value for the time to sleep:

```
% ./application sleep 60
^CGot signal:interrupt
signal: interrupt
```

We ask the `sleep` command to sleep for 60 seconds but manually abort it by pressing Ctrl+C. The error message tells us how the command was aborted.

Next, we sleep for 10 seconds:

```
% ./application sleep 10
```

As 10 seconds is lower than the context time-out for 30 seconds, it exits cleanly. Finally, let's execute the `sleep` command for 31 seconds:

```
% ./listing7 sleep 31
signal: killed
```

Now we can see that the time-out context kicks in and kills the process.

Summary

In this chapter, you learned about patterns for implementing scalable command-line applications. You learned how to implement a sub-command-based interface for your application, and you built upon it to design a scalable architecture for applications with sub-commands. Then you learned to use the `context` package to implement certain control over the runtime behavior of your applications. Finally, you used goroutines and channels to allow the user to interrupt the application using contexts and signals.

In the next chapter, we will continue our exploration into the world of writing command-line applications as you learn about writing HTTP clients. You will do so as you build out the HTTP client implementation for which we laid the foundation in this chapter.

Writing HTTP Clients

In this chapter, you are going to learn about the building blocks of writing testable HTTP clients. You will become familiar with key concepts—sending and receiving data, serialization and deserialization, and working with binary data. Once you grasp these concepts, you will be able to write stand-alone client applications and a Go client for your service's HTTP API and make HTTP API calls as part of a service-to-service communication architecture. As you progress through the chapter, you will be enhancing the `mync http` sub-command by implementing these features and techniques. Let's get started!

Downloading Data

You are likely familiar with command-line programs such as `wget` and `curl`, which are suitable for downloading data over HTTP. Let's see how you can write one using the functions and types defined in the `net/http` package. First, let's write a function that will accept an HTTP URL as a parameter and return a byte slice containing the contents at the URL and an `error` value:

```
func fetchRemoteResource(url string) ([]byte, error) {
    r, err := http.Get(url)
    if err != nil {
        return nil, err
    }
```

```
    defer r.Body.Close()
    return io.ReadAll(r.Body)


}
```

The `Get()` function defined in the `net/http` package makes a HTTP GET request to the specified `url` and returns an object of type `Response` and an error value. The `Response` object, `r`, has several fields, one of which is the `Body` field (of type `io.ReadCloser`), which contains the response body. We use a `defer` statement to close the body by calling the `Close()` method before the function returns. We then use the `ReadAll()` function from the `io` package to read the contents of the body (`r.Body`) and return both of the values we get back from it—a byte slice and an error value. Let's define a `main` function to write a buildable application. The complete listing is shown in Listing 3.1.

Listing 3.1: A basic data downloader

```go
// chap3/data-downloader/main.go

package main

import (
        "fmt"
        "io"
        "net/http"
        "os"
)

func fetchRemoteResource(url string) ([]byte, error) {
        r, err := http.Get(url)
        if err != nil {
                return nil, err
        }
        defer r.Body.Close()
        return io.ReadAll(r.Body)
}

func main() {
        if len(os.Args) != 2 {
                fmt.Fprintf(os.Stdout "Must specify a HTTP URL to get
data from")
                os.Exit(1)
        }
        body, err := fetchRemoteResource(os.Args[1])
        if err != nil {
                fmt.Fprintf(os.Stdout, "%v\n", err)
                os.Exit(1)
        }
        fmt.Fprintf(os.Stdout, "%s\n", body)
}
```

The `main()` function expects the URL to be specified as a command-line argument and implements some basic error handling. Create a new directory, `chap3/data-downloader`, and initialize a module inside it:

```
$ mkdir -p chap3/data-downloader
$ cd chap3/data-downloader
$ go mod init github.com/username/data-downloader
```

Next, save Listing 3.1 into a new file, `main.go`. Build and run the application:

```
$ go build -o application
$./application https://golang.org/pkg/net/http/
```

You will see a bunch of HTML written to your terminal. In fact, if you specify a URL that refers to an image, you will see the image data being dumped on the screen as well. We will improve this situation soon, but first let's talk about testing our data downloader.

Testing the Data Downloader

Considering the data downloader application, a test will want to verify whether the `fetchRemoteResource()` function can successfully return the data available at the specified URL. If the URL is invalid or is not reachable, it should return an error value. How do we set up a test HTTP server that will serve some test content? The `NewServer()` function in the `net/http/httptest` package will help us. The following code snippet defines a function, `startTestHTTPServer()`, which will start an HTTP server that will return the response "Hello World" to any request:

```go
func startTestHTTPServer() *httptest.Server {
        ts := httptest.NewServer(
                http.HandlerFunc(
                        func(w http.ResponseWriter, r *http.Request) {
                                fmt.Fprint(w, "Hello World")
                        }))
        return ts
}
```

The `httptest.NewServer()` function returns a `httptest.Server` object with various fields that represent the server that was created. The only argument to the function is an object of type `http.Handler` (something you will learn a lot more about in Chapter 6, "Advanced HTTP Server Applications"). This handler object allows us to set up the desired handlers for the test server. In this case, we create a catchall handler that will return the string "Hello World" to any HTTP request—not just GET requests. Implicitly, all requests to this server will receive a successful HTTP 200 status.

Using the above function, we can now write our test function, as shown in Listing 3.2.

Listing 3.2: Test for `fetchRemoteResource()` function

```go
// chap3/data-downloader/fetch_remote_resource_test.go
package main

import (
        "fmt"
        "net/http"
        "net/http/httptest"
        "testing"
)

// TODO Insert definition of startTestHTTPServer() from above

func TestFetchRemoteResource(t *testing.T) {
        ts := startTestHTTPServer()
        defer ts.Close()

        expected := "Hello World"

        data, err := fetchRemoteResource(ts.URL)
        if err != nil {
                t.Fatal(err)
        }
        if expected != string(data) {
                t.Errorf("Expected response to be: %s, Got: %s", expected,
data)
        }
}
```

The test function starts by calling the `startTestHTTPServer()` to create a test server. The returned object, `ts`, contains the data related to the test server that was started. Calling the `Close()` method in a deferred statement ensures that the server is stopped when the test completes execution. The URL field in the returned `ts` object contains a string value representing the IP address and port combination of the server. This is passed as a parameter to the `fetchRemoteResource()` function. The rest of the test then verifies whether the returned data matches the expected string, "Hello World". Save Listing 3.2 to a new file, `fetch_remote_resource_test.go`, in the same directory as Listing 3.1. Run the test using `go test`:

```
$ go test -v
=== RUN   TestFetchRemoteResource
--- PASS: TestFetchRemoteResource (0.00s)
PASS
ok      github.com/practicalgo/code/chap3/data-downloader    0.872s
```

Great. You have implemented a basic data downloader over HTTP, and you have ensured that it works by downloading data from a remote URL as well as writing a test for it.

In this chapter's first exercise, Exercise 3.1, you will enhance the mync command-line application by adding this feature.

> **EXERCISE 3.1: ENHANCE THE HTTP SUB-COMMAND TO ALLOW DATA DOWNLOADING**   In the last chapter, we implemented a command-line application, mync, with two sub-commands, http and grpc. However, we didn't implement any functionality for those commands. In this exercise, implement the functionality of the http GET sub-command. Use the solution of Exercise 2.2 as a starting point.

Deserializing Received Data

The fetchRemoteResource() function we wrote simply displays the downloaded data to the terminal. This may not serve any purpose for the application's user and will just appear as garbage for certain kinds of data—images and non-text files, for example. In most cases, you may want to do some kind of processing on the data instead. This processing is usually referred to as *unmarshalling*, or *deserializing*, the data, and it involves converting bytes of data into a data structure that your application can understand. You can then perform any operation on this data structure in your application without having to query or parse the raw bytes. The reverse operation is *marshalling*, or *serialization*, and it is an efficient way to convert a data structure into a data format that can then be stored or transmitted over the network. We will focus on unmarshalling the data in this section. In the next section, we will turn our attention to marshalling the data.

The data structure into which certain bytes of data can be deserialized is tightly coupled to the nature of the data. For example, unmarshalling bytes of language-neutral *JavaScript Object Notation (JSON)* data into a slice of struct types is a common operation. Similarly, deserializing the Go-specific *gob* (as defined by the encoding/gob package) bytes into a struct type is another deserialization operation. Depending on the data format of the bytes, the deserialization operation will vary. The encoding package and its sub-packages has support for unmarshalling (and marshalling) popular data formats such as JSON, XML, CSV, gob, and others.

Let's study an example of how we can deserialize a JSON formatted HTTP response into a map data structure. If the response is not JSON formatted, we will not perform the deserialization. The deserialization operation as implemented by the `json.Unmarshal()` function requires that we specify the type of object into which we want the data to be unmarshalled. Hence, to write such a client:

1. We need to examine the JSON data that we will deserialize.
2. We will need to create a data structure; that is, a map that is capable of representing the data.

To keep things simple and self-contained, consider a fictional HTTP server that hosts certain software packages. It has an API that returns a JSON string containing all of the available package names and their latest versions as follows:

```
[
    {"name": "package1", "version": "1.1"},
    {"name": "package2", "version": "1.2"}
]
```

Let's look at the type that we will define to deserialize the JSON data into. We will call the type `pkgData`, a struct type to represent the data for a single package:

```
type pkgData struct {
        Name    string `json:"name"`
        Version string `json:"version"`
}
```

The structure has two string fields: `Name` and `Version`. The struct tags `` `json:"name"` `` and `"json:"version"`` indicate the key identifiers for the corresponding fields in the JSON data. Now that we have defined the data structure, we can deserialize the JSON data for the packages into a slice of `pkgData` objects.

The `fetchPackageData()` function sends a GET request to the package server `url` and returns a slice of `pkgData` struct objects and an `error` value. If there is an error, or the data cannot be deserialized, an empty slice is returned along with an error value if available, as follows:

```
func fetchPackageData(url string) ([]pkgData, error) {
        var packages []pkgData
        r, err := http.Get(url)
        if err != nil {
                return nil, err
        }
        defer r.Body.Close()
        if r.Header.Get("Content-Type") != "application/json" {
                return packages, nil
        }
        data, err := io.ReadAll(r.Body)
        if err != nil {
```

```
            return packages, err
    }
    err = json.Unmarshal(data, &packages)
    return packages, err
}
```

Our fictional package server also has a web backend by which it serves the package data as an HTML page viewable via a browser. Hence, in the client code, we only attempt to deserialize the response body if it is identified as JSON data. The `Content-Type` HTTP header is used to detect whether the response body is `application/json` or not.

The response headers are available via the `Header` field—a map of type `[string]` `[]string` in the response object. Hence, to obtain the value for a specific header, we use the `Get()` method specifying the header key as the parameter.

If the header value of `Content-Type` is not found to be `application/json`, the empty slice is returned along with a `nil` error. You may design your application to return an error here, of course. If the `Content-Type` was found to be `application/json`, we read the body using the `io.ReadAll()` function. After some standard error handling, we then call the `json.Unmarshal()` function specifying the data to deserialize and the object to deserialize it into.

Listing 3.3 shows a complete implementation of the `pkgquery` package:

Listing 3.3: Querying data from the package server

```go
// chap3/pkgquery/pkgquery.go

package pkgquery

import (
        "encoding/json"
        "io"
        "net/http"
        "time"
)

type pkgData struct {
        Name    string `json:"name"`
        Version string `json:"version"`
}

// TODO Insert definition of fetchPackageData() from earlier
```

Create a new directory, `chap3/pkgquery`, and initialize a module inside it:

```
$ mkdir -p chap3/pkgquery
$ cd chap3/pkgquery
$ go mod init github.com/username/pkgquery
```

Save Listing 3.3 as a file, `pkgquery.go`.

How do we test the functionality of the `pkgquery` package? We could implement a `main` package and query an implementation of the fictional package server. Alternatively, we can implement a test HTTP server that returns JSON formatted data as introduced earlier. The function, `startTestPackageServer()`, implements such a server:

```
func startTestPackageServer() *httptest.Server {
        pkgData := `[
{"name": "package1", "version": "1.1"},
{"name": "package2", "version": "1.0"}
]`
        ts := httptest.NewServer(
                http.HandlerFunc(
                        func(w http.ResponseWriter, r *http.Request) {
                                w.Header().Set("Content-Type", "application/
json")
                                fmt.Fprint(w, pkgData)
                })))
        return ts
}
```

With the test server implemented, Listing 3.4 shows the complete test function.

Listing 3.4: Test for `pkgquery`

```
// chap3/pkgquery/pkgquery_test.go

package pkgquery

import (
        "fmt"
        "net/http"
        "net/http/httptest"
        "testing"
        "time"
)

// TODO Insert definition of startTestPackageServer() from earlier

func TestFetchPackageData(t *testing.T) {
        ts := startTestPackageServer()
        defer ts.Close()
        packages, err := fetchPackageData(ts.URL)
        if err != nil {
                t.Fatal(err)
        }
```

```
        if len(packages) != 2 {
                t.Fatalf("Expected 2 packages, Got back: %d", len(packages))
        }
}
```

We start the test HTTP server by calling the `startTestPackageServer()` function. Then we create an HTTP client object by calling the `createHTTPClientWithTimeout()` function. Next, we call the `fetchPackageData()` function passing as parameters the HTTP client object, `client`, and the URL to request.

Finally, we send a GET request to the server, which will return the JSON package data. We then assert that a `nil` error is returned, and we obtain a slice with two elements corresponding to two `pkgData` objects.

Save Listing 3.4 into a new file, `pkgquery_test.go`, in the same directory as `pkgquery.go`. Run the test:

```
$ go test -v
=== RUN    TestFetchPackageData
--- PASS: TestFetchPackageData (0.00s)
PASS
ok          github.com/practicalgo/code/chap3/pkgquery/          0.511s
```

As expected, the test passes. In a more practical scenario, you may be writing an HTTP client to consume data from someone else's server. Thus, you would have to perform the following key steps:

1. Look up the JSON API schema for the third-party server.

2. Construct the data structures to deserialize the response data into.

3. Use step 1 to implement test servers so that you can implement fully testable HTTP clients.

You saw how you can make use of the `Content-Type` header to decide whether to deserialize the data or to ignore it. You could also use it to decide whether the data is readable in the terminal or whether you would need to read it using dedicated software, such as an image viewer or a PDF (Portable Document Format) reader. In Exercise 3.2, you will implement support in the `http` sub-command so that the user has the ability to write the data downloaded into a file.

EXERCISE 3.2: WRITE DOWNLOADED DATA TO A FILE   Implement a new option for the `http` sub-command, `-output`, which will take a file path as an option. When the option is specified, the downloaded data will be written to the file instead of being shown on the terminal.

Sending Data

Let's consider the package server again. We have seen how we can view existing package data by making an HTTP GET request. Now let's say that we want to add new package data to the server. Creating or registering a new package to the server involves sending the package itself (a `.tar.gz` file) and some metadata (a name and version). For simplicity, let's assume that the package server doesn't have any state management in place, and it responds to all requests successfully if it contains the expected data in the right format. The HTTP protocol when following the *REST* specifications allows us to use a POST, PUT, or PATCH request to send data to a server. The POST method is usually the one that is used to create a new resource. To use the POST method to register a new package, we will do the following:

1. Make a HTTP POST request using the `Post` function defined in the `net/http` package, `http.Post(url, contentType, packagePayload)`. `url` is the URL to send the POST request to, `contentType` is a string containing the value to identify the value of the `Content-Type` header for the request, and finally, `packagePayload` is an object of type `io.Reader` containing the request body that we want to send.

2. The key step here will be to send both the binary package data and the metadata in a single request body. The HTTP `Content-Type` header `multipart/form-data` will come in handy here.

First, let's see how we can send a POST request containing only the metadata as a JSON body. Then we will develop it further to send the package data as well as the metadata in a `multipart/form-data` request.

Recall the JSON format that we came up with to describe a package:

```
{"name": "package1", "version": "1.1"}
```

We will use the same JSON format to describe the metadata when registering a new package. The result of a package registration is sent back as a JSON body as well, and it appears as follows:

```
{"id":"package1-1.1"}
```

The corresponding struct type would be

```
type pkgRegisterResult struct {
        ID string `json:"id"`
}
```

First, let's look at how we can send a JSON body using an HTTP POST request:

```go
func registerPackageData(url string, data pkgData) (pkgRegisterResult, error) {
        p := pkgRegisterResult{}
        b, err := json.Marshal(data)
        if err != nil {
                return p, err
        }
        reader := bytes.NewReader(b)
        r, err := client.Post(url, "application/json", reader)
        if err != nil {
                return p, err
        }
        defer r.Body.Close()

        // TODO Handle response from the server
        ...
}
```

The function takes two parameters—url is the HTTP server URL that we will send the request to, and data is an object of type pkgData that we will serialize as JSON and will be sent as the request body.

We create an object, p, of type pkgRegisterResult, which will be populated and returned as a response when a package registration is successful.

In the function, we first use the Marshal() function defined in the encoding/json package to convert the pkgData object into a byte slice—the JSON object we will send as the request body. The struct tags we defined earlier will be used as the JSON object keys. Given a pkgData object, {"Name":"package1", "Version":"1.0"}, the Marshal() function will automatically convert it to a byte slice corresponding to the JSON encoded string: {"name":"package1"," version":"1.0"}. We will then create an io.Reader object for this byte slice using the NewReader() function from the bytes package. Once we have the io .Reader object, reader, created, we will then call the Post() function as http .Post(url, "application/json", reader).

If we get a non-nil error, we return the empty pkgRegisterResult object and the error object, err. If we get a successful response of the server, we then read the body and deserialize the body into the pkgRegisterResult response object:

```go
func registerPackageData(url string, data pkgData) (pkgRegisterResult,
error) {
        // Send the request to the server as earlier
        respData, err := io.ReadAll(r.Body)
        if err != nil {
```

```
                return p, err
        }
        if r.StatusCode != http.StatusOK {
                return p, errors.New(string(respData))
        }
        err = json.Unmarshal(respData, &p)
        return p, err
}
```

If we didn't get a successful response indicated by an HTTP 200 status code, we return an error object containing the response body. Else, we unmarshal the response and return the `pkgRegisterResult` object, `p`, and any unmarshalling error, `err`.

We will create a new package, `pkgregister`, for our package registration code. Listing 3.5 shows the complete code.

Listing 3.5: Register a new package

```go
// chap3/pkgregister/pkgregister.go
package pkgregister

import (
        "bytes"
        "encoding/json"
        "io/ioutil"
        "net/http"
        "time"
)

type pkgData struct {
        Name    string `json:"name"`
        Version string `json:"version"`
}

type pkgRegisterResult struct {
        Id string `json:"id"`
}

func registerPackageData(url string, data pkgData) (pkgRegisterResult, error) {
        p := pkgRegisterResult{}
        b, err := json.Marshal(data)
        if err != nil {
                return p, err
        }
        reader := bytes.NewReader(b)
        r, err := client.Post(url, "application/json", reader)
        if err != nil {
                return p, err
        }
```

```
        defer r.Body.Close()
        respData, err := io.ReadAll(r.Body)
        if err != nil {
                return p, err
        }
        if r.StatusCode != http.StatusOK {
                return p, errors.New(string(respData))
        }
        err = json.Unmarshal(respData, &p)
        return p, err
}
```

Create a new directory, chap3/pkgregister, and initialize a module inside it:

```
$ mkdir -p chap3/pkgregister
$ cd chap3/pkgregister
$ go mod init github.com/username/pkgregister
```

Save Listing 3.5 as a new file, pkgregister.go. How do we test that this all works? We will adopt an approach similar to the one we used in the last section and implement a test server that behaves like our real package server:

1. Implement an HTTP handler function to handle POST requests.

2. Perform an unmarshal operation to convert the incoming JSON body to a pkgData object.

3. If there is an error in the unmarshal operation, or the pkgData object has an empty Name or Version, an HTTP 400 error is returned to the client.

4. Construct an artificial package ID by concatenating the Name and Version with a - separating them.

5. Create a pkgRegisterResult object specifying the ID constructed in the previous step.

6. Marshal the object, set the content header to application/json, and return the marshalled result as a string as response.

Next you can see the implementation of the above steps as a separate *handler function* as follows. (You will learn more about handler functions in Chapter 5.)

```
func packageRegHandler(w http.ResponseWriter, r *http.Request) {
        if r.Method == "POST" {
                // Incoming package data
                p := pkgData{}

                // Package registration response
                d := pkgRegisterResult{}
                defer r.Body.Close()
                data, err := io.ReadAll(r.Body)
```

```
                        if err != nil {
                                http.Error(w, err.Error(),
http.StatusInternalServerError)
                                return
                        }
                        err = json.Unmarshal(data, &p)
                        if err != nil || len(p.Name) == 0 || len(p.Version) == 0 {
                                http.Error(w, "Bad Request", http.StatusBadRequest)
                                return
                        }
                        d.ID = p.Name + "-" + p.Version
                        jsonData, err := json.Marshal(d)
                        if err != nil {
                                http.Error(w, err.Error(),
http.StatusInternalServerError)
                                return
                        }
                        w.Header().Set("Content-Type", "application/json")
                        fmt.Fprint(w, string(jsonData))
                } else {
                        http.Error(w, "Invalid HTTP method specified",
http.StatusMethodNotAllowed)
                        return
                }
        }
}
```

You can find the implementation of the test functions in Listing 3.6. We have two tests—one to test the happy path through which we are sending the expected package registration data to the package server and the other through which we are sending an empty JSON body.

Listing 3.6: Test for registering a new package

```go
// chap3/pkgregister/pkgregister_test.go
package pkgregister

// TODO Insert definition of packageRegHandler() from above
func startTestPackageServer() *httptest.Server {
        ts := httptest.NewServer(http.HandlerFunc(packageRegHandler))
        return ts
}

func TestRegisterPackageData(t *testing.T) {
        ts := startTestPackageServer()
        defer ts.Close()
        p := pkgData{
                Name:    "mypackage",
                Version: "0.1",
        }
```

```
        resp, err := registerPackageData(ts.URL, p)
        if err != nil {
                t.Fatal(err)
        }
        if resp.ID != "mypackage-0.1" {
                t.Errorf("Expected package id to be mypackage-0.1, Got: %s",
resp.ID)
        }
}

func TestRegisterEmptyPackageData(t *testing.T) {
        ts := startTestPackageServer()
        defer ts.Close()
        p := pkgData{}
        resp, err := registerPackageData(ts.URL, p)
        if err == nil {
                t.Fatal("Expected error to be non-nil, got nil")
        }
        if len(resp.ID) != 0 {
                t.Errorf("Expected package ID to be empty, got: %s", resp.ID)
        }
}
```

Save Listing 3.6 into a new file, pkgregister_test.go, in the same directory as Listing 3.5. Run the tests:

```
% go test -v
=== RUN    TestRegisterPackageData
--- PASS: TestRegisterPackageData (0.00s)
=== RUN    TestRegisterEmptyPackageData
--- PASS: TestRegisterEmptyPackageData (0.00s)
PASS
ok          github.com/practicalgo/code/chap3/pkgregister          0.540s
```

In this section, you learned how to send and receive JSON data by using marshalling and unmarshalling techniques. You will now apply that to implement support for POST requests in the mync http sub-command (Exercise 3.3).

EXERCISE 3.3: ENHANCE THE HTTP SUB-COMMAND TO SEND POST REQUESTS WITH A JSON BODY   The http sub-command only supports the GET method. Your task in this exercise is to enhance it to be able to make POST requests and accept a JSON body either from the command line as a string via the -body option or from a file via the -body-file option. For testing, you can implement a test HTTP server as we have done in this section.

The techniques you learned in this section to process JSON data also apply to another popular data format, XML, as supported via the `encoding/xml` package. Coming back to registering a new package, we have seen how we can send the package name and version as a JSON formatted body. However, we haven't seen how we can send the package data as well along with that. Let's see how we can use the `multipart/form-data` content type.

Working with Binary Data

The `multi-part/formdata` HTTP content type allows you to send a body containing key value pairs such as `name=package1` and `version=1.1` as well as other data such as contents of a file as part of an HTTP request. As you can imagine, there is a fair bit of work involved in creating this body before you can send it off to the server.

Before we learn how to create a `multipart/form-data` message, let's look at what such a message looks like:

```
--91f7de347fb9749c83cea1d596e52849fb0a95f6698459e2baab1e6c1e22
Content-Disposition: form-data; name="name"

mypackage
--91f7de347fb9749c83cea1d596e52849fb0a95f6698459e2baab1e6c1e22
Content-Disposition: form-data; name="version"

0.1
--91f7de347fb9749c83cea1d596e52849fb0a95f6698459e2baab1e6c1e22
Content-Disposition: form-data; name="filedata"; filename="mypackage-
0.1.tar.gz"
Content-Type: application/octet-stream

data
--91f7de347fb9749c83cea1d596e52849fb0a95f6698459e2baab1e6c1e22--
```

The above message contains three parts. Each part is separated by a boundary string, which is generated randomly. Here the boundary string is the line starting with `91f....`. The dashes are part of the HTTP/1.1 specifications.

The first part of the message contains a form field with the name `"name"` and value `mypackage`.

The second part contains a field with the name `"version"` and the value `0.1`.

The third part of the message contains a field with the name `"filedata"`, a field with the name `filename`, the value `"mypackage-0.1.tar.gz"`, and the value of the field itself, `data`. The third part also contains a `Content-Type` specification specifying the content to be `application/octet-stream`, which is indicative of non-plaintext data. Of course, the string `data` is a placeholder for real non-plaintext data, such as an image or a PDF file.

The standard library's `mime/multipart` package defines all of the necessary types and methods to read and write multipart bodies. Let's see how we can create a multipart body containing a package and the metadata:

1. Initialize an object, `mw`, of type `multipart.NewWriter()` with a byte buffer.

2. Use the method `mw.CreateFormField("name")` to create a form field object, `fw`, with the field name `"name"`.

3. Use the `fmt.Fprintf()` method to write the bytes representing the value of the field to the writer, `mw`.

4. Repeat the steps 2 and 3 for each form field that you want to create.

5. Use the method `mw.CreateFormFile("filedata", "filename.ext")` to create a field, `fw`, with the field name `filedata` to store the contents of a file, whose name is given by `"filename.ext"`.

6. Use the `io.Copy()` method to copy the bytes from the file to the writer, `mw`.

7. If you want to send multiple files, use the same field name (`"filedata"`), but use different filenames.

8. Finally, call the `mw.Close()` method.

Let's see how this looks in a real implementation. First, we will update the `pkgData` struct to account for the package contents:

```
type pkgData struct {
        Name     string
        Version  string
        Filename string
        Bytes    io.Reader
}
```

The `Filename` field will store the filename of the package, and the `Bytes` field is an `io.Reader` pointing to the opened file.

Given an object of type `pkgData`, we can create a multipart message as shown in Listing 3.7 to "package" the data.

Listing 3.7: Creating a multipart message

```
// chap3/pkgregister-data/form_body.go
package pkgregister

import (
        "bytes"
        "io"
        "mime/multipart"
)
```

```
func createMultiPartMessage(data pkgData) ([]byte, string, error) {
        var b bytes.Buffer
        var err error
        var fw io.Writer

        mw := multipart.NewWriter(&b)

        fw, err = mw.CreateFormField("name")
        if err != nil {
                return nil, "", err
        }
        fmt.Fprintf(fw, data.Name)

        fw, err = mw.CreateFormField("version")
        if err != nil {
                return nil, "", err
        }
        fmt.Fprintf(fw, data.Version)

        fw, err = mw.CreateFormFile("filedata", data.Filename)
        if err != nil {
                return nil, "", err
        }
        _, err = io.Copy(fw, data.Bytes)
        err = mw.Close()
        if err != nil {
                return nil, "", err
        }

        contentType := mw.FormDataContentType()
        return b.Bytes(), contentType, nil

}
```

The `multipart.NewWriter()` method is called with a new `bytes.Buffer` object, `b`, to create a new `multipart.Writer` object, `mw`. Then, we call the `CreateFormField()` method twice to create the `name` and `version` fields. Next, we call the `CreateFormFile()` method to insert the file contents. Finally, we retrieve the related bytes of the corresponding `multipart/form-data` message by calling the `b.Bytes()` method and return it. We also return two other values, the content type obtained via the `FormDataContentType()` method of the `multipart.Writer` object and a `nil` error object.

Create a new directory, `chap3/pkgregister-data`, and initialize a module inside it:

```
$ mkdir -p chap3/pkgregister-data
$ cd chap3/pkgregister-data
$ go mod init github.com/username/pkgregister-data
```

Next, save Listing 3.7 as a new file, `form_body.go`.

Next, let's look at the `registerPackageData()` function, which will call the `createMultiPartMessage()` function to create the `multipart/form-data` payload:

```go
type pkgRegisterResult struct {
        Id       string `json:"id"`
        Filename string `json:"filename"`
        Size     int64  `json:"size"`
}

func registerPackageData(
        client *http.Client, url string, data pkgData,
) (pkgRegisterResult, error) {

        p := pkgRegisterResult{}
        payload, contentType, err := createMultiPartMessage(data)
        if err != nil {
                return p, err
        }
        reader := bytes.NewReader(payload)
        r, err := http.Post(url, contentType, reader)
        if err != nil {
                return p, err
        }
        defer r.Body.Close()
        respData, err := io.ReadAll(r.Body)
        if err != nil {
                return p, err
        }
        err = json.Unmarshal(respData, &p)
        return p, err
}
```

We call the `createMultiPartMessage()` function, which gives us the multipart data, `payload`, and the content type, `contentType`. Then, we construct an `io.Reader` object to read from `payload` and send the HTTP POST request by calling the `http.Post()` function. After that we read the response and unmarshal it into the `pkgRegisterResult` object, p. Note that we have added two new fields to the `pkgRegisterResult` struct to refer to the filename of the package and the size of the file that was sent. This will allow us to validate that the server side read the data successfully.

Listing 3.8 shows the complete implementation of the `pkgregister` package, which uses the `createMultiPartMessage()` function.

Listing 3.8: Package registration using multipart message

```go
// chap3/pkgregister-data/pkgregister.go
package pkgregister
```

```
import (
        "bytes"
        "encoding/json"
        "io"
        "net/http"
        "time"
)

type pkgData struct {
        Name     string
        Version  string
        Filename string
        Bytes    io.Reader
}

type pkgRegisterResult struct {
        ID       string `json:"id"`
        Filename string `json:"filename"`
        Size     int64  `json:"size"`
}

// TODO Insert definition of registerPackageData() from earlier

func createHTTPClientWithTimeout(d time.Duration) *http.Client {
        client := http.Client{Timeout: d}
        return &client
}
```

Save Listing 3.8 as a new file, `pkgregister.go`, in the same directory as Listing 3.7. To test this package, we will implement a test server that accepts the package registration data sent in a `multipart/form-data` message and sends a JSON encoded response back. The key functionality of this test server will be implemented by the `ParseMultipartForm()` method defined for the `http` `.Request` object. This method will parse a request body, which has been encoded as a `multipart/form-data` message, and it automatically makes the embedded data available via an object of type `multipart.Form`, defined in the `mime/multipart` package. This type is defined as follows:

```
type Form struct {
    Value map[string][]string
    File  map[string][]*FileHeader
}
```

The `Value` field is a map object containing the form field names as keys and their values as a slice of strings. A form can have multiple values for a field name. The `File` field is a map whose key consists of the field name, such as `filedata`, and the slice of objects represents the data about each file as a `FileHeader` object. The `FileHeader` type is defined in the same package as follows:

```
type FileHeader struct {
    Filename string
    Header    textproto.MIMEHeader
    Size      int64
}
```

The field names are fairly self-explanatory. So, an example object of this type would be as follows:

```
{"Filename": "package1.tar.gz", "Header": map[string]string{"Content-
Type":"application/octet-stream"}, "Size": "200"}
```

How do we get the file data then? The `FileHeader` object defines the `Open()` method, which returns a `File` object. This can then be used to read the data stored in the file. Let's see the server handler function:

```
func packageRegHandler(w http.ResponseWriter, r *http.Request) {
        if r.Method == "POST" {
            d := pkgRegisterResult{}
            err := r.ParseMultipartForm(5000)
            if err != nil {
                http.Error(
                        w, err.Error(), http.StatusBadRequest,
                )
                return
            }
            mForm := r.MultipartForm
            f := mForm.File["filedata"][0]
            d.ID = fmt.Sprintf(
                "%s-%s", mForm.Value["name"][0], mForm.Value["version"]
[0],
            )
            d.Filename = f.Filename
            d.Size = f.Size
            jsonData, err := json.Marshal(d)
            if err != nil {
                http.Error(w, err.Error(), http.StatusInternalServerError)
                    return
            }
            w.Header().Set("Content-Type", "application/json")
            fmt.Fprint(w, string(jsonData))
        } else {
```

```
                http.Error(
                        w, "Invalid HTTP method specified",
        http.StatusMethodNotAllowed,
                )
                return
        }
}
```

Right off the bat we see the call to the key function: `err := r.ParseMulti partForm(5000)`, with `5000` being the maximum number of bytes that will be buffered in memory. If we get a non-`nil` error, we return with an HTTP 400 Bad Request error. If not, we proceed to access the parsed form data in the request's `MultipartForm` attribute. Subsequently, we access the form's key-value pairs and the file data, construct a package ID, set the `Filename` and `Size` attributes, marshal the data as a JSON object, and send it back as response. Okay, that's it—time to look at the test function so that we can test our code. Listing 3.9 shows the test function.

Listing 3.9: Test for package registration with multipart message

```go
// chap3/pkgregister-data/pkgregister_test.go
package pkgregister
import (
        "encoding/json"
        "fmt"
        "net/http"
        "net/http/httptest"
        "strings"
        "testing"
        "time"
)

// TODO Insert definition of packageHandler() from above


func startTestPackageServer() *httptest.Server {
        ts := httptest.NewServer(http.HandlerFunc(packageHandler))
        return ts
}

func TestRegisterPackageData(t *testing.T) {
        ts := startTestPackageServer()
        defer ts.Close()
        p := pkgData{
                Name:     "mypackage",
                Version:  "0.1",
                Filename: "mypackage-0.1.tar.gz",
                Bytes:    strings.NewReader("data"),
        }
```

```
        pResult, err := registerPackageData(ts.URL)
        if err != nil {
                t.Fatal(err)
        }

        if pResult.ID != fmt.Sprintf("%s-%s", p.Name, p.Version) {
                t.Errorf(
                        "Expected package ID to be %s-%s, Got: %s",
p.Name, p.Version, pResult.ID,
                )
        }
        if pResult.Filename != p.Filename {
                t.Errorf(
                        "Expected package filename to be %s, Got: %s",
p.Filename, pResult.Filename,
                )
                if pResult.Size != 4 {
                        t.Errorf("Expected package size to be 4, Got: %d",
pResult.Size)
                }
        }
}
```

Save Listing 3.9 as a new file, pkgregister_test.go, in the same directory
as Listing 3.8 and run the test:

```
$ go test -v
=== RUN    TestRegisterPackageData
--- PASS: TestRegisterPackageData (0.00s)
PASS
ok         github.com/practicalgo/code/chap3/pkgregister-data      0.728s
```

The mime/multipart package contains everything that you need to read and
write binary data in HTTP request bodies. You learned how to use it to send a
file from your client application. In the final exercise, you are going to implement support for sending files in the mync command-line application.

**EXERCISE 3.4: ENHANCE THE HTTP SUB-COMMAND TO SEND
POST REQUESTS WITH FORM UPLOAD**   Enhance the http sub-
command to implement a new option -upload, which will allow sending files as
part of POST requests with or without any other data. The option, -form-data, can
be used to specify any other parameters to be sent along with the file. An example
invocation would be as follows:

```
$ mync http POST -upload /path/to/file.pdf -form-data name=Package1
-form-data version=1.0.
```

Summary

You started the chapter by learning how to download data from an HTTP URL. You then learned how you can process bytes of data in the response by deserializing them into a data structure that your program recognizes. Next, you learned how to perform the reverse operation and serialize a data structure into bytes to be sent as an HTTP request body. Finally, you learned how to send and receive arbitrary files as HTTP request bodies using `multipart/form-data` messages. All throughout, you wrote tests to verify the behavior of your client.

In the next chapter, you will learn a number of advanced techniques that you will find useful when building production-ready HTTP clients.

Advanced HTTP Clients

In this chapter, you are going to do a deep dive into writing HTTP clients. The last chapter focused on performing various operations over HTTP. This chapter focuses on the techniques used to write HTTP clients that are robust and scale well. You will learn to enforce time-outs in your clients, create client middleware, and explore connection pooling. Let's get started!

Using a Custom HTTP Client

Let's consider the data downloader application that you wrote in the previous chapter. It's rare that the server with which you are communicating always behaves as expected. In fact, it's not just the server, but any of the other networking devices that your application's request is passing through may behave suboptimally. How does our client fare then? Let's find out.

Downloading from an Overloaded Server

Let's consider the following function, which will create an always overloaded test HTTP server where every response is delayed by 60 seconds:

```
func startBadTestHTTPServer() *httptest.Server {
        ts := httptest.NewServer(
```

```
                      http.HandlerFunc(
                          func(w http.ResponseWriter, r *http.Request) {
                              time.Sleep(60 * time.Second)
                              fmt.Fprint(w, "Hello World")
                      }))
          return ts
    }
```

Note the call to the `Sleep()` function from the `time` package. This will introduce a delay of 60 seconds before it sends a response to the client. Listing 4.1
shows a test function that sends an HTTP GET request to the bad test server.

Listing 4.1: Test for `fetchRemoteResource()` function with a bad server

```
// chap4/data-downloader/fetch_remote_resource_bad_server_test.go
package main

import (
        "fmt"
        "net/http"
        "net/http/httptest"
        "testing"
        "time"
)

// TODO: Insert definition of startBadTestHTTPServer() from above

func TestFetchBadRemoteResource(t *testing.T) {
        ts := startBadTestHTTPServer()
        defer ts.Close()

        data, err := fetchRemoteResource(ts.URL)
        if err != nil {
            t.Fatal(err)
        }

        expected := "Hello World"
        got := string(data)

        if expected != got {
            t.Errorf("Expected response to be: %s, Got: %s", expected, got)
        }
}
```

Create a new directory, `chap4/data-downloader`. Copy all the files from `chap3/`
`data-downloader`. Update the `go.mod` file to be as follows:

```
module github.com/username/chap4/data-downloader

go 1.16
```

Next, save Listing 4.1 into a new file, `fetch_remote_resource_bad_server_test.go`, and run the tests:

```
$ go test -v
=== RUN    TestFetchBadRemoteResource
--- PASS: TestFetchBadRemoteResource (60.00s)
=== RUN    TestFetchRemoteResource
--- PASS: TestFetchRemoteResource (0.00s)
PASS
ok         github.com/practicalgo/code/chap4/data-downloader    60.142s
```

As you can see, the `TestFetchBadRemoteResource` test now takes 60 seconds to run. In fact, if the bad server were to sleep for 600 seconds before it sent back the response, our client code in `fetchRemoteResource()` (Listing 3.1) would wait the same amount of time. As you can imagine, this will lead to a very bad user experience.

We touched upon the topic of introducing robustness into our applications in Chapter 2. Next, let's see how we can improve our data downloader function so that it doesn't wait for the response if the server takes more than a specified duration.

The answer to making our data downloader wait only for a specified maximum period of time is to use a custom HTTP client. When we used the `http.Get()` function, we implicitly used a default HTTP client that is defined in the `net/http` package. The default client is made available via the variable `DefaultClient`, which is created as `var DefaultClient = &Client{}`. The `Client` struct here is defined in the `net/http` package, and it is in its fields that we can configure various properties of the HTTP client. The one we are going to look at now is the `Timeout` field. Later on, we will look at another field, `Transport`.

The value of `Timeout` is a `time.Duration` object, which essentially specifies the maximum duration that the client will be allowed to connect to the server, make the request, and read the response. If not specified, there is no maximum duration enforced and hence the client will simply wait until the server replies or either the client or server terminates the connection.

To create an HTTP client with a 100-millisecond time-out, for example, you will use the following statement:

```
client := http.Client{Timeout: 100 * time.Millisecond}
```

This statement will allow up to 100 milliseconds for an HTTP request made via the client to complete. Using the custom client, the `fetchRemoteResource()` function will now appear as follows:

```
func fetchRemoteResource(
        client *http.Client, url string,
) ([]byte, error) {
```

```
        r, err := client.Get(url)
        if err != nil {
                return nil, err
        }
        defer r.Body.Close()
        return io.ReadAll(r.Body)
}
```

Note how instead of calling the http.Get() function, we call the Get() method of the http.Client object that was passed to the fetchRemoteResource() function. Listing 4.2 shows the complete application code.

Listing 4.2: The data downloader application with a custom HTTP client with time-out

```go
// chap4/data-downloader-timeout/main.go
package main

import (
        "fmt"
        "io"
        "net/http"
        "os"
        "time"
)

// TODO Insert definition of fetchRemoteResource() from above

func createHTTPClientWithTimeout(d time.Duration) *http.Client {
        client := http.Client{Timeout: d}
        return &client
}

func main() {
        if len(os.Args) != 2 {
                fmt.Fprintf(
                        os.Stdout,
                        "Must specify a HTTP URL to get data from",
                )
                os.Exit(1)
        }
        client := createHTTPClientWithTimeout(15 * time.Second)
        body, err := fetchRemoteResource(client, os.Args[1])
        if err != nil {
                fmt.Fprintf(os.Stdout, "%#v\n", err)
                os.Exit(1)
        }
        fmt.Fprintf(os.Stdout, "%s\n", body)
}
```

We define a new function, `createHTTPClientWithTimeout()`, to create a custom HTTP client with a specified time-out, duration of type `time.Duration`. In the `main()` function, we create a custom `client` with 15 seconds as the configured time-out and then call the `fetchRemoteResource()` function, passing the client and the specified URL. Save Listing 4.2 as a new file, `main.go`, in a new directory, `chap4/data-downloader-timeout` and initialize a module inside it:

```
$ mkdir -p chap4/data-downloader-timeout
$ go mod init github.com/username/data-downloader-timeout
```

Instead of trying to think of a bad HTTP server to test the time-out behavior, let's do so by writing a test.

Testing the Time-Out Behavior

We can update the test in Listing 4.1 to be as shown in Listing 4.3.

Listing 4.3: Test for `fetchRemoteResource()` function with a bad server

```go
// chap4/data-downloader-timeout/fetch_remote_resource_bad_server_old_
test.go
package main

import (
        "fmt"
        "net/http"
        "net/http/httptest"
        "testing"
        "time"
)

func startBadTestHTTPServerV1() *httptest.Server {
        // TODO Insert the function body of startBadTestHTTPServer from
earlier
}

func TestFetchBadRemoteResourceV1(t *testing.T) {
        ts := startBadTestHTTPServerV1()
        defer ts.Close()

        client := createHTTPClientWithTimeout(200 * time.Millisecond)
        _, err := fetchRemoteResource(client, ts.URL)
        if err == nil {
                t.Fatal("Expected non-nil error")
        }

        if !strings.Contains(err.Error(), "context deadline exceeded") {
```

```
        t.Fatalf("Expected error to contain: context deadline
    exceeded, Got: %v", err.Error())
        }
}
```

The `startBadTestHTTPServer()` (in Listing 4.1) has been renamed to `startBadTestHTTPServerV1()`. The other key changes are as follows:

1. We create a `http.Client` object by calling the `createHTTPClientWithTimeout()` function. The object is then passed on to the `fetchRemoteResource()` function call.
2. We assert that the error message contains a specific substring indicating that the client closed its end of the connection to the server.

Save Listing 4.3 as a new file, `fetch_remote_resource_bad_server_old_test.go`, in the same directory as Listing 4.2. Run the test:

```
$ go test -v
=== RUN   TestFetchBadRemoteResourceV1
2020/11/15 15:17:43 httptest.Server blocked in Close after 5 seconds,
waiting for connections:
    *net.TCPConn 0xc00018a040 127.0.0.1:65227 in state active
FAIL
exit status 1
FAIL      github.com/practicalgo/code/chap4/data-downloader-timeout/   60.357s
```

From the test output, you can see that the test function fails but the execution takes slightly more than 60 seconds. You also see messages being logged from `httptest.Server`. What's happening here? Recall that (in both Listing 4.1 and Listing 4.3), we have a call to the `Close()` function of the test server in a deferred call. After the test function completes execution, the `Close()` function is called to shut down the test server cleanly. However, this function checks to see if there are any active requests before shutting down. Hence, it only returns when the bad handler returns the response after 60 seconds. What can we do about it?

We can rewrite our bad test server as follows:

```
func startBadTestHTTPServerV2(shutdownServer chan struct{}) *httptest.Server {
        ts := httptest.NewServer(http.HandlerFunc(func(w http.ResponseWriter, r
*http.Request) {
                <-shutdownServer
                fmt.Fprint(w, "Hello World")
        }))
        return ts
}
```

We create an unbuffered channel, `shutdownServer`, and pass it to the function `startBadTestHTTPServerV2()` as a parameter. Then, inside the handler of the test server, we attempt to read from the channel, thus creating a potential point of infinitely blocking the execution of the handler. Since we do not care about the value inside the channel, the type of the channel is the empty struct, `struct{}`. Replacing the `time.Sleep()` statement via a blocking read operation allows us to have more control over the test server operation as we will see next.

We will update our test function code to be as shown in Listing 4.4.

Listing 4.4: Test for `fetchRemoteResource()` function with the updated bad server

```go
// chap4/data-downloader-timeout/fetch_remote_resource_bad_server_test.go
package main

import (
        "fmt"
        "net/http"
        "net/http/httptest"
        "strings"
        "testing"
        "time"
)

// TODO Insert definition of startBadTestHTTPServerV2 from above

func TestFetchBadRemoteResourceV2(t *testing.T) {
        shutdownServer := make(chan struct{})
        ts := startBadTestHTTPServerV2(shutdownServer)
        defer ts.Close()
        defer func() {
                shutdownServer <- struct{}{}
        }()

        client := createHTTPClientWithTimeout(200 * time.Millisecond)
        _, err := fetchRemoteResource(client, ts.URL)
        if err == nil {
                t.Log("Expected non-nil error")
                t.Fail()
        }

        if !strings.Contains(err.Error(), "context deadline exceeded") {
                t.Fatalf("Expected error to contain: context deadline
exceeded, Got: %v", err.Error())
        }

}
```

There are three key changes in the above function:

1. We create an unbuffered channel, `shutdownServer`, of type `struct{}`—an empty struct type.

2. We create a new deferred call to an anonymous function that writes an empty struct value to the channel. This call comes *after* the ts.Close() call so that it is called before the ts.Close() function.

3. We call the startBadTestHTTPServerV2() function with this channel as a parameter.

Save Listing 4.4 as a new file, fetch_remote_resource_bad_server_test.go, in the same directory as Listing 4.3 and run the following test:

```
$ go test -run TestFetchBadRemoteResourceV2 -v
=== RUN    TestFetchBadRemoteResourceV2
--- PASS: TestFetchBadRemoteResourceV2 (0.20s)
PASS
ok          github.com/practicalgo/code/chap4/data-downloader-timeout
0.335s
```

The test only runs for 0.2 seconds (or 200 milliseconds), which is the time-out that we configured for the test client. What happens now? Before the test function completes execution, the anonymous function is first called, which writes an empty struct value to the shutdownServer channel. This unblocks the test server handler. Hence, when the Close() method is called, it shuts down the test server and returns successfully. This completes the test function execution.

Configuring a time-out for your HTTP client is one way to configure your HTTP client. You will next learn another aspect that you may want to configure—what happens when the server responds with a redirect?

Configuring the Redirect Behavior

When a server issues an HTTP redirect, the default HTTP client automatically and silently *follows* the redirect up to 10 times, after which it terminates. What if you wanted to change that to, say, follow no redirects at all, or at least let you know that it is following a redirect? This can be achieved by configuring another field in the http.Client object, CheckRedirect. When set to a function following a specific signature, this object will be invoked when there is a decision to be made regarding a redirect. You can then choose to implement your custom logic there. Let's see an example of how such a function can be implemented:

```
func redirectPolicyFunc(req *http.Request, via []*http.Request) error {
        if len(via) >= 1 {
                return errors.New("stopped after 1 redirect")
        }
        return nil
}
```

The custom function to implement the redirect policy must satisfy the following signature:

```
func (req *http.Request, via []*http.Request) error
```

The first argument, req, is the request to follow the redirect response that it got back from the server; the slice, via, contains the requests that have been made so far, with the oldest request (your original request) the first element of this slice. This can be better illustrated via the following steps:

1. The HTTP client sends a request to the original URL, url.
2. The server responds with a redirect to, say, url1.
3. redirectPolicyFunc is now called with (url1, []{url}).
4. If the function returns a nil error, it will follow the redirect and send a new request for url1.
5. If there is another redirect to url2, the redirectPolicyFunc function is then called with (url2, []{url, url1}).
6. Steps 3, 4, and 5 are repeated until the redirectPolicyFunc returns a non-nil error.

Thus, if you were to use the redirectPolicyFunc() as the custom redirect policy function, it will not allow a redirect at all. How do you hook it up with a custom HTTP client? You can do so as follows:

```
func createHTTPClientWithTimeout(d time.Duration) *http.Client {
        client := http.Client{Timeout: d, CheckRedirect: redirectPolicyFunc}
        return &client
}
```

Let's see this custom redirect in action. Listing 4.5 shows a data downloader that exits with an error if it sees that a redirect has been requested by the server.

Listing 4.5: A data downloader that exits if there is a redirect attempt

```
// chap4/data-downloader-redirect/main.go
package main

import (
        "errors"
        "fmt"
        "io"
        "net/http"
        "os"
        "time"
)
```

```go
func fetchRemoteResource(client *http.Client, url string) ([]byte, error) {
        r, err := client.Get(url)
        if err != nil {
                return nil, err
        }
        defer r.Body.Close()
        return io.ReadAll(r.Body)
}

// TODO Insert definition of redirectPolicyFunc from above

// TODO Insert definition of createHTTPClientWithTimeout from above

func main() {
        if len(os.Args) != 2 {
                fmt.Fprintf(os.Stdout, "Must specify a HTTP URL to get
data from")
                os.Exit(1)
        }
        client := createHTTPClientWithTimeout(15 * time.Second)
        body, err := fetchRemoteResource(client, os.Args[1])
        if err != nil {
                fmt.Fprintf(os.Stdout, "%v\n", err)
                os.Exit(1)
        }
        fmt.Fprintf(os.Stdout, "%s\n", body)
}
```

Create a new directory, chap4/data-downloader-redirect, and initialize a module inside it:

```
$ mkdir -p chap4/data-downloader-redirect
$ cd chap4/data-downloader-redirect
$ go mod init github.com/username/data-downloader-redirect
```

Next, save Listing 4.5 as a new file, main.go, in it. Build it and run it passing http://github.com as the first argument; you will see the following:

```
$ go build -o application
$ ./application http://github.com
Get "https://github.com/": Attempted redirect to https://github.com/
```

If you try it with the https URL directly, https://github.com, you will see that it dumps the content of the page. Great.

You have learned how to customize the redirect behavior of a http.Client object which leads us nicely to our first exercise of this chapter, Exercise 4.1.

EXERCISE 4.1: ENHANCE THE HTTP SUB-COMMAND TO ALLOW CONFIGURING REDIRECT BEHAVIOR   In the last chapter, you implemented the HTTP GET functionality in the `mync http` sub-command. Add a Boolean flag, `-disable-redirect`, to the sub-command so that the user has the ability to disable the default redirect behavior.

Customizing Your Requests

You have seen how to create a custom HTTP client. Furthermore, you have used methods such as `Get()` on the `Client` object to make requests. Similarly, you would use the `Post()` method to make POST requests. Underneath, the client is using a default request object of type `http.Request` that is defined in the standard library. Now you will learn how to customize this object.

Customizing the `http.Request` object allows you to add headers or cookies or simply set the time-out for a request. Creating a new request is done by calling the `NewRequest()` function. The `NewRequestWithContext()` function has the exact same purpose, but additionally it allows passing a context to the request. In your applications, it is thus preferred to use the `NewRequestWithContext()` function to create new requests:

```
req, err := http.NewRequestWithContext(ctx, "GET", url, nil)
```

The first argument to the function is the context object. The second parameter is the HTTP method, for which we are creating the request. `url` points to the URL of the resource to which we are going to make the request. The last argument is an `io.Reader` object pointing to the body, which in the case of a GET request will in most cases likely be empty. To create a request for a POST request, with `io.Reader` and `body`, you would make the following function call:

```
req, err := http.NewRequestWithContext(ctx, "POST", url, body)
```

Once you create the request object, you can then add a header using the following:

```
req.Header().Add("X-AUTH-HASH", "authhash")
```

This will add a header X-AUTH-HASH with the value `authhash` to the outgoing request. You can encapsulate this logic in a function that creates a custom `http.Request` object for making a GET request with headers:

```
func createHTTPGetRequest(ctx context.Context, url string, headers
map[string]string) (*http.Request, error) {
        req, err := http.NewRequestWithContext(ctx, "GET", url, nil)
        if err != nil {
                return nil, err
        }
```

```
        for k, v := range headers {
                req.Header.Add(k, v)
        }
        return req, err
}
```

To create a custom HTTP client and send a customized GET request, you will then write something like this:

```
client := createHTTPClientWithTimeout(20 * time.Millisecond)
ctx, cancel := context.WithTimeout(context.Background(), 15*time.
Millisecond)
defer cancel()

req, err := createHTTPGetRequest(ctx, ts.URL+"/api/packages", nil)
resp, err := client.Do(req)
```

The client's Do() method is used to send a custom HTTP request encapsulated by the http.Request object, req.

A key point of interest in the above code is the two time-out configurations—one at the client level and the other at the request level. Of course, ideally your request time-out (if using the time-out context) should be lower than your client time-out else your client may time out before your request times out.

Customization of a request object is not limited to adding headers. You can add cookies and basic auth information as well. This leads us nicely to Exercise 4.2.

EXERCISE 4.2: ENHANCE THE HTTP SUB-COMMAND TO ALLOW ADDING HEADERS AND BASIC AUTH CREDENTIALS   Enhance the http sub-command to recognize a new option, -header, which will add a header to the outgoing request. This option may be specified multiple times to add multiple headers, as in the following example:

```
-header key1=value1 -header key1=value2
```

Enhance the http sub-command to define a new option, -basicauth. You should be able to add basic auth information to requests using the SetBasicAuth() method of the request object, as in this example:

```
-basicauth user:password
```

Implementing Client Middleware

The term *middleware* (or *interceptor*) is used for custom code that can be configured to be executed along with the core operation in a network server or client application. In a server application, it would be code that gets executed when the server is processing a request from a client. In a client application, it would be code that is executed when making an HTTP request to a server application.

In the following sections, you will see how to implement custom middleware by customizing the client object. First, let's look into a specific field in the Client struct type, Transport.

Understanding the RoundTripper Interface

The http.Client struct defines a field, Transport, as follows:

```
type Client struct {
    Transport RoundTripper

    // Other fields
}
```

The RoundTripper interface defined in the net/http package defines a type that will carry an HTTP request from the client to the remote server and carry the response back to the client. The only method this type needs to implement is RoundTrip():

```
type RoundTripper interface {
    RoundTrip(*Request) (*Response, error)
}
```

When the Transport object is not specified while creating a client, a predefined object of type Transport, DefaultTransport is used. It is defined as follows (with fields omitted):

```
var DefaultTransport RoundTripper = &Transport{
    // fields omitted
}
```

The Transport type defined in the net/http package implements the RoundTrip() method as required by the RoundTripper interface. It is responsible for creating and managing the underlying Transmission Control Protocol (TCP) connections over which an HTTP request-response transaction occurs:

1. You create a Client object.
2. You create an HTTP Request.
3. The HTTP request is then "carried over" the RoundTripper implementation (for instance, over a TCP connection) to the server, and the response is carried back.
4. If you make more than one request with the same client, step 2 and step 3 will be repeated.

To implement a client middleware, we will write a custom type that will encapsulate the `DefaultTransport`'s `RoundTripper` implementation. Let's see how.

A Logging Middleware

The first middleware that you will write will log a message before sending a request. It will log another message when a response is received. We first define a `LoggingClient` struct type with a `*log.Logger` field:

```
type LoggingClient struct {
        log *log.Logger
}
```

To satisfy the `RoundTripper` interface, we implement the `RoundTrip()` method:

```
func (c LoggingClient) RoundTrip(
        r *http.Request,
) (*http.Response, error) {
        c.log.Printf(
                "Sending a %s request to %s over %s\n",
                r.Method, r.URL, r.Proto,
        )
        resp, err := http.DefaultTransport.RoundTrip(r)
        c.log.Printf("Got back a response over %s\n", resp.Proto)

        return resp, err
}
```

When the `RoundTrip()` method of our `RoundTripper` implementation is called, we do the following:

1. Log the outgoing request, r.
2. Call the `DefaultTransport`'s `RoundTrip()` method passing it the outgoing request, r.
3. Log the response and error returned by the `RoundTrip()` call.
4. Return the response and error returned.

Great. You have defined you own custom `RoundTripper`. Now how do you use it? Create a `Client` object, and set the `Transport` field to a `LoggingClient` object:

```
myTransport := LoggingClient{}
client := http.Client{
        Timeout:   10 * time.Second,
        Transport: &myTransport,
}
```

Listing 4.6 is a modified version of the data downloader program (Listing 4.2) to use this custom RoundTripper implementation.

Listing 4.6: A data downloader with a custom logging middleware

```go
// chap4/logging-middleware/main.go

package main

import (
        "fmt"
        "log"
        "net/http"
        "os"
        "time"
)


type LoggingClient struct {
        log *log.Logger
}

// TODO Insert definition of RoundTrip() function from above

func main() {
        if len(os.Args) != 2 {
                fmt.Fprintf(os.Stdout, "Must specify a HTTP URL to get
data from")
                os.Exit(1)
        }
        myTransport := LoggingClient{}
        l := log.New(os.Stdout, "", log.LstdFlags)
        myTransport.log = l

        client := createHTTPClientWithTimeout(15 * time.Second)
        client.Transport = &myTransport

        body, err := fetchRemoteResource(client, os.Args[1])
        if err != nil {
                fmt.Fprintf(os.Stdout, "%#v\n", err)
                os.Exit(1)
        }
        fmt.Fprintf(os.Stdout, "Bytes in response: %d\n", len(body))
}
```

The key modifications are highlighted. First, we create a new LoggingClient object. Then, we create a new log.Logger object by calling the log.New() function. The first parameter to the function is a io.Writer object to which the logs will be written. Here we use `os.Stdout`. The second parameter to the function is the prefix string to add to each log statement—an empty string is specified here. The last parameter to the function is a flag—text to prefix to each log line. Here we use `log.LstdFlags`, which will display the date and time. We then assign the `log.Logger` object to the `l` field of the `myTransport` object. Finally, we set `client.Transport` to `&myTransport`.

Create a new subdirectory, `chap4/logging-middleware`, and save Listing 4.6 to a new file, `main.go`. Build and run it, passing an HTTP server URL as a command-line argument:

```
$ go build -o application
$ ./application https://www.google.com
2020/11/25 22:03:40 Sending a GET request to https://www.google.com over
HTTP/1.1
2020/11/25 22:03:40 Got back a response over HTTP/2.0
Bytes in response: 13583
```

As expected, the logging statements appear first and then the response is printed. You would use a similar custom `RoundTripper` implementation to emit metrics such as request latency or non-200 errors. What else could you use a custom `RoundTripper` for? You could write a `RoundTripper` implementation to look up the request in a cache automatically, for example, to avoid making the call at all.

There are two things you will have to keep in mind while implementing a custom `RoundTripper`:

1. The `RoundTripper` must be implemented with the assumption that there may be more than one instance of it running at any given point of time. Hence, if you are manipulating any data structure, the data structure must be concurrency safe.

2. The `RoundTripper` must not mutate the request or response or return an error.

Add a Header to All Requests

Let's look an example of implementing a middleware that will add one or more HTTP headers to every outgoing request. You will likely end up needing this functionality in various scenarios—sending an authentication header, propagating a request ID, and so on.

We will first define a new type for our middleware:

```
type AddHeadersMiddleware struct {
        headers map[string]string
}
```

The headers field is a map containing the HTTP headers that we want to add in the RoundTripper implementation:

```
func (h AddHeadersMiddleware) RoundTrip(r *http.Request) (*http.Response,
error) {
        reqCopy := r.Clone(r.Context())
        for k, v := range h.headers {
                reqCopy.Header.Add(k, v)
        }
        return http.DefaultTransport.RoundTrip(reqCopy)
}
```

This middleware will modify the original request by adding headers to it. However, instead of modifying it in place, we clone the request using the Clone() method and add headers to it. We then call the DefaultTransport's RoundTrip() implementation with the new request.

Listing 4.7 shows the implementation of an HTTP client with this middleware.

Listing 4.7: An HTTP client with a middleware to add custom headers

```
// chap4/header-middleware/client.go
package client

import (
        "net/http"
)

type AddHeadersMiddleware struct {
        headers map[string]string
}

// TODO Insert RoundTrip() implementation from above

func createClient(headers map[string]string) *http.Client {
        h := AddHeadersMiddleware{
                headers: headers,
        }
        client := http.Client{
                Transport: &h,
        }
        return &client
}
```

Create a new directory, chap4/header-middleware, and initialize a module inside it:

```
$ mkdir -p chap4/header-middleware
$ cd chap4/header-middleware
$ go mod init github.com/username/header-middleware
```

Next, save Listing 4.7 as a new file, `client.go`. To test whether the specified headers get added to the outgoing request, we will write a test server that sends back the request headers as response headers:

```
func startHTTPServer() *httptest.Server {
        ts := httptest.NewServer(http.HandlerFunc(func(w http.ResponseWriter,
r *http.Request) {
                for k, v := range r.Header {
                        w.Header().Set(k, v[0])
                }
                fmt.Fprint(w, "I am the Request Header echoing program")
        }))
        return ts
}
```

Listing 4.8 shows the test function using the above test server.

Listing 4.8: Test for middleware to add headers

```
// chap4/header-middleware/header_middleware_test.go

package client

import (
        "fmt"
        "net/http"
        "net/http/httptest"
        "testing"
)

// TODO Insert startHTTPServer() from above

func TestAddHeaderMiddleware(t *testing.T) {
        testHeaders := map[string]string{
                "X-Client-Id": "test-client",
                "X-Auth-Hash": "random$string",
        }
        client := createClient(testHeaders)

        ts := startHTTPServer()
        defer ts.Close()

        resp, err := client.Get(ts.URL)
        if err != nil {
                t.Fatalf("Expected non-nil [AU: "nil"—JA] error, got: %v", err)
        }
```

```
        for k, v := range testHeaders {
            if resp.Header.Get(k) != testHeaders[k] {
                t.Fatalf("Expected header: %s:%s, Got: %s:%s", k, v, k,
testHeaders[k])
            }
        }

}
```

We create a map, `testHeaders`, to specify the headers that we want to add to the outgoing request. The `createClient()` function is then called, passing the map as a parameter. As you can see in Listing 4.7, this function also creates an `AddHeaderMiddleware` object, which is then set as the `Transport` when creating the `http.Client` object.

Save Listing 4.8 into a new file, `header_middleware_test.go`, in the same directory as Listing 4.7 and run the test:

```
% go test -v
=== RUN    TestAddHeaderMiddleware
--- PASS: TestAddHeaderMiddleware (0.00s)
PASS
ok          github.com/practicalgo/code/chap4/header-middleware      0.472s
```

While writing this middleware, you have seen an example of how to create a client middleware that modifies the incoming request by creating a copy, modifying it, and then handing it over to the `DefaultTransport`.

Exercise 4.3 will give you an opportunity to implement a middleware to log request latencies.

> **EXERCISE 4.3: A MIDDLEWARE FOR CALCULATING REQUEST LATENCIES**   Similar to how we implemented the logging middleware, implement a middleware to log how long a request took to complete (in seconds). The logging should be implemented as an optional feature in the `mync http` subcommand, which will be enabled using the `-report` option.

Connection Pooling

In the previous section, you learned that the default `RoundTripper` interface implementation carries an HTTP request to the remote server and then carries the response back.

One of the underlying steps that occurs is that a new TCP connection is established for your request. This connection setup process is expensive. You may not notice it when you are making a single request. However, when you are making HTTP requests as part of a service-oriented architecture, for example, you are usually making multiple requests in a short time window—either in bursts or continuously. In such a scenario, it is expensive to perform the TCP connection setup for every request. Hence, the net/http library maintains a *connection pool* where it automatically tries to reuse an existing TCP connection to send your HTTP requests.

Let's first understand how the connection pooling works and then learn how we can configure the pool itself. The net/http/httptrace package will help us delve into the internals of connection pooling. One of the things that you can see using this package is whether a connection is being reused or whether a new one was established for making an HTTP request. In fact, it does a bit more, but we will only use it to demonstrate connection reuse.

Consider the following function definition,

```
createHTTPGetRequestWithTrace():
func createHTTPGetRequestWithTrace(ctx context.Context, url string)
(*http.Request, error) {
        req, err := http.NewRequestWithContext(ctx, "GET", url, nil)
        if err != nil {
                return nil, err
        }
        trace := &httptrace.ClientTrace{
                DNSDone: func(dnsInfo httptrace.DNSDoneInfo) {
                        fmt.Printf("DNS Info: %+v\n", dnsInfo)
                },
                GotConn: func(connInfo httptrace.GotConnInfo) {
                        fmt.Printf("Got Conn: %+v\n", connInfo)
                },
        }
        ctxTrace := httptrace.WithClientTrace(req.Context(), trace)
        req = req.WithContext(ctxTrace)
        return req, err

}
```

The httptrace.ClientTrace struct type defines functions that will be called when certain events in a request's life cycle happen. We are interested in two events here:

- The DNSDone event happens when the DNS lookup for a hostname has completed.

- The GotConn event happens when a connection has been obtained to send the request over.

To define a function to be called when the DNSDone event happens, we specify the function as the value of the field when creating the struct object. This function must accept an object of type httptrace.DNSDoneInfo as a parameter and not return any value. Similarly, we define a function to be called when the GotConn event happens. This function must accept an object of type httptrace .GotConnInfo as a parameter and not return any value. In both the functions, we print the object to standard output.

Once the ClientTrace object, trace, is created, you create a new context by calling the httptrace.WithClientTrace() function, passing it the original request's context and the trace object.

Finally, you create a new Request object by adding this context as its context and return this object.

Listing 4.9 is a program that uses the createHTTPGetRequestWithTrace() function to send an HTTP GET request to a remote server.

Listing 4.9: A program to illustrate connection pooling

```go
// chap4/connection-pool-demo/main.go
package main

import (
        "context"
        "fmt"
        "log"
        "net/http"
        "net/http/httptrace"
        "os"
        "time"
)

func createHTTPClientWithTimeout(d time.Duration) *http.Client {
        client := http.Client{Timeout: d}
        return &client
}

// TODO Insert definition of createHTTPGetRequestWithTrace() function
from earlier

func main() {
        d := 5 * time.Second
        ctx := context.Background()
        client := createHTTPClientWithTimeout(d)

        req, err := createHTTPGetRequestWithTrace(ctx, os.Args[1])
        if err != nil {
                log.Fatal(err)
        }
```

```
    for {
            client.Do(req)
            time.Sleep(1 * time.Second)
            fmt.Println("--------")
    }
}
```

Note that we have an infinite loop that sends the same request with a sleep of 1 second in between. You will have to terminate the program using the Ctrl+C key combination.

Create a new directory, chap4/connection-pool-demo, and initialize a module inside it:

```
$ mkdir -p chap4/connection-pool-demo
$ cd chap4/ connection-pool-demo
$ go mod init github.com/username/connection-pool-demo
```

Next, save Listing 4.9 as a new file, main.go. Build and run it specifying an HTTP server hostname as a command-line argument.

```
$ go build -o application
$./application https://www.google.com
DNS Info: {Addrs:[{IP:216.58.200.100 Zone:} {IP:2404:6800:4006:810::2004
Zone:}] Err:<nil> Coalesced:false}
TLS HandShake Start
TLS HandShake Done
Got Conn: {Conn:0xc000096000 Reused:false WasIdle:false IdleTime:0s}
Resp protocol: "HTTP/2.0"
--------
Got Conn: {Conn:0xc000096000 Reused:true WasIdle:true IdleTime:1.003019133s}
Resp protocol: "HTTP/2.0"
--------
Got Conn: {Conn:0xc000096000 Reused:true WasIdle:true IdleTime:1.005444969s}
Resp protocol: "HTTP/2.0"
--------
Got Conn: {Conn:0xc000096000 Reused:true WasIdle:true IdleTime:1.005472933s}
Resp protocol: "HTTP/2.0"
^C
```

First, we see the output from the DNSDone function. The details are not important, but we notice that we only see it once. Then we see the output from the GotConn function. We can see that it is called every time that we make the request. We also see that for the first request, the value of Reused was false. The value of WasIdle was false, and IdleTime was 0s. This tells us that for the first request, a new connection was created and it wasn't idle. For all subsequent requests, we see that the values of these fields are true, true and a non-zero idle time—close to 1 second. Of course, 1 second is the duration that we sleep between requests, and hence we see that as the time for which a connection was in the idle state.

Configuring the Connection Pool

Connection pooling saves the cost of creating a new connection for every request. However, in real life there are various kinds of issues about which you would want to be aware that may happen with the default connection pool.

First up, let's consider the DNS lookup for your hostname. Since, in most cases, you are dealing with hostnames rather than IP addresses directly, it is worth considering that DNS records can change—especially in the dynamic world of cloud-hosted services. Now, what happens to our connection pool implementation when an underlying IP address with which a connection was established is no longer available? Will the connection pool implementation realize that it is no longer available and create a new connection to the new IP address? Yes, in fact, it will. When you attempt to make a new request, a new connection will be opened to the remote server.

Next, let's consider the situation where you always want to force a new connection to be made for every HTTP request when 10 seconds or more has expired. To do so, you will create a Transport object as follows:

```
transport := &http.Transport{
        IdleConnTimeout: 10 * time.Second,
}
Then, create a client as follows:
client := http.Client{
        Timeout:    d,
        Transport: transport,
}
```

With the above configuration, an idle connection will be kept around for a maximum of 10 seconds. Hence, if you make two requests using a client with an interval of 11 seconds in between them, the second request will trigger a new connection to be created.

Besides the time-out, you can also configure two other related parameters:

MaxIdleConns: This represents the maximum number of idle connections to be kept in the pool. By default, this is 0, which enforces no upper limit.

MaxIdleConnsPerHost: This is the maximum number of idle connections per host. By default, this is set to the value of DefaultMaxIdleConnsPerHost, which as of Go 1.16 is 2.

Exercise 4.4 asks you to implement support for configuring the connection pooling behavior in mync's http sub-command.

> **EXERCISE 4.4: SUPPORT FOR ENABLING CONNECTION POOLING**
>
> **BEHAVIOR**   Add a new option, `-num-requests`, which accepts an integer as a value to the `http` sub-command, which will make the same request to a server the specified number of times.
>
> Add a new option, `-max-idle-conns`, which accepts an integer to configure the maximum number of idle connections in the pool.

Summary

We started this chapter by learning how to implement time-out behavior in an HTTP client. Time-out behavior, together with request contexts, allows you to enforce an upper bound on how long the client will wait for a request to complete. This allows you to implement robustness in your application. Then you learned about implementing client middleware, which allows you to develop a variety of functionality in your applications—logging, exporting metrics, and caching, for example. Finally, you learned about connection pooling and how you can configure it.

In the next chapter, you will continue your journey in the world of writing HTTP applications where you will learn to write scalable and robust HTTP server applications.

## CHAPTER 5

Building HTTP Servers

In this chapter, you will dive into the basics of writing HTTP servers. You will learn how handler functions work, discover more about processing requests, and study how to read and write streaming data. You scratched the surface of these topics a bit in the previous chapter. Now it's time to dive in.

Your First HTTP Server

The net/http package gives us the building blocks for writing an HTTP server. A server running on your computer, available at http://localhost:8080, would process a request as follows (see Figure 5.1):

1. The server receives a client request at a certain path, say /api.

2. The server checks if it can handle this request.

3. If the answer is yes, the server calls a handler function to process the request and return the response. If not, it returns an HTTP error as a response to the client.

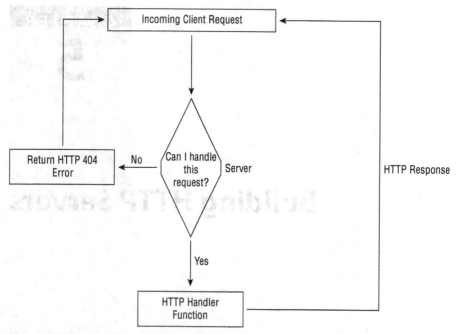

Figure 5.1: Request processing by an HTTP server

Listing 5.1 shows the simplest web server that you can write.

Listing 5.1: A basic HTTP server

```
// chap5/basic-http-server/server.go
package main

import (
        "log"
        "net/http"
        "os"
)

func main() {
        listenAddr := os.Getenv("LISTEN_ADDR")
        if len(listenAddr) == 0 {
                listenAddr = ":8080"
        }

        log.Fatal(http.ListenAndServe(listenAddr, nil))
}
```

The ListenAndServe() function in the net/http package starts an HTTP server at a given network address. It is a good idea to make this address configurable.

Thus, in the `main()` function, the following lines check if the `LISTEN_ADDR` environment variable has been specified, and if not, it defaults to `":8080"`:

```
listenAddr := os.Getenv("LISTEN_ADDR")
if len(listenAddr) == 0 {
        listenAddr = ":8080"
}
```

The `Getenv()` function defined in the `os` package looks for the value of an environment variable. If an environment variable `LISTEN_ADDR` is found, its value is returned as a string. If no such environment variable exists, an empty string is returned. The `len()` function thus can be used to check if the `LISTEN_ADDR` environment variable has been specified or not. The default value of `":8080"` means that the server will listen on all network interfaces on the port 8080. If you wanted the server only to be reachable on the computer where your application is running, you would set the environment variable `LISTEN_ADDR` to `"127.0.0.1:8080"` and then start the application.

Next, we call the `ListenAndServe()` function specifying the address to listen on (`listenAddr`) and the *handler* for the server. We will specify `nil` as the value for the handler and thus our function call to `ListenAndServe` is as follows:

```
log.Fatal(http.ListenAndServe(listenAddr, nil))
```

The `ListenAndServe()` returns immediately with an error value if there is an error when starting the server. If the server has started correctly, the function only returns when the server is terminated. In either case, the `log.Fatal()` function will log the error value if there is one.

Create a new directory, `chap5/basic-http-server`, and initialize a module inside it:

```
$ mkdir -p chap5/basic-http-server
$ cd chap5/basic-http-server
$ go mod init github.com/username/basic-http-server
```

Next, save Listing 5.1 as a new file, `server.go`. Build and run it:

```
$ go build -o server
$ ./server
```

Great, your first HTTP server is running!

How do you make requests to it? You can use your Internet browser, but we will use the `curl` command-line HTTP client. Start a new terminal session, and run the following:

```
$ curl -X GET localhost:8080/api
404 page not found
```

We make an HTTP GET request to our HTTP server at the path /api, and we get back a 404 page not found response. This means that the server receives the incoming request, looks at it, and returns an HTTP 404 response, meaning that it cannot find the resource, /api, which we are requesting. Next, let's see how we can fix this. To terminate the server, press Ctrl+C in the terminal where you started the server.

Setting Up Request Handlers

When you specified nil as the second argument to the ListenAndServe() function, you asked the function to use the default handler, DefaultServeMux. It serves as the default registry of how to handle a request path. DefaultServeMux is an object of type ServeMux defined in the http package. It is a global object, which means that any other code you may be using in your application can also register handler functions with your server. There is absolutely nothing preventing a third-party rogue package from exposing an HTTP path without you even knowing it (see Figure 5.2). Additionally, as with any other global object, this opens your code up to unforeseen concurrency bugs and non-robust behavior. Hence, we are not going to use it. Instead, we will create a new ServeMux object:

```
mux := http.NewServeMux()
```

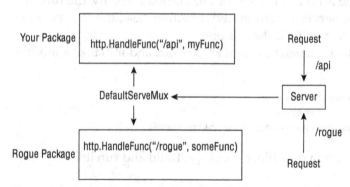

Figure 5.2: Any package can register a handler function with the DefaultServeMux object.

The ServeMux object contains, among other fields, a map data structure containing a mapping of the paths that you want your server to handle and the corresponding handler function. To solve the HTTP 404 issue that you encountered in the previous section, you will need to register a special function called a *handler function* for the path. You may recall that we wrote handler functions to implement test servers in Chapter 3, "Writing HTTP Clients." Let's now study them in detail.

Handler Functions

A handler function must be of type `func(http.ResponseWriter, *http.Request)`, where `http.ResponseWriter` and `http.Request` are two `struct` types defined in the `net/http` package. The object of type `http.Request` represents the incoming HTTP request and the `http.ResponseWriter` object is used to write back the response to the client making the request. The following is an example of a handler function:

```
func apiHandler(w http.ResponseWriter, r *http.Request) {
        fmt.Fprintf(w, "Hello World")
}
```

Note that there is no need to return from this function. Anything you write to the `ResponseWriter` object, `w`, is sent back as a response to the client. Here we send the string `"Hello World"` using the `fmt.Fprintf()` function. Note how the `Fprintf()` function, which we used to write a string to the standard output, is equally applicable to send back a string as an HTTP response thanks to the power of the `io.Writer` interface. Of course, you could use any other library function here instead of `fmt.Fprintf()` – `io.WriteString()`, for example.

You are not limited to writing strings as responses. For example, you can use the `w.Write()` method directly to send a slice of bytes as the response.

Once you have written your handler function, the next step is to register it with the `ServeMux` object that you created earlier:

```
mux.HandleFunc("/api", apiHandler)
```

This creates a mapping in the `mux` object so that any request for the `/api` path is now handled by the `apiHandler()` function. Finally, we will call the `ListenAndServe()` function specifying this `ServeMux` object:

```
err := http.ListenAndServe(listenAddr, mux)
```

Listing 5.2 shows the updated code for the HTTP server. It registers handler functions for two paths: `/api` and `/healthz`.

Listing 5.2: An HTTP server using a dedicated `ServeMux` object

```
// chap5/http-serve-mux/server.go
package main

import (
        "fmt"
        "log"
        "net/http"
        "os"
)
```

```go
func apiHandler(w http.ResponseWriter, req *http.Request) {
        fmt.Fprintf(w, "Hello, world!")
}

func healthCheckHandler(w http.ResponseWriter, req *http.Request) {
        fmt.Fprintf(w, "ok")
}

func setupHandlers(mux *http.ServeMux) {
        mux.HandleFunc("/healthz", healthCheckHandler)
        mux.HandleFunc("/api", apiHandler)

}

func main() {

        listenAddr := os.Getenv("LISTEN_ADDR")
        if len(listenAddr) == 0 {
                listenAddr = ":8080"
        }

        mux := http.NewServeMux()
        setupHandlers(mux)

        log.Fatal(http.ListenAndServe(listenAddr, mux))

}
```

We create a new ServeMux object, mux, via a call to the NewServeMux() function and then call the setupHandlers() function passing mux as a parameter. In the setupHandlers() function, we call the HandleFunc() functions to register the two paths and their corresponding handler functions. Then we call the ListenAndServe() function passing mux as the handler to use.

Create a new directory, chap5/http-serve-mux, and initialize a new module inside it:

```
$ mkdir -p chap5/http-serve-mux
$ cd chap5/http-serve-mux
$ go mod init github.com/username/http-serve-mux
```

Next, save Listing 5.2 as a new file, server.go. Build and run the server:

```
$ go build -o server
$ ./server
```

From a new terminal, use curl to make HTTP requests to the server. For the /api and /healthz paths, you will see the Hello, world! and ok responses respectively.

```
$ curl localhost:8080/api
Hello, world!

$ curl localhost:8080/healthz
ok
```

However, if you make a request to any other path, such as /healtz/ or the / path, you will get a "404 page not found":

```
$ curl localhost:8080/healtz/
404 page not found

$ curl localhost:8080/
404 page not found
```

When a request comes in and a handler function is available to handle it, the handler function is executed in a separate goroutine. Once the processing completes, the goroutine is terminated (see Figure 5.3).

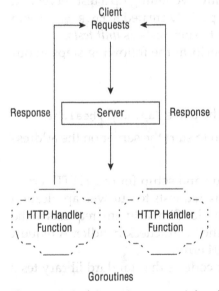

Figure 5.3: Each incoming request is handled by a new goroutine.

This ensures that the server is capable of processing multiple requests concurrently. As a desirable side effect, this also means that if there is a runtime exception while handling one request, this doesn't have any effect on other requests being handled.

Testing Your Server

Manually testing your server by invoking requests via `curl` works for preliminary testing and validation of your server, but it doesn't scale. Thus, you need to build an automated procedure for testing your server so that these tests are easy to run. The Go standard library's `httptest` package (imported as `net/http/httptest`) provides us with various features to enable writing tests for HTTP servers. Broadly speaking, there are two categories of HTTP application behavior that you will end up testing:

- Server startup and initialization behavior
- Handler function logic—user-facing functionality of your web applications

The tests we write for the first category of behavior will rely on starting a test HTTP server and then making HTTP requests against the test server. We will refer to such tests as *integration tests*.

The tests for the second category will not involve setting up a test server and will instead call the handler functions with specially created `http.Request` and `http.ResponseWriter` objects. We will refer to such tests as *unit tests*.

Consider our server in Listing 5.2. We perform the following steps in our `main()` function:

1. We create a new `ServeMux` object.
2. We register the handler functions for the paths `/api` and `/healthz`.
3. We call the `ListenAndServe()` function to start the server on the address specified in the `listenAddr`.

The above steps comprise the initialization and setup for our HTTP server. For steps 1 and 2, we want to verify that any requests to our web application for the `/api` path is forwarded to the `/api` handler. Similarly, any requests to the `/healthz` handler should be forwarded to the healthcheck handler. A request to any other path should return an HTTP 404 error.

We don't have to test step 3 of the server code as the standard library tests already cover it.

Next, consider the two HTTP handler functions in Listing 5.2. The `apiHandler` function responds with the text `"Hello, world!"` as a response. The `healthcheckHandler` function responds with the text `"ok"` as a response. Thus, our tests should verify that these handler functions are returning the expected text as responses.

Enough theory. Listing 5.3 shows the test function to test our server and handler functions.

Listing 5.3: A test for the HTTP server

```go
// chap5/http-serve-mux/server_test.go
package main

import (
        "io"
        "log"
        "net/http"
        "net/http/httptest"
        "testing"
)

func TestServer(t *testing.T) {

        tests := []struct {
                name     string
                path     string
                expected string
        }{
                {
                        name:     "index",
                        path:     "/api",
                        expected: "Hello, world!",
                },
                {     name:     "healthcheck",
                      path:     "/healthz",
                      expected: "ok",
                },
        }

        mux := http.NewServeMux()
        setupHandlers(mux)

        ts := httptest.NewServer(mux)
        defer ts.Close()

        for _, tc := range tests {
                t.Run(tc.name, func(t *testing.T) {
                        resp, err := http.Get(ts.URL + tc.path)
                        respBody, err := io.ReadAll(resp.Body)
                        resp.Body.Close()
                        if err != nil {
                                log.Fatal(err)
                        }
                        if string(respBody) != tc.expected {
                                t.Errorf(
                                        "Expected: %s, Got: %s",
                                        tc.expected, string(respBody),
                                )
                        }
                })
        }
```

We first define a slice of test cases. Each test case consists of a name of the config, path for the request we want to make, and the expected response—all string values.

We create a new `ServeMux` object by calling the `NewServeMux()` function. Then it invokes the `setupHandlers()` function with the created `mux` object.

Next it calls the `NewServer()` function to start the server passing the created `ServeMux` object, `mux`. This function returns a `httptest.Server` object containing the details of the server that is started. Of our interest here is the URL field that contains the IP address and port combination of the server. Usually, this is `http://127.0.0.1:<some port>`.

The deferred call to the `ts.Close()` function ensures that the server is shut down cleanly before the test function exits.

For each of the test configurations, we make an HTTP GET request using the `http.Get()` function. The server path is constructed by concatenating the `ts.URL` and `path` strings. We then verify if the returned response body matches the expected response body.

Save Listing 5.3 as a new file, `server_test.go`, in the same directory as Listing 5.2. Run the test:

```
$ go test -v
=== RUN    TestServer
=== RUN    TestServer/index
=== RUN    TestServer/healthcheck
--- PASS: TestServer (0.00s)
    --- PASS: TestServer/index (0.00s)
    --- PASS: TestServer/healthcheck (0.00s)
PASS
ok          github.com/practicalgo/code/chap5/http-serve-mux          0.577s
```

Great. You have written your first HTTP server and learned how to test it using the facilities provided by the `httptest` package. In upcoming chapters, you will learn techniques to test more complicated server applications. Next, you will learn more about the `Request` struct.

The Request Struct

An HTTP handler function accepts two parameters: a value of type `http.ResponseWriter` and a pointer to a value of type `http.Request`. The pointer object of `http.Request` type (defined in the `net/http` package) describes the incoming request. You will recall from Chapter 4, "Advanced HTTP Clients," that this type is also used to define an outgoing HTTP request. `Request` is a `struct` type defined in the `net/http` package. Some key fields and methods in the `struct` type that are relevant in the context of an incoming request are described next.

Method

This is a `string` and its value represents the HTTP method of the request being processed. In the previous section, you used this field for dedicated handler functions for different types of HTTP requests.

URL

This is a pointer to a value of type `url.URL` (defined in the `net/url` package) representing the path of the request. It is best understood with an example. Let's say that we make a request to our HTTP server using the URL `http://example .com/api/?name=jane&age=25#page1`. When a handler function processes this request, the URL object's fields are set as follows:

- Path: `/api/`
- RawQuery: `name=jane&age=25`
- Fragment: `page1`

To access a specific individual query parameter and its value, you use the `Query()` method. This method returns an object of type `Values`, which is defined as `map[string][]string`. For the above URL, calling the `Query()` method will return the following:

```
url.Values{"age":[]string{"25"}, "name":[]string{"jane"}}
```

If a query parameter is specified more than once, for example `http://example .com/api/?name=jane&age=25&name=john#page1`, the returned value of `Query()` would be

```
url.Values{"age":[]string{"25"}, "name":[]string{"jane", "john"}}"
```

If your server accepts an HTTP basic authentication, then the request URL would be of the form `http://user:pass@example.com/api/?name=jane&age= 25&name=john`. In this case, the `User` field contains the details of the username and password specified in the request. To obtain the username, call the `User()` method. To obtain the password, call the `Password()` method.

NOTE   The URL struct contains other fields, but the above are the only ones that are relevant in the context of processing a request.

Proto, ProtoMajor, and ProtoMinor

These fields identify the HTTP protocol over which the client and server are communicating. Proto is a string identifying the protocol and the version (for example "HTTP /1.1"). ProtoMajor and ProtoMinor are integers identifying the major and minor protocol versions, respectively. For HTTP /1.1, the major and minor protocol versions are both 1.

Header

This is a map of type map[string][]string, and it contains the incoming headers.

Host

This is a string containing the hostname and port combination (example.com:8080) or the IP address and port combination (127.0.0.1:8080) that the client used to make a request to the server.

Body

This is a value of type io.ReadCloser, which refers to the request body. You can use any function that understands the io.Reader interface to read the body. For example, you could use the io.ReadAll() method to read the entire request body. The function returns a byte slice containing the entire request body, and then you can process the slice of bytes according to your handler's functionality requirements. In the next section, you will see how to process the request body without reading the entire body into memory.

A related field is ContentLength, which is the maximum number of bytes available to be read from the request body.

Form, PostForm

If your handler function is processing an HTML form submission, then instead of reading the body directly, you can call the ParseForm() method of the request object. Calling this method will read the request and populate the Form and PostForm fields with the submitted form data. These two fields get populated differently based on the type of HTTP request method used to submit the form. If a GET request was used to submit the form, only the Form field gets populated. If a POST, PUT, or PATCH method was used to submit the form, the PostForm field gets populated. Both the fields are of type url.Values (defined in the net/url package), which is defined as map[string][]string. Hence, to access any form field, you would use the same approach as you would for accessing a key in a map.

MultipartForm

If you are handling form uploads containing `multipart/form-encoded` data, usually containing files (as you did in Chapter 3), calling the `ParseMultipartForm()` method will read the request body and populate the `MultipartForm` field with the submitted data. The field is of type `multipart.Form` (defined in the `mime/multipart`) package:

```
type Form struct {
    Value map[string][]string
    File  map[string][]*FileHeader
}
```

`Value` contains the submitted form text fields and `File` contains the data related to the submitted files. The key in this map is the form field name, and the data related to the file is stored in an object of type `FileHeader`. The `FileHeader` type is defined in the `mime/multipart` package as follows:

```
type FileHeader struct {
    Filename string
    Header   textproto.MIMEHeader
    Size     int64


}
```

The fields and their description are as follows:

Filename: A `string` value containing the original filename of the uploaded file

Header: A value of type `MIMEHeader` defined in the `net/textproto` package describing the file type

Size: An int64 value containing the size of the file in bytes

The `FileHeader` also defines a method, `Open()`, which returns a value of type `File` (defined in the `mime/multipart` package). This value can then be used to read the file contents in the handler function. Often, you will need to access some of the fields in the incoming `Request` object to debug problems in your server application. The next exercise gives you an opportunity to implement a request logger.

> **EXERCISE 5.1: A REQUEST LOGGER** A useful functionality to have in a server is a log of all incoming requests. Update the application in Listing 5.2 so that every incoming request detail is logged. Key details to log are URL, Request type, Request body size, and Protocol. Each log line should be a JSON formatted string.

Attaching Metadata to a Request

Every incoming request processed by a handler function is associated with a *context*. The context for a request, `r`, can be obtained by calling the `Context()` method. The life cycle of this context is the same as that of the request (see Figure 5.4).

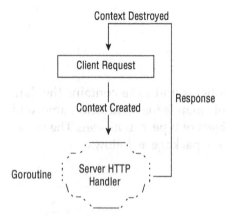

Figure 5.4: A context is created for every incoming request and destroyed when the request processing completes.

A context can have values attached to it. This is useful to associate request-specific and request-scoped data, such as, for example, a unique ID identifying the request that can be passed on to different parts of your application. To attach metadata to a request's context, we will need to do the following:

1. Retrieve the current context using `r.Context()`.

2. Create a new context with the desired data as a key-value pair using the `context.WithValue()` method.

The `context.WithValue()` expects three parameters:

- A parent `Context` object identifying the context in which to store the value
- An `interface{}` object identifying the key for the data
- An `interface{}` object containing the data

This essentially means that what you can store in the context is completely determined by the users of the `WithValue()` function. There are a couple of conventions to stick to, though:

- The key shouldn't be one of the basic types, such as `string`.

- A package should define its own custom unexported `struct` type to use as the key. An unexported data type ensures that this type is not accidentally used outside your package. For example, define an empty struct, type `requestContextKey struct{}`. This ensures that there is no accidental use of the same context key across different packages.

- Only request-scoped data should be stored in the context.

Let's see an example where we attach a request identifier before we start processing the request. First, we will define two struct types: `requestContextKey` for the key and `requestContextValue` for the value:

```
type requestContextKey struct{}
type requestContextValue struct {
        requestID string
}
```

Then, we will define a helper function to store a request identifier in a request's context:

```
func addRequestID(r *http.Request, requestID string) *http.Request {
        c := requestContextValue{
                requestID: requestID,
        }
        currentCtx := r.Context()
        newCtx := context.WithValue(currentCtx, requestContextKey{}, c)
        return r.WithContext(newCtx)
}
```

Next, in a handler function, we will call this function to store the request identifier before we process it:

```
func apiHandler(w http.ResponseWriter, r *http.Request) {
        requestID := "request-123-abc"
        r = addRequestID(r, requestID)
        processRequest(w, r)
}
```

We will define a second helper function to retrieve and log the `requestID`:

```
func logRequest(r *http.Request) {
        ctx := r.Context()
        v := ctx.Value(requestContextKey{})

        if m, ok := v.(requestContextValue); ok {
                log.Printf("Processing request: %s", m.requestID)
        }
}
```

We retrieve the value of the request context by calling the `ctx.Value()` method with the corresponding key. Recall that we used the empty `requestContextKey` object as the key when adding the value. The method returns an object of type `interface{}`. Hence, we perform a type assertion on the value obtained to ensure that it is of the `requestContextValue` type. If the type assertion is successful, we log the `requestID`.

The `processRequest()` function then calls the `logRequest()` function to log the `requestID`:

```
func processRequest(w http.ResponseWriter, r *http.Request) {
        logRequest(r)
        fmt.Fprintf(w, "Request processed")
}
```

Listing 5.4 shows a runnable server application that attaches a request identifier for every request and then logs it before processing it.

Listing 5.4: Attaching metadata to a request

```
// chap5/context-metadata/server.go
package main

import (
        "context"
        "fmt"
        "log"
        "net/http"
        "os"
)

type requestContextKey struct{}
type requestContextValue struct {
        requestID string
}

// TODO: Insert func addRequestID() function from earlier
// TODO: Insert logRequest() function from earlier
// TODO: Insert processRequest() function from earlier
// TODO: Insert apiHandler() function from earlier

func main() {

        listenAddr := os.Getenv("LISTEN_ADDR")
        if len(listenAddr) == 0 {
                listenAddr = ":8080"
        }
        mux := http.NewServeMux()
        mux.HandleFunc("/api", apiHandler)
        log.Fatal(http.ListenAndServe(listenAddr, mux))

}
```

Create a new directory, `chap5/context-metadata`, and initialize a module inside it:

```
$ mkdir -p chap5/context-metadata
$ cd chap5/ context-metadata
$ go mod init github.com/username/context-metadata
```

Next, save Listing 5.4 as a new file, `server.go`. Build and run the server:

```
$ go build -o server
$ ./server
```

From another terminal, make a request to the server, `curl localhost:8080/api`. On the terminal where you started the server, you will see the following:

```
2021/01/14 18:26:54 Processing request: request-123-abc
```

Attaching metadata, such as a request ID to an incoming request before processing it further, is a good practice to follow. However, imagine calling the `addRequestID()` function from all of your handler functions. You will learn a better way to attach metadata to the request object in Chapter 6, "Advanced HTTP Server Applications," by implementing middleware in your server applications.

Processing Streaming Requests

In Chapter 3, you first learned how to unmarshal JSON data when writing the test package server. In addition to the `Unmarshal()` function, the `encoding/json` package gives us another, more flexible approach to decode JSON data. Let's consider an example HTTP server that acts as a log collector. It does just two things:

- It receives logs via a HTTP POST request. The request body contains the logs encoded as one or more JSON objects. This is commonly referred to as a *JSON stream* as the client continuously sends the logs as part of the same request.

- It prints those logs once it has decoded them successfully.

  An example request body that the server may receive is as follows:

  ```
  {"user_ip": "172.121.19.21", "event":
  "click_on_add_cart"}{"user_ip": "172.121.19.21",
  "event": "click_on_checkout"}
  ```

Note how we have two individual logs encoded as JSON objects, one after the other. How do we unmarshal this request body?

You learned to unmarshal a JSON encoded request body of an incoming request, r, into an object, p, using the following steps:

1. Read the request body: `data, err := io.ReadAll(r.Body)`.

2. Decode the JSON data into the object: `json.Unmarshal(data, &p)`.

This approach works if the request body describes a single JSON object or an array of JSON objects. What if the body had multiple JSON objects as in the above sample request? `Unmarshal()` will fail to decode the data. To be able to decode the above data successfully, you will have to look at the `json.NewDecoder()` function.

The `json.NewDecoder()` function reads from any object that implements the `io.Reader` interface. Instead of expecting to read a fully formed JSON object (or an array of JSON objects), the `NewDecoder()` function adopts an incremental token-based approach to reading the data. Recall from the previous section that the `Body` field of the request object implements the `io.Reader` interface. Thus, by feeding the request body directly to the `NewDecoder()` function, you are able to decode JSON objects on the fly instead of needing all of the data available as required for the `json.Unmarshal()` function.

Let's write the HTTP handler function that will successfully process the logs being sent to our server. First, we will define the `struct` type to unmarshal a single log entry into the following:

```
type logLine struct {
        UserIP string `json:"user_ip"`
        Event  string `json:"event"`
}
```

Next, we write the handler function:

```
func decodeHandler(w http.ResponseWriter, r *http.Request) {

    dec := json.NewDecoder(r.Body)

    for {
        var l logLine
        err := dec.Decode(&l)
        if err == io.EOF {
            break
        }
        if err != nil {
                http.Error(w, err.Error(), http.StatusBadRequest)
            return
        }
        fmt.Println(l.UserIP, l.Event)
    }
    fmt.Fprintf(w, "OK")
}
```

We initialize a json.Decoder object, dec, by calling the NewDecoder() function, passing it r.Body. Then, in an infinite for loop, we execute the following steps:

1. We declare an object, l of type logLine, which will be used to store a single decoded log entry sent to the server.

2. We call the Decode() method defined on the dec object to read a JSON object. The Decode() function will read from the reader in r.Body until it finds the first valid JSON object and deserialize it into the l object.

3. If the error returned is io.EOF, there is nothing to read anymore and hence we break from the loop.

4. If the error was non-nil but something else, we stop any further processing and send back an HTTP Bad Request error response, else go to next step.

5. If there was no error, we print the fields of the object.

6. Go back to step 1.

When the loop exits, an OK response is sent back to the client.

Listing 5.5 shows a HTTP server that registers a path decode with the handler function decodeHandler, shown earlier.

Listing 5.5: Decoding JSON data using Decode()

```
// chap5/streaming-decode/server.go

package main

import (
        "encoding/json"
        "fmt"
        "io"
        "net/http"
)

type logLine struct {
        UserIP string `json:"user_ip"`
        Event  string `json:"event"`
}

// TODO: Insert definition of decodeHandler() from earlier

func main() {

        mux := http.NewServeMux()
        mux.HandleFunc("/decode", decodeHandler)

        http.ListenAndServe(":8080", mux)
}
```

Create a new directory, `chap5/streaming-decode/`, and initialize a module inside it:

```
$ mkdir -p chap5/streaming-decode
$ cd chap5/streaming-decode
$ go mod init github.com/username/streaming-decode
```

Next, save Listing 5.5 as a new file, `server.go`. Build and run it:

```
$ go build -o server
$ ./server
```

From a new terminal session, make a request to the server using `curl`:

```
$ curl -X POST http://localhost:8080/decode \
-d '
{"user_ip": "172.121.19.21", "event": "click_on_add_cart"}
{"user_ip": "172.121.19.21", "event": "click_on_checkout"}
'
OK
```

On the terminal where you ran the server, you should see the following output:

```
172.121.19.21 click_on_add_cart
172.121.19.21 click_on_checkout
```

The `Decode()` function will return an error in two scenarios, whichever happens first:

- It encounters an invalid character in the JSON data that it is reading. This is position dependent. A { character before a matching } character or vice versa is an invalid character.

- An error occurs in the conversion of the data being read into the specific object.

An example of the first scenario can be seen by making the following request (note the extra { before the second JSON object):

```
$ curl -X POST http://localhost:8080/decode \
-d '
{"user_ip": "172.121.19.21", "event": "click_on_add_cart"}{{"user_ip":
"172.121.19.21", "event": "click_on_checkout"}'
```

You will get the following response:

```
invalid character '{' looking for beginning of object key string
```

However, on the server side, you will see the following:

```
172.121.19.21 click_on_add_cart
```

This output tells us that the first JSON object was successfully decoded. This is essentially due to the nature of how `Decode()` works—it will keep reading the input stream until it encounters an error.

Now let's see an error of the second kind. Make the following request (note the wrong data type for `event` in the second JSON object):

```
$ curl -X POST http://localhost:8080/decode \
-d '
{"user_ip": "172.121.19.21","event": "click_on_add_cart"}
{"user_ip": "172.121.19.21", "event": 1}
'
```

The response you will get is as follows:

```
json: cannot unmarshal number into Go struct field
logLine.event of type string
```

If you wanted to introduce a bit more robustness into your handler function, where you want to ignore the unmarshalling errors and continue processing the JSON stream, you can do so using small changes to the `decodeHandler()` function (highlighted):

```
func decodeHandler(w http.ResponseWriter, r *http.Request) {
        dec := json.NewDecoder(r.Body)

        var e *json.UnmarshalTypeError

        for {
                var l logLine
                err := dec.Decode(&l)
                if err == io.EOF {
                        break
                }
                if errors.As(err, &e) {
                        log.Println(err)
                        continue
                }
                if err != nil {
                        http.Error(w, err.Error(), http.StatusBadRequest)
                        return
                }
                fmt.Println(l.UserIP, l.Event)
        }
        fmt.Fprintf(w, "OK")
}
```

When there is an error in the unmarshalling step, a specific type of error, UnmarshalTypeError (defined in the encoding/json) package, is returned. Thus, by checking whether the error returned by the Decode() function is of this type or not, we can choose to ignore the unmarshalling error and continue with the rest of the stream. With the above change, the server will log the unmarshalling error and continue with the rest of the stream.

To see it in action, make the following request:

```
$ curl -X POST http://localhost:8080/decode \
-d '
{"user_ip": "172.121.19.21","event": "click_on_add_cart"}
{"user_ip": "172.121.19.21", "event": 1}
{"user_ip": "172.121.21.22", "event": "click_on_checkout"}'
OK%
```

On the server with the above change, you will see the following:

```
172.121.19.21 click_on_add_cart
2020/12/30 16:42:30 json: cannot unmarshal number into Go struct field
logLine.event of type string
172.121.21.22 click_on_checkout
```

The json.NewDecoder() function coupled with the Decode() method is a flexible approach to parsing JSON data. It is most useful when parsing a stream of JSON data as we have seen here. Of course, you will have to be mindful that flexibility also brings with it more error handling responsibility on the application creator's part. In the next exercise, you will implement a more robust JSON decoding in your application to reject data with any unknown fields.

> **EXERCISE 5.2: STRICTER JSON DECODING**   If you send the following request body to the /decode endpoint above, the Decode() function will ignore the extra field user_data in the log.
>
> ```
> {"user_ip": "172.121.19.21","event":
> "click_on_add_cart", "user_data": "some_data"}
> ```
>
> Update Listing 5.5 so that the Decode() function will now throw an error if an unknown field is specified in the JSON stream.

Streaming Data as Responses

You have seen how to send a response to the server using functions such as fmt .Fprintf(). You have also seen how to set custom headers using w.Headers() .Add() for the http.ResponseWriter object, w. In this section, you will learn about sending responses when you don't have all the data available to be sent as a response and you want to send the data as it becomes available. This is commonly referred to as *streaming* the response. An example scenario where this may happen is when a long-running job is triggered as part of a client request and the result of the processing is sent as a response as more data becomes available (see Figure 5.5).

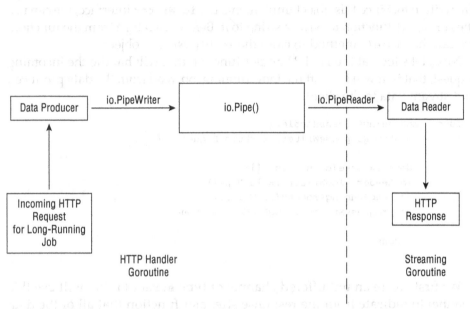

Figure 5.5: From left to right: An incoming HTTP request triggers a long-running job. The result of the job processing is sent as it becomes available.

The *data producer* creates a continuous stream of bytes that is read by the *data reader* and sent as an HTTP response. This continues until the data producer has stopped producing the data. How do we get the data from the producer to the consumer efficiently? The io.Pipe() function provides one way. Calling this function returns two objects: an io.PipeReader and an io.PipeWriter. The data producer will write to the io.PipeWriter object, and the data consumer will read from the io.PipeReader object.

Consider a sample data producer function, longRunningProcess(), which produces a line of log every second to produce a total of 21 log lines:

```
func longRunningProcess(logWriter *io.PipeWriter) {
        for i := 0; i <= 20; i++ {
                fmt.Fprintf(
                    logWriter,
                    `{"id": %d, "user_ip": "172.121.19.21", "event":
"click_on_add_cart" }`, i,
                )
                fmt.Fprintln(logWriter)
```

```
                        time.Sleep(1 * time.Second)
        }
        logWriter.Close()
}
```

The function is called with an `io.PipeWriter` object, which is where the logs are written to. Since this object implements the `io.Writer` interface, we can use the `Fprintf()` function to write a string to it. Before we return from the function, we call the `Close()` method to close the `io.PipeWriter` object.

Next, let's look at the HTTP handler function that will handle the incoming request; that is, it will kick off the long-running job, read from the data producer, and stream data to the client:

```
func longRunningProcessHandler(
        w http.ResponseWriter, r *http.Request) {

        done := make(chan struct{})
        logReader, logWriter := io.Pipe()
        go longRunningProcess(logWriter)
        go progressStreamer(logReader, w, done)

        <-done
}
```

We first create an unbuffered channel of type `struct{}`. We will use this channel to indicate from the response streamer function that all of the data has been sent. Then, we call the `io.Pipe()` function to give us back an `io .PipeReader` and an `io.PipeWriter` object.

Next, we spawn a goroutine to run the `longRunningProcess()` function, calling the function with the `io.PipeWriter` object. Then, we spawn another goroutine—our data reader and streamer implemented in the `progressStreamer()` function. Finally, we wait for data to be available on the `done` channel before we exit from the handler function. The `progressStreamer()` function is defined as follows:

```
func progressStreamer(
        logReader *io.PipeReader, w http.ResponseWriter,
        done chan struct{}) {

        buf := make([]byte, 500)

        f, flushSupported := w.(http.Flusher)

        defer logReader.Close()
        w.Header().Set("Content-Type", "text/plain")
        w.Header().Set("X-Content-Type-Options", "nosniff")

        for {
```

```
        n, err := logReader.Read(buf)
        if err == io.EOF {
                break
        }
        w.Write(buf[:n])
        if flushSupported {
                f.Flush()
        }
    }
    done <- struct{}{}
}
```

First, we create a buffer object, buf, to store 500 bytes. This is the maximum amount of data that we will read from the pipe at any given point of time.

Since we want the response data to be immediately available to the client, we will explicitly call the Flush() method of the ResponseWriter object after writing to the ResponseWriter. However, we first have to check if the ResponseWriter object, w, implements the http.Flusher interface. We do so using the following statement:

```
f, flushSupported := w.(http.Flusher)
```

If w implements the http.Flusher interface, f will contain a http.Flusher object and flushSupported will be set to true.

Next, we set up a deferred call to ensure that the io.PipeReader object is closed before we return from the function.

We set two response headers. We set the Content-Type header to text/plain to indicate to the client that we will be sending plaintext data. We also set the X-Content-Type-Options header to nosniff to instruct browsers not to buffer any data on their side before displaying it to the user.

Next, we start an infinite for loop to read data from the io.PipeReader object. If we get an io.EOF error indicating that the writer has finished writing to the pipe, we break out of the loop. If not, we call the Write() method to send the data we just read. If flushSupported is true, we call the Flush() method on the http.Flusher object, f.

Once the loop finishes, we write an empty struct object, struct{}{}, to the done channel.

Listing 5.6 shows an HTTP server that registers a single path, /job, and registers longRunningProcessHandler as the handler function.

Listing 5.6: Streaming response

```
// chap5/streaming-response/server.go
package main

import (
        "fmt"
```

```
        "io"
        "log"
        "net/http"
        "os"
        "time"
)

// TODO Insert definition of longRunningProcess function
// TODO Insert definition of progressStreamer function
// TODO Insert definition of longRunningProcessHandler function

func main() {
        listenAddr := os.Getenv("LISTEN_ADDR")
        if len(listenAddr) == 0 {
                listenAddr = ":8080"
        }

        mux := http.NewServeMux()
        mux.HandleFunc("/job", longRunningProcessHandler)
        log.Fatal(http.ListenAndServe(listenAddr, mux))
}
```

Create a new directory, chap5/streaming-response, and initialize a module inside it:

```
$ mkdir -p chap5/streaming-response
$ cd chap5/streaming-response
$ go mod init github.com/username/chap5/streaming-response
```

Next, save Listing 5.6 as a new file, server.go. Build and run the server:

```
$ go build -o server
$ ./server
```

Open a new terminal session and make a request using curl. You will see the response arriving every second:

```
$ curl localhost:8080/job

{"id": 0, "user_ip": "172.121.19.21", "event": "click_on_add_cart" }
{"id": 1, "user_ip": "172.121.19.21", "event": "click_on_add_cart" }
{"id": 2, "user_ip": "172.121.19.21", "event": "click_on_add_cart" }
{"id": 3, "user_ip": "172.121.19.21", "event": "click_on_add_cart" }
{"id": 4, "user_ip": "172.121.19.21", "event": "click_on_add_cart" }
...
{"id": 20, "user_ip": "172.121.19.21", "event": "click_on_add_cart" }
```

Next, execute `curl` adding the `--verbose` flag, and you will see the following response headers:

```
Content-Type: text/plain
X-Content-Type-Options: nosniff
Date: Thu, 14 Jan 2021 06:02:13 GMT
Transfer-Encoding: chunked
```

Of course, we set the `Content-Type` and `X-Content-Type-Options` headers when writing the response. The `Transfer-Encoding: chunked` header is automatically set by the call to the `Flush()` method. This indicates to the client that data is being streamed from the server and that it should keep reading until the connection is closed by the server.

The approach illustrated above using `io.Pipe()` establishes a clean separation from the data production and the consumption processes. It is important to note that you don't *need* to create `PipeReader` and `PipeWriter` objects to send streaming responses in all cases.

You can directly stream data by writing to the `ResponseWriter` if you have control over the streaming data generation process. Then you can periodically call the `Flush()` method of the `ResponseWriter` object in between the write calls. For example, if you wanted to send a large file as a response to a user request, you could periodically read a fixed number of bytes and send it to the client and repeat the process until the complete file was read. In this case, you don't even have to call the `Flush()` method, since a partial file is useless to the user. Fortunately, you don't have to do all that yourself. The `io.Copy()` function allows us to achieve this without writing any custom code. First, open the file for reading:

```
f, err := os.Open(fileName)
defer f.Close()
```

To stream the data over as the response over the `ResponseWriter` object, w:

```
io.Copy(w, f)
```

This will read the file data in chunks—32 KB as of Go 1.16—and directly write the data into the `ResponseWriter`. In the last exercise in this chapter, Exercise 5.3, you will use this technique to implement a file download server.

EXERCISE 5.3: FILE DOWNLOAD SERVER   Implement an HTTP server that will perform the role of file download server. Users will be able to make a request to the `/download` path specifying a filename via the `fileName` query parameter and then get back the file contents. Your server should be able to look up a custom directory for the file.

Make sure that you set the `Content-Type` header appropriately to indicate the file contents.

Summary

You had already started the journey into writing HTTP servers in Chapter 3 when writing test servers for clients. In this chapter, you dove deeper into doing that. You learned how a server handles incoming requests, why using `DefaultServeMux` is a bad idea, and how you can use your own `ServeMux` object. You wrote handler functions to process streaming data, and finally, you learned to use goroutines and channels in your servers to send streaming responses.

In the next chapter, you will continue your journey into the world of building production-ready HTTP server applications.

Advanced HTTP Server Applications

In this chapter, you will learn techniques that will be useful when you are writing production-quality HTTP server applications. You will start by learning about the `http.Handler` type, and you will use it to share data across handler functions. Then you will learn how to implement common server functionality as middleware. You will learn about the `http.HandlerFunc` type and use it to define and chain together middleware. You will end the chapter by looking at a strategy to organize your server application and test the various components. Let's get started!

The Handler Type

In this section, you will learn about the `http.Handler` type — a fundamental mechanism that enables how HTTP server works in Go. You are now familiar with the `http.ListenAndServe()` function that starts an HTTP server. Formally, the signature of this function is as follows:

```
func ListenAndServe(addr string, handler Handler)
```

The first argument is the network address on which to listen, and the second object is a value of type `http.Handler` defined in the `net/http` package as follows:

```
type Handler interface {
        ServeHTTP(ResponseWriter, *Request)
}
```

Thus, the second parameter of the `http.ListenAndServe()` function can be *any* object that implements the `http.Handler` interface. How do we create such an object? You are now familiar with the following pattern for building an HTTP server application:

```
mux := http.NewServeMux()
// register handlers with mux
http.ListenAndServe(addr, mux)
```

Recall that the `http.NewServeMux()` function returns a value of type `http.ServeMux`. As it turns out, this value satisfies the `Handler` interface by defining a `ServeHTTP()` method. When an HTTP server application gets a request, the `ServeHTTP()` method of the `ServeMux` object is called, which then routes the request to the specific handler function, if one is found.

As with any other interface, you can define your own type to satisfy the `http.Handler` interface as follows:

```
type myType struct {}
(t *myType) func ServeHTTP(w http.ResponseWriter, r *http.Request) {
        fmt.Printf(w, "Hello World")
}
http.ListenAndServe(":8080", myType{})
```

When you make a request to a server defined as above, the `ServeHTTP()` method defined on the `myType` object is called and a response is sent. When might you want to implement a custom `http.Handler` type? One situation is when you want to share data across all of your handler functions. For example, you may initialize an object only once at startup and then share it across all of your handler functions instead of using a global object. Next, let's see how you can combine a custom handler type with an `http.ServeMux` object in order to share data across handler functions.

Sharing Data across Handler Functions

In the previous chapter, you learned that you could use a request's context to store data across the lifetime of a request. This is useful for storing request scoped data, such as a request identifier, a user identifier after authentication, and so on. There is another category of data that you need to store in a typical server application, such as an initialized logger object or an open database connection object. These objects are initialized once the server starts and then accessed across all of the HTTP handler functions.

Let's define a struct type, appConfig, to contain the configuration data for a server application:

```
type appConfig struct {
        logger *log.Logger
}
```

The struct type contains a field, logger, of type *log.Logger. Define another struct type, app, to be the custom http.Handler type:

```
type app struct {
        config  appConfig
        handler func(
                w http.ResponseWriter,r *http.Request,config appConfig,
        )
}
```

An app object will contain an object of type appConfig and a function with signature func(http.ResponseWriter, *http.Request, config appConfig). This function will be a standard HTTP handler function, but it accepts an additional parameter—a value of type appConfig. This is how we *inject* the configuration values into the handler function. Since the app type will implement the http .Handler interface, we will define a ServeHTTP() method as follows:

```
func (a app) ServeHTTP(w http.ResponseWriter, r *http.Request) {
        a.handler(w, r, a.config)
}
```

We have implemented a custom http.Handler type and laid the foundation for sharing data across handler functions. Let's take an example handler function:

```
func healthCheckHandler(w http.ResponseWriter, r *http.Request, config
appConfig) {
        if r.Method != http.MethodGet {
                http.Error(w, "Method not allowed",
http.StatusMethodNotAllowed)
                return
        }
        config.logger.Println("Handling healthcheck request")
        fmt.Fprintf(w, "ok")
}
```

Inside the handler function, we process the request. If the request method is anything other than GET, we send an error response. Otherwise, we use the configured logger available in the `config` object to log a sample message and send a response back.

To register this handler function, we will use the following pattern:

```
config := appConfig{
        logger: log.New(
                os.Stdout, "", log.Ldate|log.Ltime|log.Lshortfile,
        ),
}
mux := http.NewServeMux()
setupHandlers(mux, config)
```

We create a value of type `appConfig`. Here we configure a logger that logs to `stdout` and set it up to log the date, time, filename, and line number. Then we create a new `http.ServeMux` object by calling `http.NewServeMux()`. Next, we call the `setupHandlers()` function with the created `ServeMux` object and the `appConfig` object. The definition of `setupHandlers()` is as follows:

```
func setupHandlers(mux *http.ServeMux, config appConfig) {
        mux.Handle("/healthz", &app{config: config, handler:
healthCheckHandler})
        mux.Handle("/api", &app{config: config, handler: apiHandler})
}
```

We call the `Handle()` method of the `http.ServeMux` object, `mux`, with two arguments. The first argument is the request path to handle, and the second argument is an object of type `app`—our custom `http.Handler` type. Each path and handler function registration thus involves creating a new app object. The `Handle()` method is similar to the `HandleFunc()` method that you have been using so far to register a request handler, except for the second argument. Whereas the `HandleFunc()` method takes any function with the signature `func(http.ResponseWriter, *http.Request)` as argument, the `Handle()` method requires the second argument to be an object that implements the `http.Handler` interface.

Figure 6.1 demonstrates how the `http.ServeMux` object and a custom handler type work together to handle a request.

To summarize, for an incoming request, the `http.ServeMux` object's `ServeHTTP()` method checks to see if there is a valid handler object registered for the path. If one is found, the corresponding `ServeHTTP()` method of the handler object is called, which then calls the registered handler function. The handler function processes the request and sends a response, and then the control is returned back to the `ServeHTTP()` method of the handler object. Listing 6.1 shows a complete HTTP server application using a custom type.

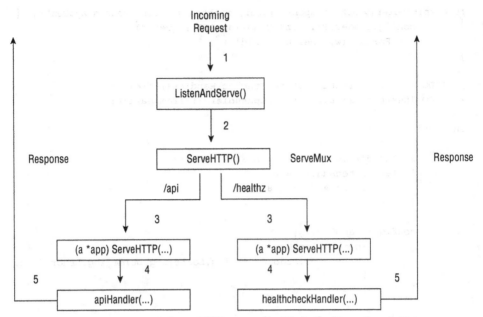

Figure 6.1: Request processing by an HTTP server when using a custom handler type

Listing 6.1: An HTTP server using a custom handler type

```go
// chap6/http-handler-type/server.go
package main

import (
        "fmt"
        "log"
        "net/http"
        "os"
)

type appConfig struct {
        logger *log.Logger
}

type app struct {
        config  appConfig
        handler func(
                w http.ResponseWriter,r *http.Request,config appConfig,
        )
}

func (a *app) ServeHTTP(w http.ResponseWriter, r *http.Request) {
        a.handler(w, r, a.config)
}
```

```go
func apiHandler(w http.ResponseWriter, r *http.Request, config appConfig) {
        config.logger.Println("Handling API request")
        fmt.Fprintf(w, "Hello, world!")
}

// TODO Insert definition of healthcheckHandler() from earlier
// TODO Insert definition of setupHandlers() from earlier

func main() {

        listenAddr := os.Getenv("LISTEN_ADDR")
        if len(listenAddr) == 0 {
                listenAddr = ":8080"
        }

        config := appConfig{
                logger: log.New(
                        os.Stdout, "" log.Ldate|log.Ltime|log.Lshortfile,
                ),
        }

        mux := http.NewServeMux()
        setupHandlers(mux, config)

        log.Fatal(http.ListenAndServe(listenAddr, mux))


}
```

Create a new directory, chap6/http-handler-type, and initialize a module inside it:

```
$ mkdir -p chap6/http-handler-type
$ cd chap6/http-handler-type
$ go mod init github.com/username/http-handler-type
```

Next, save Listing 6.1 as a new file, server.go. Build and run the server:

```
$ go build -o server
$ ./server
```

In a new terminal session, make an HTTP request using curl:

```
$ curl localhost:8080/api
Hello, world!
```

On the server's terminal, you will see a log message showing the API request:

```
2021/03/08 10:31:00 server.go:24: Handling API request
```

You will see a similar log message if you make a request to the /healthz API endpoint.

Great. You now know how to share a logger object across handler functions. In real-life applications, you will need to share other objects, such as an initialized client for a remote service or a database connection object, and you will be able to use this technique to do so. It is more robust than using globally scoped values, and it automatically results in testing-friendly servers.

A point worth noting here is that a custom `http.Handler` type also allows you to implement other patterns in your server application, such as a centralized error-reporting mechanism. Exercise 6.1 gives you an opportunity to implement this.

EXERCISE 6.1: CENTRALIZED ERROR HANDLING

Define the app type as follows:

```
type app struct {
        config  appConfig
        h func(w http.ResponseWriter,r *http.Request,conf appConfig) error
}
```

Next you define your handler functions (defined as per the field h) to return an error value instead of reporting an error directly to the client. In the ServeHTTP() method of the app object, you can report or log the error to an error tracking service and then send back the original error to the client.

Next you will learn how to implement an oft-used pattern when handling HTTP requests in a server—implementing common operations as server middleware.

Writing Server Middleware

Server-side middleware allows you to run common operations automatically while processing a request. For example, you may want to log every request, add a request identifier to each request, or check if the request has the associated authentication credentials specified. Instead of duplicating the logic in every HTTP handler function, the server itself takes responsibility for invoking the corresponding operation. The handler functions can focus on the business logic. You will learn two patterns for implementing middleware: First, you will learn how to implement middleware using a custom `http.Handler` type, and then you will learn how to do it using the `HandlerFunc` technique.

Custom HTTP Handler Technique

In the previous section, you learned how to define a custom handler type to share data across handler functions. The `ServeHTTP()` method of the custom type, `app`, was implemented as follows:

```
func (a *app) ServeHTTP(w http.ResponseWriter, r *http.Request) {
        a.handler(w, r, a.config)
}
```

If you update the above method to something like the following, you will have implemented a *middleware* to log how long it took to process a request:

```
func (a *app) ServeHTTP(w http.ResponseWriter, r *http.Request) {
        startTime := time.Now()
        a.handler(w, r, a.config)
        a.config.logger.Printf(
                "path=%s method=%s duration=%f", r.URL.Path, r.Method,
                time.Now().Sub(startTime).Seconds(),
        )
}
```

When you replace the `ServeHTTP()` method in Listing 6.1 with the above code and make a request to the `/api` or the `/healthz` endpoint, you will see logs like the following (all in a single line):

```
2021/03/09 08:47:27 server.go:23: path=/healthz method=GET
duration=0.000327
```

If you make a request to a path that is not registered, you will not see any logs, however. Recall that the `ServeHTTP()` method of the app type is only called when there is a handler registered for the path. To fix that, we will instead create a middleware such that it *wraps* the `ServeMux` object.

The HandlerFunc Technique

`http.HandlerFunc` is a type defined in the standard library as follows:

```
type HandlerFunc func(ResponseWriter, *Request)
```

The type also implements a `ServeHTTP()` method and thus implements the `http.Handler` interface. As with any other type, we can convert any function that has the signature `func(w http.ResponseWriter, r *http.Request)` into a value that satisfies the `http.Handler` interface using the expression `HandlerFunc(func(w http.ResponseWriter, r *http.Request))`. Figure 6.2 demonstrates how a request is handled by a function that has been *converted* to an `http.HandlerFunc` type.

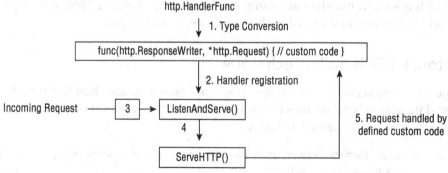

Figure 6.2: Request processing by an HTTP server when using an `http.HandlerFunc` type

Why do we need such a type at all? It enables us to write a function that *wraps* around *any* other `http.Handler` value, h, and returns another `http.Handler`. Let's say that we wanted to implement a logging middleware using this technique. Here is how we would write one:

```
func loggingMiddleware(h http.Handler) http.Handler {
        return http.HandlerFunc(
                func(w http.ResponseWriter, r *http.Request) {
                        startTime := time.Now()
                        h.ServeHTTP(w, r)
                        log.Printf(
                                "path=%s method=%s duration=%f",
                                r.URL.Path, r.Method, time.Now()
.Sub(startTime).Seconds(),
                        )
                })
}
```

Then we will create a `ServeMux` object and use it with the `ListenAndServe()` function as follows:

```
mux := http.NewServeMux()
setupHandlers(mux, config)
m := loggingMiddleware(mux)
http.ListenAndServe(listenAddr, m)
```

We create the `ServeMux` object and register the request handlers. Then we call the `loggingMiddleware()` function, passing the `ServeMux` object as a parameter. This is how we wrap the `ServeMux` object inside the `loggingMiddleware` function. Since the value returned by the `loggingMiddleware()` function implements the `http.Handler` interface, we specify that as the handler when calling the `ListenAndServe()` function.

Figure 6.3 demonstrates how a request is processed when we wrap the `http.ServeMux` object with an outer `http.Handler` type, `loggingMiddleware`. We will refer to the `http.ServeMux` object as the *wrapped* handler.

When a request comes in, it is first processed by the `ServeHTTP()` method implemented by `http.HandlerFunc`. As part of the processing, this method calls the function returned by the `loggingMiddleware()` function. Inside the body of this function, a timer is started and then the wrapped handler's `serveHTTP()` method is called, which then invokes the request handlers. After the request handlers have finished processing the request, the execution returns to the function returned by the `loggingMiddleware()` function where the request details are logged.

Since the `http.HandlerFunc` type enables us to write a function that *wraps* around *any* other `http.Handler` value, h, and returns another `http.Handler`, we can set up a *chain* of middleware, as you will learn next.

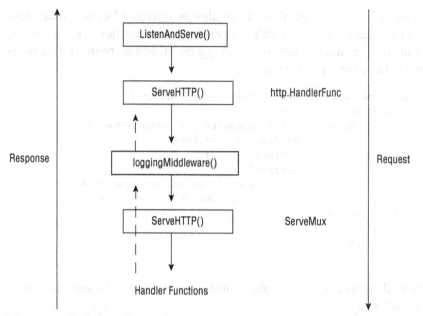

Figure 6.3: Request processing by an HTTP server when using a wrapped `ServeMux`

Chaining Middleware

Implementing common functionalities for your server application as middleware enables good separation of concerns between the business logic in your server and the other aspects such as logging, error handling, and authentication. This often results in being able to process a request through multiple middleware. The `http.HandlerFunc` type makes it easy to set up multiple middleware to process requests. A scenario where you may find this technique useful is to be able to call the `recover()` function in case there is an unexpected call to the `panic()` function when processing a request. A call to the `panic()` function may be initiated by application code that you have written, in a package that you are using, or it may have been initiated by the go runtime. Once this function is called, the request processing is terminated. However, when you set up a middleware that has defined a `recover()` function, you can log the details of the panic or continue the execution of any other middleware that you have configured in your server. First, we will implement a panic-handling middleware and then implement a server that will chain together the logging middleware implemented in the previous section and the panic-handling middleware.

The panic-handling middleware is as follows:

```
func panicMiddleware(h http.Handler) http.Handler {
        return http.HandlerFunc(
                func(w http.ResponseWriter, r *http.Request) {
```

```
            defer func() {
                    if rValue := recover(); rValue != nil {
                            log.Println("panic detected", rValue)
                            w.WriteHeader(http.StatusInternalServerError)
                            fmt.Fprintf(w, "Unexpected server error")
                    }
            }()
            h.ServeHTTP(w, r)
    })
}
```

We set up a deferred function call where we use the `recover()` function to probe if there was a panic when handling a request. If there was one, we log a message, set the HTTP status to 500, and send an "Unexpected server error" response. This is because there is a reasonably good chance that something bad happened when handling the request, and it's likely the handler didn't successfully send any response to the client. After we set up the deferred call, we call the *wrapped* handler's `ServeHTTP()` method.

Next, let's see how we will set up the server so that it combines both the logging middleware and the panic-handling middleware:

```
config := appConfig{
        logger: log.New(
                os.Stdout, "", log.Ldate|log.Ltime|log.Lshortfile,
        ),
}
mux := http.NewServeMux()
setupHandlers(mux, &config)
m := loggingMiddleware(panicMiddleware(mux))
err := http.ListenAndServe(listenAddr, m)
```

The key statement above is highlighted. First, we call the `panicMiddleware()` function to wrap the `ServeMux` object. The returned `http.Handler` value is then passed as a parameter to the `loggingMiddleware()` function. The returned value from this call is then configured as the handler to the `ListenAndServe()` call. Figure 6.4 shows how an incoming request flows through the configured middleware to the `ServeMux` object's `ServeHTTP()` method.

When chaining middleware, the innermost middleware is the one that's executed first when processing your request (and response from a handler function), and the outermost middleware is the one executed last.

Listing 6.2 shows a complete server application to illustrate chaining middleware using the `http.HandlerFunc` type.

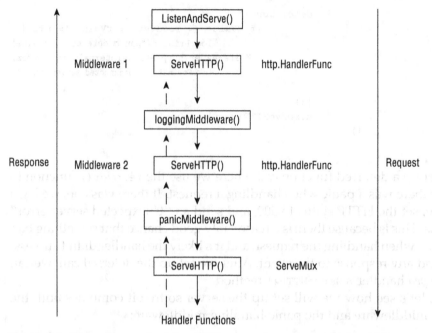

Figure 6.4: Request processing by an HTTP server when using multiple middleware

Listing 6.2: Chaining middleware using `http.HandleFunc`

```
// chap6/middleware-chaining/server.go
package main

import (
        "fmt"
        "log"
        "net/http"
        "os"
        "time"
)

type appConfig struct {
        logger *log.Logger
}

type app struct {
        config  appConfig
        handler func(
                w http.ResponseWriter,r *http.Request,config appConfig,
        )
}
```

```go
func (a app) ServeHTTP(w http.ResponseWriter, r *http.Request) {
        a.handler(w, r, a.config)
}

// TODO Insert definition of apiHandler() from Listing 6.1
// TODO Insert definition of healthCheckHandler() from Listing 6.1

func panicHandler(
        w http.ResponseWriter, r *http.Request,config appConfig,
) {

        panic("I panicked")
}

func setupHandlers(mux *http.ServeMux, config appConfig) {
        mux.Handle(
                "/healthz",
                &app{config: config, handler: healthCheckHandler},
        )
        mux.Handle("/api", &app{config: config, handler: apiHandler})
        mux.Handle("/panic",
                &app{config: config, handler: panicHandler},
        )

}

// TODO Insert definition of loggingMiddleware() from earlier
// TODO Insert definition of panicMiddleware() from earlier

func main() {

        listenAddr := os.Getenv("LISTEN_ADDR")
        if len(listenAddr) == 0 {
                listenAddr = ":8080"
        }

        config := appConfig{
                logger: log.New(
                        os.Stdout, "", log.Ldate|log.Ltime|log.Lshortfile,
                ),
        }

        mux := http.NewServeMux()
        setupHandlers(mux, config)

        m := loggingMiddleware(panicMiddleware(mux))

        log.Fatal(http.ListenAndServe(listenAddr, m))
}
```

We define a new handler function, `panicHandler()`, to handle any request for the `/panic` path. To illustrate the workings of the panic-handling middleware, `panicMiddleware()`, all we need to do in this handler function is to call the `panic()` function with some text. This is the value that will be recovered by the `recover()` function in the middleware. We then set up the middleware chain in `main()` and call the `ListenAndServe()` function with the handler returned by the `loggingMiddleware()` function.

Create a new directory, `middleware-chaining`, and initialize a module inside it:

```
$ mkdir -p chap6/middleware-chaining
$ cd chap6/ middleware-chaining
$ go mod init github.com/username/middleware-chaining
```

Next, save Listing 6.2 as a new file, `server.go`. Build and run the server as follows:

```
$ go build -o server
$ ./server
```

From a separate terminal, make a request to the `/panic` endpoint of your server using curl or another HTTP client:

```
$ curl http://localhost:8080/panic
Unexpected server error occurred
```

On the terminal where the server application is open, you will see logs similar to the following (all on the same line):

```
2021/03/16 14:17:34 panic detected I panicked
2021/03/16 14:17:34 protocol=HTTP/1.1 path=/panic method=GET
duration=0.001575
```

You can see that the value recovered is "I panicked," which is the string that you called with the `panic()` function. Thus, you have verified that the panic-handling middleware is working. It recovers the panic that occurred in the handler function, logs it, and sets the response appropriately. Once it has finished doing its work, the response then passes through the logging middleware to the client.

Great. Now that you know how to set up a middleware chain, it's time to test your understanding in Exercise 6.2.

> **EXERCISE 6.2: ATTACH REQUEST IDENTIFIER IN A MIDDLE-WARE**   In Listing 5.4 in the previous chapter, you learned how you can store a request identifier in the context of a request. You called the `addRequestID()` function from *every* request handler to do so.
>
> You now know that a middleware is the more appropriate place to perform such an operation. Write a middleware that will associate a request ID to every request. Update the server application in Listing 6.2 to log the request ID as well.

So far in this chapter, you have learned a number of new patterns for implementing the functionality in our server application. You have seen how to use the custom handler type to share data across handlers and also implement middleware. Moreover, to be able to wrap the `ServeMux` object, you learned about a new technique for implementing middleware using the `HandlerFunc` type. Couldn't you just use a custom handler type to achieve the same? Yes, but that would involve more work. However, if your middleware implements a complicated piece of your server functionality, using a custom handler type to implement it is a good approach. You can separate out your middleware functionality into a custom type with data and methods. You will still be able to set up a middleware chain using the approach that we applied here.

For complex server applications, it is vital to start thinking about how to organize the various components, which brings us to our next section. You will learn about a way to organize the server code and write automated tests for the different components.

Writing Tests for Complex Server Applications

In Chapter 5, "Building HTTP Servers," the server applications that you wrote were composed of three main functionalities: writing handler functions, registering the handlers with a `ServeMux` object, and calling `ListenAndServe()` to start the server. All of the functionalities were implemented in the `main` package, and that's a good starting point for very simple server applications. However, as you start writing more complicated servers, you will find that breaking down the application into multiple packages is a more practical approach.

One way to do this is to have a separate package for each area of concern of the application: configuration management, middleware and handler functions, and the `main` package orchestrating them all together, finally calling `ListenAndServe()` function to start the server. Let's do that next.

Code Organization

We will now rewrite the server application in Listing 6.2 so that we have four packages: `main`, `config`, `handlers`, and `middleware`. Create a new directory, `complex-server`, and initialize a new module using `go mod init` inside it:

```
$ mkdir complex-server
$ cd complex-server
$ go mod init github.com/username/chap6/complex-server
```

Create three subdirectories, `config`, `handlers`, and `middleware`, in the module directory.

Save Listing 6.3 as `config.go` inside the `config` directory.

Listing 6.3: Managing application configuration

```
// chap6/complex-server/config/config.go
package config

import (
        "io"
        "log"
)

type AppConfig struct {
        Logger *log.Logger
}

func InitConfig(w io.Writer) AppConfig {
        return AppConfig{
                Logger: log.New(
                        w, "", log.Ldate|log.Ltime|log.Lshortfile,
                ),
        }
}
```

We rename the `appConfig` struct to `AppConfig` so that we can access it from outside the package. We also add an `InitConfig()` method that accepts an `io.Writer` value that we use to initialize the logger, and it returns an `AppConfig` value.

Next, save Listing 6.4 as `handlers.go` inside the `handlers` subdirectory.

Listing 6.4: Request handlers

```
// chap6/complex-server/handlers/handlers.go
package handlers

import (
        "fmt"
        "net/http"

        "github.com/username/chap6/complex-server/config"
)

type app struct {
        conf    config.AppConfig
        handler func(
                w http.ResponseWriter,
                r *http.Request,
                conf config.AppConfig,
        )
}
```

```
func (a app) ServeHTTP(w http.ResponseWriter, r *http.Request) {
        a.handler(w, r, a.conf)
}

func apiHandler(
        w http.ResponseWriter,
        r *http.Request,
        conf config.AppConfig,
) {

        fmt.Fprintf(w, "Hello, world!")

}

func healthCheckHandler(
        w http.ResponseWriter,
        r *http.Request,
        conf config.AppConfig,
) {

        if r.Method != "GET" {
                conf.Logger.Printf("error=\"Invalid request\" path=%s
method=%s", r.URL.Path, r.Method)
                http.Error(
                        w,
                        "Method not allowed",
                        http.StatusMethodNotAllowed,
                )
                return
        }
        fmt.Fprintf(w, "ok")

}

func panicHandler(
        w http.ResponseWriter,
        r *http.Request,
        conf config.AppConfig,
) {

        panic("I panicked")

}
```

We import the config package using the import path `"github.com/username/chap6/complex-server/config"`, and we define the app type and handler functions. You will notice that we have done away with the request logging inside the handler functions, which is of course due to the logging middleware that our server will now have. In most production scenarios, however, you will need to log messages or access other configuration data, hence the config parameter has been kept as it was first introduced.

Save Listing 6.5 as `register.go` inside the `handlers` subdirectory as well.

Listing 6.5: Setting up the request handlers

```go
// chap6/complex-server/handlers/register.go
package handlers

import (
        "net/http"
        "github.com/username/chap6/complex-server/config"
)

func Register(mux *http.ServeMux, conf config.AppConfig) {
        mux.Handle(
                "/healthz",
                &app{conf: conf, handler: healthCheckHandler},
        )
        mux.Handle(
                "/api",
                &app{conf: conf, handler: apiHandler},
        )
        mux.Handle(
                "/panic",
                &app{conf: conf, handler: panicHandler},
        )
}
```

The `Register()` function accepts a `ServeMux` object and a `config.AppConfig` value, and it registers the request handlers.

Next, save Listing 6.6 as `middleware.go` inside the `middleware` directory. Here we define the middleware for the server. Note how we also pass the configuration object into the middleware now so that we can access the configured `Logger`.

Listing 6.6: Logging and panic-handling middleware

```go
// chap6/complex-server/middleware/middleware.go
package middleware
import (
        "fmt"
        "log"
        "net/http"
        "time"
        "github.com/username/chap6/complex-server/config"
)

func loggingMiddleware(
        h http.Handler, c config.AppConfig,
) http.Handler {
        return http.HandlerFunc(
                func(w http.ResponseWriter, r *http.Request) {
                        t1 := time.Now()
                        h.ServeHTTP(w, r)
```

```
                    requestDuration := time.Now().Sub(t1).Seconds()
                    c.Logger.Printf(
                            "protocol=%s path=%s method=%s
                            duration=%f",
                            r.Proto, r.URL.Path,
                            r.Method, requestDuration,
                    )
        })
}


func panicMiddleware(h http.Handler, c config.AppConfig) http.Handler {
        return http.HandlerFunc(func(w http.ResponseWriter, r *http.Request) {
                defer func() {
                        if rValue := recover(); rValue != nil {
                                c.Logger.Println("panic detected", rValue)
                                w.WriteHeader(http.StatusInternalServerError)
                                fmt.Fprintf(w, "Unexpected server error
occurred")
                        }
                }()
                h.ServeHTTP(w, r)
        })
}
```

Next, save Listing 6.7 as `register.go` inside the `middleware` subdirectory as well.

Listing 6.7: Middleware registration

```
// chap6/complex-server/middleware/register.go
package middleware
import (
        "net/http"
        "github.com/username/chap6/complex-server/config"
)

func RegisterMiddleware(
        mux *http.ServeMux,
        c config.AppConfig,
) http.Handler {
        return loggingMiddleware(panicMiddleware(mux, c), c)
}
```

The `RegisterMiddleware()` function sets up the middleware chain for the specific `ServeMux` object.

Finally, save Listing 6.8 as `server.go` at the root of the module directory.

Listing 6.8: Main server

```go
// chap6/complex-server/server.go
package main

import (
        "io"
        "log"
        "net/http"
        "os"

        "github.com/username/chap6/complex-server/config"
        "github.com/username/chap6/complex-server/handlers"
        "github.com/username/chap6/complex-server/middleware"
)

func setupServer(mux *http.ServeMux, w io.Writer) http.Handler {
        conf := config.InitConfig(w)

        handlers.Register(mux, conf)
        return middleware.RegisterMiddleware(mux, conf)
}

func main() {

        listenAddr := os.Getenv("LISTEN_ADDR")
        if len(listenAddr) == 0 {
                listenAddr = ":8080"
        }

        mux := http.NewServeMux()
        wrappedMux := setupServer(mux, os.Stdout)

        log.Fatal(http.ListenAndServe(listenAddr, wrappedMux))
}
```

The `setupServer()` function initializes the configuration for the application by calling the `config.InitConfig()` function. Then it registers the handler functions with the `ServeMux` object, `mux`, by calling the `handlers.Register()` function. Finally, it registers the middleware and then returns the wrapped `handler.Handler` value. In the `main()` function, we create a `ServeMux` object, call the `setupServer()` function, and then finally call the `ListenAndServe()` function.

Build and run the server from the `complex-server` directory:

```
$ go build -o server
$ ./server
```

From a separate terminal session, make a few requests to the server in order to ensure that it is still operating as expected. Once you have done that, let's move on to writing automated tests.

Testing the Handler Functions

There are two approaches to testing handler functions. One approach involves starting a test HTTP server using `httptest.NewServer()` and then making requests against this test server. You followed that approach to test your handler functions in Chapter 5. The second approach involves testing the handler functions directly without starting a test server. This technique is useful when you want to test the handler functions in isolation—ignoring the rest of the server application. In any large server application, this is the recommended approach. Let's consider the `apiHandler()` function defined as follows:

```
func apiHandler(
        w http.ResponseWriter,
        r *http.Request,
        conf config.AppConfig,
) {
        fmt.Fprintf(w, "Hello, world!")
}
```

To test this handler function in isolation, we will create a test response writer, a test request, and an `AppConfig` value.

To create a test response writer, we will use the `httptest.NewRecorder()` function. This function returns a value of type `httptest.ResponseRecorder`, which implements the `http.ResponseWriter` interface:

```
w := httptest.NewRecorder()
```

To create a test request, we will use the `httptest.NewRequest()` function:

```
r := httptest.NewRequest("GET", "/api", nil)
```

The first parameter of the `httptest.NewRequest()` function is the HTTP request type—GET, POST, and so on. The second parameter can either be a URL, like `http://my.host.domain/api`, or a path, like `/api`. The third parameter is the request body, which is `nil` here. Create an `AppConfig` value:

```
b := new(bytes.Buffer)
c := config.InitConfig(b)
```

Then call the `apiHandler()` function:

```
apiHandler(w, r, c)
```

The recorded response in `w` is obtained using `w.Result()`. It returns a value of type `*http.Response`. Listing 6.9 shows the test function.

Listing 6.9: Test for the API handler function

```go
// chap6/complex-server/handlers/handler_test.go
package handlers

import (
        "bytes"
        "io"
        "net/http"
        "net/http/httptest"
        "testing"

        "github.com/username/chap6/complex-server/config"
)

func TestApiHandler(t *testing.T) {
        r := httptest.NewRequest("GET", "/api", nil)
        w := httptest.NewRecorder()

        b := new(bytes.Buffer)
        c := config.InitConfig(b)

        apiHandler(w, r, c)

        resp := w.Result()
        body, err := io.ReadAll(resp.Body)
        if err != nil {
                t.Fatalf("Error reading response body: %v", err)
        }

        if resp.StatusCode != http.StatusOK {
                t.Errorf(
                        "Expected response status: %v, Got: %v\n",
                        http.StatusOK, resp.StatusCode,
                )
        }

        expectedResponseBody := "Hello, world!"

        if string(body) != expectedResponseBody {
                t.Errorf(
                        "Expected response: %s, Got: %s\n",
                        expectedResponseBody, string(body),
                )
        }
}
```

After retrieving the response, using w.Result(), we retrieve the status code via the StatusCode field and the body via resp.Body. We compare them against the expected values. Save Listing 6.9 as handlers_test.go in the handlers subdirectory, and run the following test:

```
$ go test  -v
=== RUN    TestApiHandler
--- PASS: TestApiHandler (0.00s)
PASS
ok         github.com/practicalgo/code/chap6/complex-server/handlers
0.576s
```

Similarly, you can write a test for each of the other handler functions. For the healthCheckHandler() function, you would want to test the behavior when an HTTP request other than GET is received by the handler. Exercise 6.3 gives you the opportunity to do just that.

> **EXERCISE 6.3: TESTING THE** HEALTHCHECKHANDLER
> **FUNCTION**   Define a test function for the healthCheckHandler()
> function. It should test the behavior for GET and other HTTP request types.

What about testing the panicHandler() function? Since we know that all this function does is call the panic() function, the more useful component to test here is the panic-handling middleware. Let's see how we can go about testing middleware for our server applications.

Testing the Middleware

Let's consider the panicMiddleware() function signature: func panicMiddleware(h http.Handler, c config.AppConfig) http.Handler. The parameters of the function are a handler value, h; the handler to be wrapped; and a config .AppConfig value:

```
b := new(bytes.Buffer)
c := config.InitConfig(b)
m := http.NewServeMux()
handlers.Register(m, c)
h := panicMiddleware(m, c)
```

We create an http.ServeMux object, register the handler functions, and then call the panicMiddleware() function. The returned value, another http.Handler value, will then be either wrapped by another middleware or passed on to the `http.ListenAndServe()` function call for the *real* server. To test the middleware, though, we will instead call the `ServeHTTP()` method of the handler directly:

```
r := httptest.NewRequest("GET", "/panic", nil)
w := httptest.NewRecorder()
h.ServeHTTP(w, r)
```

Listing 6.10 shows the complete test function.

Listing 6.10: Test for panic-handling middleware

```go
// chap6/complex-server/middleware/middleware_test.go
package middleware

import (
        "bytes"
        "io"
        "net/http"
        "net/http/httptest"
        "testing"

        "github.com/username/chap6/complex-server/config"
        "github.com/username/chap6/complex-server/handlers"
)

func TestPanicMiddleware(t *testing.T) {
        b := new(bytes.Buffer)
        c := config.InitConfig(b)

        m := http.NewServeMux()
        handlers.Register(m, c)

        h := panicMiddleware(m, c)

        r := httptest.NewRequest("GET", "/panic", nil)
        w := httptest.NewRecorder()
        h.ServeHTTP(w, r)

        resp := w.Result()

        body, err := io.ReadAll(resp.Body)
        if err != nil {
                t.Fatalf("Error reading response body: %v", err)
        }

        if resp.StatusCode != http.StatusInternalServerError {
                t.Errorf(
                        "Expected response status: %v, Got: %v\n",
                        http.StatusOK,
                        resp.StatusCode,
                )
        }
```

```
        expectedResponseBody := "Unexpected server error occurred"

        if string(body) != expectedResponseBody {
                t.Errorf(
                        "Expected response: %s, Got: %s\n",
                        expectedResponseBody,
                        string(body),
                )
        }
}
```

Calling the `ServeHTTP()` method of the returned handler from `panicMiddle ware()` simulates the behavior of the `ListenAndServe()` function while testing the behavior of the panic handler in isolation. Save Listing 6.10 as `middleware_test. go` in the `middleware` subdirectory and run the following test:

```
$ go test -v
=== RUN    TestPanicMiddleware
--- PASS: TestPanicMiddleware (0.00s)
PASS
ok          github.com/practicalgo/code/chap6/complex-server/middleware
0.615s
```

This technique is useful for testing middleware in isolation. What if you wanted to test whether your entire middleware chain is working as expected? Let's write a test for that next.

Testing the Server Startup

For the server application in Listing 6.8, the function `setupServer()` creates the server configuration and registers request handlers and the middleware chain. Thus, testing the server startup behavior will boil down to testing this function.

First, we will create new `http.ServeMux` and `bytes.Buffer` objects and call the `setupServer()` function:

```
b := new(bytes.Buffer)
mux := http.NewServeMux()
wrappedMux := setupServer(mux, b)
```

Then we will use the `httptest.NewServer()` function to start a test HTTP server and specify `wrappedMux` as the handler:

```
ts := httptest.NewServer(wrappedMux)
defer ts.Close()
```

Once we have the test server running, we will send HTTP requests and verify the following:

1. The response status and body contents are as expected

2. The logging middleware and the panic-handling middleware are working as expected

Listing 6.11 shows the test function for verifying the server setup.

Listing 6.11: Test for server setup

```go
// chap6/complex-server/server_test.go
package main

import (
        "bytes"
        "io"
        "net/http"
        "net/http/httptest"
        "strings"
        "testing"
)

func TestSetupServer(t *testing.T) {
        b := new(bytes.Buffer)
        mux := http.NewServeMux()
        wrappedMux := setupServer(mux, b)
        ts := httptest.NewServer(wrappedMux)
        defer ts.Close()

        resp, err := http.Get(ts.URL + "/panic")
        if err != nil {
                t.Fatal(err)
        }
        defer resp.Body.Close()
        _, err = io.ReadAll(resp.Body)
        if err != nil {
                t.Error(err)
        }
        if resp.StatusCode != http.StatusInternalServerError {
                t.Errorf(
                        "Expected response status to be: %v, Got: %v",
                        http.StatusInternalServerError,
                        resp.StatusCode,
                )
        }

        logs := b.String()
        expectedLogFragments := []string{
```

```
                    "path=/panic method=GET duration=",
                    "panic detected",
        }
        for _, log := range expectedLogFragments {
                if !strings.Contains(logs, log) {
                        t.Errorf(
                                "Expected logs to contain: %s, Got: %s",
                                log, logs,
                        )
                }
        }
}
```

In the test function, we start up the test server after calling the setupServer() function and make an HTTP request to the /panic endpoint. Then we verify that the response status is 500 Internal Server Error. In the rest of the test, we verify whether the expected logs have been written to the configured io.Writer, b. Save Listing 6.11 as server_test.go in the same directory as server.go (where Listing 6.8 is stored) and run the test:

```
$ go test -v
=== RUN TestSetupServer
--- PASS: TestSetupServer (0.00s)
PASS
ok          github.com/practicalgo/code/chap6/complex-server          0.711s
```

The above test function tests the server setup, including the functioning of your middleware chain. When writing tests for server applications, it is always a good idea to test components in isolation and then test which tests verify the integration of the components. For handlers and middleware, you wrote unit tests to test them in isolation without starting an HTTP server. For the final server setup test, you started a test HTTP server to test the integration of the request handlers and the middleware.

Summary

You began this chapter by learning about the http.Handler interface. You learned how http.ServeMux is a type that implements this interface and then wrote your own type to implement the same. You saw how you can integrate a ServeMux object with your own handler implementation in order to share data across handler functions.

Next you learned to write server middleware, first by implementing a custom Handler type and then using the http.HandlerFunc type. You also learned how to chain together middleware in your server so that you could implement common server functionality as independent plug-and-play components.

Finally, you learned about a way to organize and test a server application along with its various components.

In the next chapter, "Production Ready HTTP Servers," you will explore techniques to make your HTTP server application ready for deployment.

Production-Ready HTTP Servers

In this chapter, you will learn about techniques to improve the robustness and stability of HTTP server applications. You will learn how to implement timeouts at various points of your server's request handling life cycle, abort request processing to preserve server resources, and implement graceful shutdowns. Finally, you will learn how to configure your HTTP server so that there is a secure communication channel between a client and your server. Let's get started!

Aborting Request Handling

Consider a specific functionality that your web application provides—say, allowing the user to perform a search over a large dataset based on certain parameters. Before you made this feature available to the users, you performed extensive testing and found out that a search request completes within 500 milliseconds for all of your test scenarios. However, once users started making use of the feature in their applications, you found that, for certain search criteria, the requests may take up to 30 seconds to be completed, sometimes without success. What's worse is that the same search would complete successfully within 500 milliseconds when retried. You are now concerned that this may result in your application being exploited, as multiple such requests can make

it incapable of serving *any* request—operating system resources are finite—
open file descriptors, memory, and so on. Sounds familiar? This is how denial
of service (DoS) attacks are accomplished!

When you start to look into this strange behavior to come up with a fix, you
want to insert a safety mechanism into your server. To do so, you will enforce a
time-out on the handler for this request. If this operation is taking longer than
10 seconds, you will abort the request processing and return an error response.
Doing this will achieve two goals: Your server's resources are not tied up with
these requests, which takes longer than expected, and your client gets a fast
response telling them that their request couldn't be completed. They can then
simply retry and likely obtain a successful response. Let's see how we can
implement this behavior in an HTTP server application.

The `http.TimeoutHandler()` function is middleware defined in the `net/`
`http` package that creates a new `http.Handler` object wrapping another `http.`
`Handler` object in such a manner that if the internal handler doesn't complete
within a specified duration of time, a 503 Service Unavailable HTTP response
is sent to the client. Let's consider a handler function:

```
func handleUserAPI(w http.ResponseWriter, r *http.Request) {
        log.Println("I started processing the request")
        time.Sleep(15 * time.Second)
        fmt.Fprintf(w, "Hello world!")
        log.Println("I finished processing the request")
}
```

We have a call to the `time.Sleep()` function to simulate a 15-second delay
in processing a request. After 15 seconds have passed, it will send a response
`Hello world!` to the client. The logs will help us understand the interaction
of the handler function with the time-out handler better, as you will soon see.

Next, we will use the `http.TimeoutHandler()` function to wrap the
`handleUsersAPI()` function so that an HTTP 503 response will be sent to the
client after 14 seconds—just before the handler function wakes up from its
sleep. The `http.TimeoutHandler()` function's signature is defined as follows:

```
func TimeoutHandler(h Handler, dt time.Duration, msg string) Handler
```

Its parameters are an object, `h`, the *incoming* handler that satisfies the `http.`
`Handler` interface; a `time.Duration` object, `dt`, which contains the maximum
duration (in milliseconds or seconds) that we want the client to wait for the
handler to complete; and a string value containing the message that will
be sent to the client along with the HTTP 503 response. Thus, to wrap the
`handleUsersAPI()` handler function, we will first convert it to a value that
satisfies the `http.Handler` interface:

```
userHandler := http.HandlerFunc(handleUserAPI)
```

Then we call the `http.TimeoutHandler()` function with a time-out duration of 14 seconds:

```
timeoutDuration := 14 * time.Second
hTimeout := http.TimeoutHandler(
        userHandler, timeoutDuration, "I ran out of time",
)
```

The returned object, `hTimeout`, satisfies the `http.Handler` interface and wraps the incoming handler, `userHandler`, with this time-out logic implemented. It can then be registered with a `ServeMux` object to handle requests directly or as part of a middleware chain, as in the following example:

```
mux := http.NewServeMux()
mux.Handle("/api/users/", hTimeout)
```

Listing 7.1 shows a complete example of a runnable HTTP server showing the integration of the `handleUserAPI` handler and the `http.TimeoutHandler()` function.

Listing 7.1: Enforcing time-out on a handler function

```go
// chap7/handle-func-timeout/server.go
package main

import (
        "fmt"
        "log"
        "net/http"
        "time"
)

// TODO Insert handleUserAPI() function from above

func main() {

        listenAddr := os.Getenv("LISTEN_ADDR")
        if len(listenAddr) == 0 {
                listenAddr = ":8080"
        }

        timeoutDuration := 14 * time.Second

        userHandler := http.HandlerFunc(handleUserAPI)
        hTimeout := http.TimeoutHandler(
                userHandler,
                timeoutDuration,
                "I ran out of time",
        )
```

```
mux := http.NewServeMux()
mux.Handle("/api/users/", hTimeout)

log.Fatal(http.ListenAndServe(listenAddr, mux))
}
```

Create a new directory, chap7/handle-func-timeout, and initialize a module inside it:

```
$ mkdir -p chap7/handle-func-timeout
$ cd chap7/http-handler-type
$ go mod init github.com/username/handle-func-timeout
```

Next, save Listing 7.1 as server.go. Build and run the application:

```
$ go build -o server
$ ./server
```

From a separate terminal, make a request to the /api/users/ endpoint using curl (adding the -v option):

```
$ curl -v localhost:8080/api/users/
# output snipped #
>
< HTTP/1.1 503 Service Unavailable
# output snipped #

I ran out of time
```

The client gets a 503 Service Unavailable response along with a message "I ran out of time." On the terminal on which you ran the server, you will see logs as follows:

```
2021/04/24 09:26:19 I started processing the request
2021/04/24 09:26:34 I finished processing the request
```

The above logs show that handler function, usersAPIHandler, continues executing even though the client has already been sent an HTTP 503 response, thus terminating the connection. In this case, it's not a deal breaker to let the handler function complete and then let the runtime handle the cleanup. However, in the scenario where we will implement this time-out, such as for the search feature stated in the beginning, allowing the handler to continue running may defeat the purpose of enforcing the time-out in the first place. It will continue consuming resources on the server. Thus, we will need to do a bit of work to ensure that the handler stops doing any further processing once the time-out handler has kicked in. Let's examine a way to do this next.

Strategies to Abort Request Processing

You learned in Chapter 5 that an incoming request processed by a handler function has an associated context. This context is canceled when the client's connection is closed. Thus, on the server side, if we check whether the context has been canceled before continuing to process the request, we can abort the processing when the http.TimeoutHandler() has already sent back the HTTP 503 response to the client. Figure 7.1 illustrates this graphically.

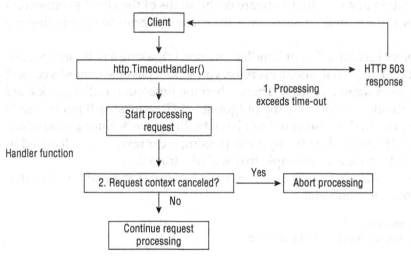

Figure 7.1: Aborting the request processing when the time-out handler has kicked in

Let's consider an updated version of the handleUserAPI() function:

```go
func handleUserAPI(w http.ResponseWriter, r *http.Request) {
        log.Println("I started processing the request")
        time.Sleep(15 * time.Second)

        log.Println(
                "Before continuing, i will check if the timeout
                has already expired",
        )
        if r.Context().Err() != nil {
                log.Printf(
                        "Aborting further processing: %v\n",
                        r.Context().Err(),
                )
                return
        }
        fmt.Fprintf(w, "Hello world!")
        log.Println("I finished processing the request")
}
```

After the call to the `time.Sleep()` function, we retrieve the request's context using the `r.Context()` method. Then we check if a call to the `Err()` method returns a non-nil error value. If a non-nil error value is returned, the client connection is closed now and so we return from the handler function. Since the client has already gone away, we save system resources or prevent unpredictable behavior by aborting the request processing. You can find a runnable server with the above handler function in the `chap7/abort-processing-timeout` directory of this book's source code repository. This strategy requires you to write your handler function in a way that is aware of the status of the client's connection and then uses that to make a decision as to whether to continue processing the request.

In a different scenario, if your handler function is making a network request, such as an HTTP request to another service, you should pass the request's context along with the outgoing request. Then, when the time-out handler has kicked in (thus canceling the context), the outgoing HTTP request will not be made at all. Of course, in this case you don't have to do the work since the standard library's HTTP client already supports passing a context, as you learned in Chapter 4. Let's review an example that will illustrate this.

Consider a function `doSomeWork()`, which is a proxy for a real function that takes 2 seconds to complete:

```
func doSomeWork() {
        time.Sleep(2 * time.Second)
}
```

Next, consider an updated `handleUserAPI()` function that calls the `doSomeWork()` function:

```
func handleUserAPI(w http.ResponseWriter, r *http.Request) {
        log.Println("I started processing the request")

        doSomeWork()

        req, err := http.NewRequestWithContext(
                        r.Context(),
                        "GET",
                        "http://localhost:8080/ping", nil,
                )
        if err != nil {
                http.Error(
                        w, err.Error(),
                        http.StatusInternalServerError,
                )
                return
        }
        client := &http.Client{}
```

```
        log.Println("Outgoing HTTP request")

        resp, err := client.Do(req)
        if err != nil {
                log.Printf("Error making request: %v\n", err)
                http.Error(
                        w, err.Error(),
                        http.StatusInternalServerError,
                )
                return
        }
        defer resp.Body.Close()
        data, _ := io.ReadAll(resp.Body)

        fmt.Fprint(w, string(data))
        log.Println("I finished processing the request")
}
```

The handleUserAPI() function first calls the doSomeWork() function and then makes an HTTP GET request on the /ping path for another HTTP application—in this case, the same application for simplicity. It uses the http.NewRequest WithContext() function to construct the HTTP request, asking it to use the context of the current request being handled as its context. The obtained response from the GET request is then sent back as the response. We expect that if the time-out handler aborts the request processing, this request will not be made. Listing 7.2 shows a runnable server application.

Listing 7.2: Enforcing time-out on a handler function

```
// chap7/network-request-timeout/server.go
package main

import (
        "fmt"
        "io"
        "log"
        "net/http"
        "time"
)

func handlePing(w http.ResponseWriter, r *http.Request) {
        log.Println("ping: Got a request")
        fmt.Fprintf(w, "pong")
}

func doSomeOtherWork() {
        time.Sleep(2 * time.Second)
}
```

```
// TODO Insert the updated handleUserAPI() function from earlier

func main() {
        listenAddr := os.Getenv("LISTEN_ADDR")
        if len(listenAddr) == 0 {
                listenAddr = ":8080"
        }

        timeoutDuration := 1 * time.Second

        userHandler := http.HandlerFunc(handleUserAPI)
        hTimeout := http.TimeoutHandler(
                userHandler,
                timeoutDuration,
                "I ran out of time"                ,
        )

        mux := http.NewServeMux()
        mux.Handle("/api/users/", hTimeout)
        mux.HandleFunc("/ping", handlePing)

        log.Fatal(http.ListenAndServe(listenAddr, mux))
}
```

We call the `http.TimeoutHandler()` function now with the `userHandler`
object and set up a time-out of 1 second. The `doSomeWork()` function takes 2
seconds to complete.

Create a new directory, `chap7/network-request-timeout`, and initialize a
module inside it:

```
$ mkdir -p chap7/network-request-timeout
$ cd chap7/network-request-timeout
$ go mod init github.com/username/network-request-timeout
```

Next, save Listing 7.2 as `server.go`. Build and run the application:

```
$ go build -o server
$ ./server
```

In a separate terminal, make a request to the application on the `/api/users/`
path using `curl` (adding the `-v` option):

```
$ curl -v localhost:8080/api/users/
# output snipped #
>
< HTTP/1.1 503 Service Unavailable
# output snipped #

I ran out of time
```

The client gets a 503 Service Unavailable response along with a message "I ran out of time." The more interesting behavior can be observed in the server logs:

```
2021/04/25 17:43:41 I started processing the request
2021/04/25 17:43:43 Outgoing HTTP request
2021/04/25 17:43:43 Error making request: Get
"http://localhost:8080/ping": context deadline exceeded
```

The `handleUserAPI()` function starts processing the request. Then, 2 seconds later it attempts to make the HTTP GET request. During this attempt, we get an error saying that the context deadline has been exceeded and hence the request processing is aborted.

You may be curious when exactly is the outgoing HTTP GET request aborted. Was it after the DNS lookup or was it after the TCP connection was made to the server? Exercise 7.1 gives you an opportunity to find out.

EXERCISE 7.1: TRACING THE OUTGOING CLIENT BEHAVIOR

In Chapter 4, you used the `net/http/httptrace` package to learn about connection pooling behavior in the HTTP client. The `httptrace.ClientTrace` struct has a number of other fields, such as `ConnectStart` when the TCP connection establishment starts and `WroteRequest` when the HTTP request is completed. You can use these fields to probe into the different stages of the HTTP request. For this exercise, update Listing 7.2 to integrate the `httptrace.ClientTrace` struct into your HTTP client so that it logs the different stages for the outgoing request.

Once you have integrated `httptrace.ClientTrace`, experiment with changing the time-out duration to be greater than the sleep duration in the `doSomeWork()` function.

In this section, you have seen two strategies to abort the request processing when using the `http.TimeoutHandler()` function. The first strategy is useful when you have to check for the time-out explicitly, and the second strategy is useful when you are using a standard library function that understands contexts. These strategies are useful when the server has initiated the client disconnection. In the next section, you will learn how to handle the scenario when a client has initiated a disconnect.

Handling Client Disconnects

Consider the scenario of the search feature earlier in this chapter. You have now enforced a maximum time-out on the operation of the handler function. Upon further analysis, you realize that for now, the search operation for certain specific cases is going to be expensive and hence the time taken will be more than in the other cases. Thus, you want your user to wait for the operation to complete in those cases. However, you now see a behavior in your users that they will make a request for an expensive search operation and then terminate their connection since they think it's not going to complete. Then they try again. This leads to a number of such requests that your server is processing, but the results are of no use since the client has disconnected already. So, we don't want to continue processing a request in this scenario.

To respond to the client disconnecting, you will once again make use of the request's context. In fact, the `handleUserAPI()` function in Listing 7.2 is already written in this manner. The difference is that the client will initiate the disconnect rather than the server. We are going to modify the function now to explore another pattern for detecting a client disconnect using the request context:

```go
func handleUserAPI(w http.ResponseWriter, r *http.Request) {
        done := make(chan bool)

        log.Println("I started processing the request")

        // TODO Make the outgoing request as earlier in Listing 7.2

        data, _ := io.ReadAll(resp.Body)

        log.Println("Processing the response i got")

        go func() {
                doSomeWork(data)
                done <- true
        }()

        select {
        case <-done:
                log.Println(
                        "doSomeWork done:Continuing request processing",
                )
        case <-r.Context().Done():
                log.Printf(
                        "Aborting request processing: %v\n",
                        r.Context().Err(),
                )
                return
        }

        fmt.Fprint(w, string(data))
        log.Println("I finished processing the request")
}
```

Upon receiving a request, the handler function makes an outgoing HTTP GET call. As seen earlier, we will pass the incoming request's context as part of this request. Once it receives the response, it calls the doSomeWork() function in a goroutine. Once the function returns, we write true to the done channel. Then we have a select..case block where we are waiting on two channels — done and the channel returned via a call to the r.Context.Done() method. If we get value on the done channel first, we continue the processing of the request. If we get a value on the second channel first, the context has been canceled and we abort the request processing by returning from the handler function. We will make a few changes to the other parts of the server as well. Listing 7.3 shows the server with these changes implemented.

Listing 7.3: Handling client disconnects

```go
// chap7/client-disconnect-handling/server.go
package main

import (
        "fmt"
        "io"
        "log"
        "net/http"
        "time"
)

func handlePing(w http.ResponseWriter, r *http.Request) {
        log.Println("ping: Got a request")
        time.Sleep(10 * time.Second)
        fmt.Fprintf(w, "pong")
}

func doSomeWork(data []byte) {
        time.Sleep(15 * time.Second)
}

// TODO Insert the modified handleUserAPI function

func main() {

        listenAddr := os.Getenv("LISTEN_ADDR")
        if len(listenAddr) == 0 {
                listenAddr = ":8080"
        }


        timeoutDuration := 30 * time.Second

        userHandler := http.HandlerFunc(handleUserAPI)
        hTimeout := http.TimeoutHandler(
                userHandler,
                timeoutDuration,
```

```
            "I ran out of time",
    )

        mux := http.NewServeMux()
        mux.Handle("/api/users/", hTimeout)
        mux.HandleFunc("/ping", handlePing)

        log.Fatal(http.ListenAndServe(listenAddr, mux))
}
```

We have increased the duration of the sleep in doSomeWork() to be 15 seconds and introduced a sleep for 10 seconds in the handlePing() function. We have also increased the duration of the time-out handler to 30 seconds. These changes have been done to reflect the new findings related to the performance of the search functionality. Thus, in this version of the server, the time-out handler will *not* abort the request processing—this is intentional.

Create a new directory, chap7/client-disconnect-handling, and initialize a module inside it:

```
$ mkdir -p chap7/client-disconnect-handling
$ cd chap7/client-disconnect-handling
$ go mod init github.com/username/client-disconnect-handling
```

Next, save Listing 7.3 as server.go. Build and run the application:

```
$ go build -o server
$ ./server
```

In a separate terminal, make a request to the application on the /api/users/ path using curl, and before 10 seconds has elapsed, press Ctrl+C to abort the request:

```
$ curl -v localhost:8080/api/users/
..
* Connected to localhost (::1) port 8080 (#0)
..
^C
```

On the terminal on which you ran the server, you will see the following logs:

```
2021/04/26 09:25:17 I started processing the request
2021/04/26 09:25:17 Outgoing HTTP request
2021/04/26 09:25:17 ping: Got a request
2021/04/26 09:25:18 Error making request: Get "http://localhost:8080/
ping": context canceled
```

From the logs, you can see that the `handlePing()` function got the request, but it was canceled before finishing execution in response to you aborting the request. Note the log message now says `context canceled` (and not `context deadline exceeded`). Experiment with aborting the request after 10 seconds but before another 15 seconds have elapsed.

You have learned to implement techniques to abort request processing in your server applications in response to a configured time-out or a client. The goal of implementing this pattern is to introduce predictability around the behavior when an unexpected situation happens. However, these techniques were focused on individual handler functions. Next, we will look at implementing robustness from the point of view of the entire server application. Before doing that, however, you have an exercise to attempt (Exercise 7.2).

EXERCISE 7.2: TESTING THE REQUEST ABORTING BEHAVIOR

You just learned to abort the processing of a request when a client disconnect has been detected. Write a test to verify this behavior. Verifying the server logs as implemented in Listing 7.3 is sufficient as a test. To simulate a client disconnect in the test, you will find it useful to refer to the HTTP client time-out configuration in Chapter 4.

Server-Wide Time-Outs

We will start by looking at implementing a global time-out for all handler functions. Then we will go one level up, looking at the network communication that happens before a request reaches a handler function and learning how to introduce robustness at various stages of the request-response process.

Implement a Time-Out for All Handler Functions

Even before you notice a specific issue with any of your applications running in production, you may want to implement a hard time-out on all the handler functions. This will provide an upper bound on the latency across all of your request handlers and prevent unforeseen circumstances from tying up your server resources. To do so, you will once again make use of the `http.TimeoutHandler()` function. You will recall that the signature for the function is as follows:

```
func TimeoutHandler(h Handler, dt time.Duration, msg string) Handler
```

A key observation to be made here is that the wrapped handler object, h, must satisfy the `http.Handler` interface. Also, you learned in Chapter 6 that a value of type http.ServeMux satisfies the same interface. Thus, to implement a global time-out across all of the handler functions, all you need to do is to call the http.TimeoutHandler() function with the ServeMux object as the handler value and then call http.ListenAndServe() with the returned handler:

```
mux := http.ServeMux()
mux.HandleFunc("/api/users/", userAPIHandler)
mux.HandleFunc("/healthz", healthcheckHandler)
mTimeout := http.TimeoutHandler(mux, 5*time.Second, "I ran out of time")
http.ListenAndServe(":8080", mTimeout)
```

With the above setup in place, all request handlers registered will have a maximum of five seconds before the time-out handler kicks in and aborts the request processing. You can find a runnable example demonstrating global handler time-outs in the chap7/global-handler-timeout directory of this book's source code distribution. Of course, you can combine global handler time-outs with handler-specific time-outs as well to implement more granular time-outs. Integrating global handler time-outs with strategies to abort processing requests ensures that your server is more equipped to *fail fast* when there is an unexpected scenario in your application.

Next, we will go one level up from handler time-outs and look at making a server immune to issues that can happen beyond the request handlers.

Implementing Server Time-Out

When a client makes a request to a HTTP application, the following steps occur at a high level (ignoring any registered middleware):

1. The client connection is *accepted* by the server's main goroutine; that is, where the call to the http.ListenAndServe() function is made.

2. The request is partially *read* by the server to figure out the path for the request, for example, /api/users/ or /healthz.

3. If there is a handler registered for the path, the server routine creates a http.Request object containing the request headers and all of the information related to the request, as you learned in Chapter 5.

4. The handler is then invoked to process the request, which processes it and then *writes* the response back to the client. Depending on the logic of the handler, it may or may not *read* the request body.

Under normal circumstances, all of the above steps happen in a reasonably short period of time—milliseconds or, depending on the request, tens of seconds. However, our goal here is to think about the unusual scenarios when bad network connections or malicious actors are involved. Consider a scenario where the handler starts reading the request (in step 4) above, but the client maliciously never stops sending the data. A similar scenario is applicable when the server is writing the response to the client but the client is maliciously reading it slowly so that the server takes way longer than it would otherwise. In both scenarios, many such clients can continue consuming the server resources and thus render the server unable to perform any functionality. To provide some level of safety for your server applications in such scenarios, you can configure your server with read and write time-out values.

Figure 7.2 shows the different time-outs in the context of handling a request. You have already learned about the time-out that is configurable per handler using the `http.TimeoutHandler()` function. So why do we need the other time-outs? For the incoming request flow, the time-out enforced by configuring the `http.TimeoutHandler()` function is only applicable once the request has reached the configured HTTP handler function for a path. The time-out doesn't come into effect before that. For the outgoing response flow, the time-out enforced by this function doesn't help at all since the `http.TimeoutHandler()` function by design will write a response to the client after the time-out and hence can be affected by a malicious client or network equally. Next, you will learn how to configure server-level read and write time-outs.

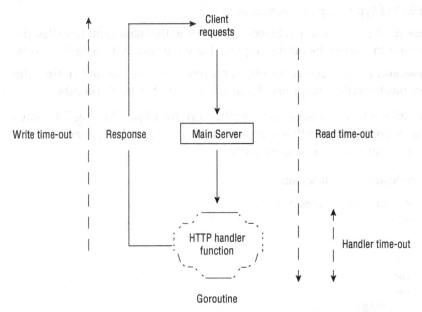

Figure 7.2: The different time-outs that play a role when handling an HTTP request

The `http.ListenAndServe()` function that starts an HTTP server is defined as follows (as of Go 1.16):

```
func ListenAndServe(addr string, handler Handler) error {
    server := &Server{Addr: addr, Handler: handler}
    return server.ListenAndServe()
}
```

It creates an object of type `http.Server`, which is a `struct` type defined in the `net/http` package. Then it calls the `ListenAndServe()` method on it. To configure the server further, for example to add read and write time-outs, we thus have to create a customized `Server` object ourselves and call the `ListenAndServe()` method:

```
s := http.Server{
        Addr:        ":8080",
        Handler:     mux,
        ReadTimeout: 5 * time.Second,
        WriteTimeout: 5 * time.Second,
}
log.Fatal(s.ListenAndServe())
```

We create an `http.Server` object, s, specifying a few fields:

Addr: A string corresponding to the address on which we want the server to listen. Here we want the server to listen on the address `":8080"`.

Handler: An object that satisfies the `http.Handler` interface. Here we specify an object of type `http.ServeMux`, mux.

ReadTimeout: A `time.Duration` object representing the maximum time that the server has to read an incoming request. Here we specify it to be 5 seconds.

WriteTimeout: A `time.Duration` object representing the maximum time the server has to write a response. Here we specify it to be 5 seconds.

Then we call the `ListenAndServe()` method on this object. Listing 7.4 shows a server that is configured with a read and write time-out. It registers a single request handler for the `/api/users/` path.

Listing 7.4: Configuring server time-outs

```
// chap7/server-timeouts/server.go
package main

import (
        "fmt"
        "io"
        "log"
        "net/http"
        "os"
        "time"
)

func handleUserAPI(w http.ResponseWriter, r *http.Request) {
        log.Println("I started processing the request")
        defer r.Body.Close()
```

```go
        data, err := io.ReadAll(r.Body)
        if err != nil {
                log.Printf("Error reading body: %v\n", err)
                http.Error(
                        w, "Error reading body",
                        http.StatusInternalServerError,
                )
                return
        }
        log.Println(string(data))
        fmt.Fprintf(w, "Hello world!")
        log.Println("I finished processing the request")
}

func main() {
        listenAddr := os.Getenv("LISTEN_ADDR")
        if len(listenAddr) == 0 {
                listenAddr = ":8080"
        }

        mux := http.NewServeMux()
        mux.HandleFunc("/api/users/", handleUserAPI)

        s := http.Server{
                Addr:         listenAddr,
                Handler:      mux,
                ReadTimeout:  5 * time.Second,
                WriteTimeout: 5 * time.Second,
        }
        log.Fatal(s.ListenAndServe())
}
```

The `handleUsersAPI()` function is expecting that requests to it will have a body. We have added various log statements inside it to ensure that we can understand how the configured time-outs affect the server behavior. It will read the body, log it, and then send a response "Hello world!" to the client. If there is an error while reading the body, it will log that and then send an error back to the client. Create a new directory, `chap7/server-timeout`, and initialize a module inside it:

```
$ mkdir -p chap7/server-timeout
$ cd chap7/server-timeout
$ go mod init github.com/username/server-timeout
```

Next, save Listing 7.4 as `server.go`. Build and run the application:

```
$ go build -o server
$ ./server
```

In a separate terminal, make the following request to it using `curl`:

```
$ curl --request POST http://localhost:8080/api/users/ \
    --data "Hello server"
Hello world!
```

The above `curl` command makes an HTTP POST request with "Hello server" as the request body. On the server side, you will see the following log statements:

```
2021/05/02 14:03:08 I started processing the request
2021/05/02 14:03:08 Hello server
2021/05/02 14:03:08 I finished processing the request
```

This was the behavior of the server under *normal* circumstances. Keep the server running.

Using some of the techniques that you learned in the Chapter 5 section entitled "Streaming Data as Responses," you can implement an HTTP client that is sending the request body very slowly. You can find the client code in the `chap7/client-slow-write` directory of the source code repository. Inside the `main.go` file, you will see the `longRunningProcess()` function, which writes the same string to the write end of an `io.Pipe`, with the read end connected to the HTTP request being sent in a for loop with a 1 second sleep in between each iteration:

```go
func longRunningProcess(w *io.PipeWriter) {
        for i := 0; i <= 10; i++ {
                fmt.Fprintf(w, "hello")
                time.Sleep(1 * time.Second)
        }
        w.Close()
}
```

As long as the loop continues execution, the server is going to continue to read the request body. Since the server's read time-out is set to 5 seconds, we expect that the request handler will never complete reading the complete request. Let's verify that.

Build the client and run it as follows (while you have the server running):

```
$ go build -o client-slow-write

$ ./client-slow-write
2021/05/02 15:37:32 Starting client request
2021/05/02 15:37:37 Error when sending the request: Post
"http://localhost:8080/api/users/": write tcp
[::1]:52195->[::1]:8080: use of closed network connection
```

The key in the error above is that the client is sending data over a closed network connection, and we see that we get the error just after 5 seconds has elapsed, which is the server's read time-out.

On the server side, you will see log statements as follows:

```
2021/05/02 15:37:32 I started processing the request
2021/05/02 15:37:37 Error reading body: read tcp
[::1]:8080->[::1]:52195: i/o timeout
```

The handler started processing the request. It starts reading the request body, and just after 5 seconds, it gets an error while doing so since the read time-out has expired.

Thus, read and write time-outs in servers and request handlers have some interesting implications in the context of streaming requests and responses. When a server is configured with a ReadTimeout, it will close the client connection and thus abort any request that is currently being handled. This of course means that setting a read time-out value for a server that will read *streaming* requests (Chapter 5) from a client is not possible as theoretically the client could continue sending the data forever. In such a scenario, where one or more of your request handlers are expecting to handle streaming requests, you may want instead to set the ReadHeaderTimeout configuration, which only enforces a time-out on reading the headers. That at least makes your server globally immune to some malicious and undesirable client requests. Similarly, if your server is sending its response as a stream, the WriteTimeout becomes impossible to enforce unless you have an estimated upper bound over the time it may take for the streaming to be completed. Reading (or writing) streaming data makes enforcing time-outs using the http.TimeoutHandler() function tricky to implement as well. By default, none of the standard library's input/output functions support cancellation as of Go 1.16. Hence, a time-out expiration event doesn't cancel any ongoing input or output in your handler function, and it is only detected after the operation completes.

So far, you have looked at techniques to improve the robustness of your server applications when faced with unexpected behavior that is common for any program that is exposed over a computer network. Next, you are going to look at implementing techniques that introduce predictability when your server is undergoing a planned termination, such as deployment of a new version of your server or as part of a scaling operation in a cloud infrastructure.

Implementing Graceful Shutdown

Shutting down an HTTP server *gracefully* means that an attempt is made to not interrupt any ongoing request processing before the server is stopped. Essentially, there are two things that go into implementing a graceful server shutdown:

1. Stop receiving any new requests.
2. Don't terminate any requests that are already being processed.

Luckily, the `net/http` library already makes this facility available via the `Shutdown()` method defined on the `http.Server` object. When this method is called, the server stops receiving any new requests, terminates any idle connections, and then waits for any running request handler function to complete processing before returning. You can control how long it will wait by passing a `context.Context` object. Let's first write a function that will set up a signal handler (similar to how you implemented it for command-line applications in Chapter 2) and call the `Shutdown()` method on the defined server object, s, when a SIGINT or SIGTERM signal is received:

```
func shutDown(
        ctx context.Context,
        s *http.Server,
        waitForShutdownCompletion chan struct{},
) {
        sigch := make(chan os.Signal, 1)
        signal.Notify(sigch, syscall.SIGINT, syscall.SIGTERM)
        sig := <-sigch
        log.Printf("Got signal: %v . Server shutting down.", sig)
        if err := s.Shutdown(ctx); err != nil {
                log.Printf("Error during shutdown: %v", err)
        }
        waitForShutdownCompletion <- struct{}{}
}
```

The `shutDown()` function is called with three parameters:

ctx: A `context.Context` object that allows you to control how long the `Shutdown()` method waits for the existing request processing to be completed

s: A `http.Server` object representing the server, which will be shut down when a signal is received

waitForShutdownCompletion: A channel of type `struct{}`

When one of SIGINT or SIGTERM is received by the program, it will call the `Shutdown()` method. When the call returns, `struct{}{}` will be written to the `waitForShutdownCompletion` channel. This will indicate to the main server routine that the shutdown process has been completed and it can go ahead and terminate itself.

Figure 7.3 illustrates graphically how the `Shutdown()` and `ListenAndServe()` methods interact. Listing 7.5 shows a server that implements graceful shutdown.

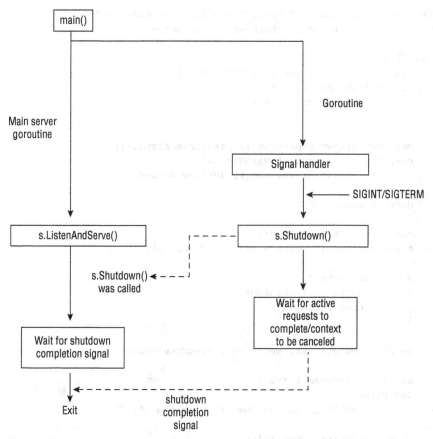

Figure 7.3: Interaction between the `Shutdown()` and `ListenAndServe()` methods

Listing 7.5: Implementing graceful shutdown in a server

```go
// chap7/graceful-shutdown/server.go
package main

import (
        "context"
        "fmt"
        "io"
        "log"
        "net/http"
        "os"
        "os/signal"
        "syscall"
        "time"
)
```

```
// TODO Insert definition of handleUserAPI() from Listing 7.4
// TODO Insert definition of shutDown() from above

func main() {
        listenAddr := os.Getenv("LISTEN_ADDR")
        if len(listenAddr) == 0 {
                listenAddr = ":8080"
        }

        waitForShutdownCompletion := make(chan struct{})
        ctx, cancel := context.WithTimeout(
                context.Background(), 30*time.Second,
        )
        defer cancel()

        mux := http.NewServeMux()
        mux.HandleFunc("/api/users/", handleUserAPI)

        s := http.Server{
                Addr:    listenAddr,
                Handler: mux,
        }

        go shutDown(ctx, &s, waitForShutdownCompletion)

        err := s.ListenAndServe()
        log.Print(
                "Waiting for shutdown to complete..",
        )
        <-waitForShutdownCompletion
        log.Fatal(err)
}
```

The waitForShutdownCompletion channel will help us orchestrate the main server goroutine and the goroutine that runs the shutDown() function. We create a context with the context.WithTimeout() function, which will be canceled after 30 seconds. This configures the maximum amount of time that the server's Shutdown() method will wait for all existing requests to be processed.

We then call the shutDown() function in a goroutine and call the s.ListenAndServe() function. Note that we don't call this function inside a call to log.Fatal(). This is because when the Shutdown() method is called, the ListenAndServe() function will immediately return and hence the server will exit without waiting for the Shutdown() method to return. Thus, we store the returned error value in err, log a message, and wait until a value has been written to the waitForShutdownCompletion channel, which blocks the server termination. Once we have received a value on this channel, we log the error and exit.

Create a new directory, chap7/graceful-shutdown, and initialize a module inside it:

```
$ mkdir -p chap7/graceful-shutdown
$ cd chap7/graceful-shutdown
$ go mod init github.com/username/graceful-shutdown
```

Next, save Listing 7.5 as server.go. Build and run the application:

```
$ go build -o server
$ ./server
```

To make a request to this server, we will use the custom client, which you can find in the chap7/client-slow-write directory of the source code repository. Build the client and run it as follows (while you have the server running):

```
$ go build -o client-slow-write

$ ./client-slow-write
2021/05/02 20:28:25 Starting client request
```

Now, once you have seen the log message above, switch back to the terminal where you have your server running and press Ctrl+C. You will see the following log statements:

```
2021/05/02 20:28:25 I started processing the request
^C2021/05/02 20:28:28 Got signal: interrupt . Server shutting down.
2021/05/02 20:28:28 Waiting for shutdown to complete..
2021/05/02 20:28:36 hellohellohellohellohellohellohello
hellohellohellohello
2021/05/02 20:28:36 I finished processing the request
2021/05/02 20:28:36 http: Server closed
```

Note that after you pressed Ctrl+C, the Shutdown() method waited for the entire body to be read, or for the request in progress to be completed, and only then did the server exit. On the client side, you will see that it got back the Hello world! response.

Great. You have now learned to implement a mechanism for terminating a server application in a way that in-flight requests are not terminated. In fact, you can use this mechanism to run various other complex cleanup operations that you may need to perform, such as notifying any open clients with long-lived connections so that they can send a reconnection request or shut down any open connections to databases and so on.

In the last section of the chapter, you will learn how to implement another essential ability to execute when running servers in production—configuring a secure communication channel with the client.

Securing Communication with TLS

Entire book chapters can be devoted to talking about *Transport Layer Security (TLS)* as it applies to securing network communication. TLS helps secure the communication between a server and a client using cryptographic protocols. More commonly, it allows you to implement secure web servers so that client-server communication happens over Hypertext Transfer Protocol Secure (HTTPS) rather than *plain* HTTP. To start an HTTPS server, you will use the `http.ListenAndServeTLS()` function or the `srv.ListenAndServeTLS()` method, where `srv` is a custom `http.Server` object. The signature of the `ListenAndServeTLS()` function is as follows:

```
func ListenAndServeTLS(addr, certFile, keyFile string, handler Handler)
```

If you compare `ListenAndServeTLS()` to the `ListenAndServe()` function, it takes two additional arguments—the second and third argument are string values containing the path to the TLS certificate and key files. These files contain the data required to transmit data securely between the server and a client using encryption and decryption techniques. You can either generate TLS certificates yourself (so called *self-signed certificates*) or ask somebody else—that is, a *certificate authority (CA)*—to generate one for you. Self-signed certificates can be used to secure the communication only within a certain well-defined perimeter, such as, for example, within an organization. However, if you were to use such a certificate in your server and then ask anyone outside your organization to access your server, they would get an error saying that the certificate is not recognized and thus no secure communication will take place. On the other hand, a certificate generated via a CA will be trusted by clients inside or outside the organization. Large organizations will generally use a mix of both, self-signed certificates for internal services where the consumers are also internal and certificates issued via a CA for public-facing services. In other words, for private domains you would use self-signed certificates and a CA-issued certificate for public domains. In fact, you could also run a certificate authority inside your organization to help with the use of self-signed certificates. Next, you will learn how to configure a secure HTTP server using self-signed certificates.

Configuring TLS and HTTP/2

First, you will create a self-signed certificate and key using the command-line program `openssl`. If you are using MacOS or Linux, the program should already be installed. For Windows, please see this book's website for instructions and links to other helpful resources.

Create a new directory, `chap7/tls-server`, and initialize a module inside it:

```
$ mkdir -p chap7/tls-server
$ cd chap7/tls-server
$ go mod init github.com/username/tls-server
```

To create a self-signed certificate using `openssl`, run the following command:

```
$ openssl req -x509 -newkey rsa:4096 -keyout server.key -out server.crt
-days 365 -subj "/C=AU/ST=NSW/L=Sydney/O=Echorand/OU=Org/CN=localhost" -nodes
```

The above command should finish executing with the following output:

```
Generating a 4096 bit RSA private key
..................................................
..................................................
........++
....................................................................++
writing new private key to 'server.key'
-----
```

You will see two files created inside the `chap7/tls-server` directory: `server.key` and `server.crt`. These are the key file and the certificate that we will specify when calling the `ListenAndServeTLS()` function, respectively. Delving into the details of the above command is out of scope here, but two points to note are as follows:

- The above certificates are only suitable for testing purposes because clients do not trust self-signed certificates by default.
- The above certificates will allow you to connect securely to your server using the `localhost` domain only.

Configuring and starting up an HTTPS server then appears as follows:

```
func main() {
        # ...

        tlsCertFile := os.Getenv("TLS_CERT_FILE_PATH")
        tlsKeyFile := os.Getenv("TLS_KEY_FILE_PATH")

        if len(tlsCertFile) == 0 || len(tlsKeyFile) == 0 {
                log.Fatal(
                        "TLS_CERT_FILE_PATH and TLS_KEY_FILE_PATH
must be specified")
        }
```

```
# ...

        log.Fatal(
                http.ListenAndServeTLS(
                        listenAddr,
                        tlsCertFile,
                        tlsKeyFile,
                        m,
                ),
        )
}
```

The server expects that the path to the certificate and the key file will be specified as environment variables: TLS_CERT_FILE_PATH and TLS_KEY_FILE_PATH, respectively. Listing 7.6 shows a complete example of an HTTP server that uses TLS certificates.

Listing 7.6: Securing an HTTP server using TLS

```go
// chap7/tls-server/server.go
package main

import (
        "fmt"
        "log"
        "net/http"
        "os"
        "time"
)

func apiHandler(w http.ResponseWriter, r *http.Request) {
        fmt.Fprintf(w, "Hello, world!")
}

func setupHandlers(mux *http.ServeMux) {
        mux.HandleFunc("/api", apiHandler)
}

func loggingMiddleware(h http.Handler) http.Handler {
        return http.HandlerFunc(
                func(w http.ResponseWriter, r *http.Request) {
                        startTime := time.Now()
                        h.ServeHTTP(w, r)
                        log.Printf(
                                "protocol=%s path=%s
                                 method=%s duration=%f",
                                r.Proto, r.URL.Path, r.Method,
                                time.Now().Sub(startTime).Seconds(),
                        )
                })
}
```

```go
func main() {
        listenAddr := os.Getenv("LISTEN_ADDR")
        if len(listenAddr) == 0 {
                listenAddr = ":8443"
        }

        tlsCertFile := os.Getenv("TLS_CERT_FILE_PATH")
        tlsKeyFile := os.Getenv("TLS_KEY_FILE_PATH")

        if len(tlsCertFile) == 0 || len(tlsKeyFile) == 0 {
                log.Fatal(
                        "TLS_CERT_FILE_PATH and TLS_KEY_FILE_PATH
                        must be specified")
        }

        mux := http.NewServeMux()
        setupHandlers(mux)
        m := loggingMiddleware(mux)

        log.Fatal(
                http.ListenAndServeTLS(
                        listenAddr,
                        tlsCertFile,
                        tlsKeyFile, m,
                ),
        )
}
```

We have added the logging middleware from Chapter 5 to the server and registered a single request handler for the /api path. Note that we have also changed the default value of listenAddr to ":8443", as it is more conventional for non-public-facing HTTPS servers. Save Listing 7.6 as server.go inside the chap7/tls-server directory. Build and run the server as follows:

```
$ go build -o server
$ TLS_CERT_FILE_PATH=./server.crt TLS_KEY_FILE_PATH=./server.key \
    ./server
```

If you are using Windows, you will have to specify the environment variables differently. For PowerShell, the following command will work:

```
C:\> $env:TLS_CERT_FILE_PATH=./server.crt; `
    $env: TLS_KEY_FILE_PATH=./server.key ./server
```

Once you have your server running, use curl to make a request:

```
$ curl https://localhost:8443/api
```

You will get the following error:

```
curl: (60) SSL certificate problem: self signed certificate
```

This is because `curl` doesn't trust your self-signed certificate. To get curl to test your certificate, specify the `server.crt` file that you indicated to the server:

```
$ curl --cacert ./server.crt https://localhost:8443/api
Hello, world!
```

On the server side, you will see the following message being logged:

```
2021/05/05 08:17:55 protocol=HTTP/2.0 path=/api method=GET
duration=0.000055
```

By manually specifying the server certificate to `curl`, you have successfully been able to communicate securely with your server. Note that the protocol now is logged as `HTTP/2.0`. This is because when you start a TLS-enabled HTTP server, Go automatically switches to using HTTP/2 instead of HTTP /1.1 if the client supports it, which `curl` does. In fact, the HTTP clients that you wrote in Chapter 3 and Chapter 4 will also automatically use HTTP/2 when the server supports it as well.

Testing TLS Servers

Once you have set up your server to use TLS, you will want to ensure that you're also communicating with the server over TLS even when testing your handler functions or middleware. In Listing 7.7, let's now tweak the TLS-enabled HTTP server in Listing 7.6 slightly to configure the logging middleware.

Listing 7.7: Securing an HTTP server using TLS with a configurable logger

```go
// chap7/tls-server-test/server.go
package main

import (
        "fmt"
        "log"
        "net/http"
        "os"
        "time"
)

// TODO: Insert apiHandler() from Listing 7.6

func setupHandlersAndMiddleware(
        mux *http.ServeMux, l *log.Logger,
) http.Handler {
        mux.HandleFunc("/api", apiHandler)
        return loggingMiddleware(mux, l)
```

```
    }

    func loggingMiddleware(h http.Handler, l *log.Logger) http.Handler {
            return http.HandlerFunc(
                    func(w http.ResponseWriter, r *http.Request,
                    ) {
                    startTime := time.Now()
                    h.ServeHTTP(w, r)
                    l.Printf(
                            "protocol=%s path=%s method=%s duration=%f",
                            r.Proto, r.URL.Path, r.Method,
                            time.Now().Sub(startTime).Seconds(),
                    )
                    })
    }

    func main() {
            # TODO: Insert the setup code as per Listing 7.6
            mux := http.NewServeMux()
            l := log.New(
                    os.Stdout, "tls-server",
                    log.Lshortfile|log.LstdFlags,
            )
            m := setupHandlersAndMiddleware(mux, l)

            log.Fatal(
                    http.ListenAndServeTLS(
                            listenAddr, tlsCertFile, tlsKeyFile, m,
                    ),
            )
    }
```

The key changes are highlighted in Listing 7.7. We combine the handler and the middleware registration code into a single function, setupHandlersAnd Middleware(). In the main() function, we create a new log.Logger object, configured to log to os.Stdout, and then call the setupHandlersAndMiddleware() function, passing the ServeMux and log.Logger object. This will allow us to configure the logger when writing the test function. Create a new directory, chap7/tls-server-test, and initialize a module inside it:

```
$ mkdir -p chap7/tls-server-test
$ cd chap7/tls-server-test
$ go mod init github.com/username/tls-server-test
```

Save Listing 7.7 as server.go inside the chap7/tls-server-test directory and copy the server.crt and server.key files from the chap7/tls-server directory into the chap7/tls-server-test directory.

Next, let's write a test to verify that the logging middleware works properly. To start a test HTTP server with TLS and HTTP/2 enabled, you will once again make use of facilities made available by the `net/http/httptest` package:

```
ts := httptest.NewUnstartedServer(m)
ts.EnableHTTP2 = true
ts.StartTLS()
```

First, we create a server configuration by calling the `httptest.New` `UnstartedServer()`. This returns an object of type `*httptest.Server`, a struct type defined in the `net/http/httptest` package. We then enable HTTP/2 by setting the `EnableHTTP2` field to true. This is to ensure that the test server is as close to the "real" server as possible. Finally, we call the `StartTLS()` method. This automatically generates a TLS certificate and key pair and starts an HTTPS server. To communicate with this test HTTPS server, we will need to use a specially constructed client:

```
client := ts.Client()
resp, err := client.Get(ts.URL + "/api")
```

The `http.Client` object that we obtain from calling the `Client()` method of the test server object is automatically configured to trust the TLS certificates that are generated for testing. Listing 7.8 shows a test that verifies the functioning of the logging middleware.

Listing 7.8: Verify middleware behavior in a TLS-enabled HTTP server

```go
// chap7/tls-server-test/middleware_test.go
package main
import (
        "bytes"
        "log"
        "net/http"
        "net/http/httptest"
        "strings"
        "testing"
)

func TestMiddleware(t *testing.T) {
        var buf bytes.Buffer
        mux := http.NewServeMux()
        l := log.New(
                &buf, "test-tls-server",
                log.Lshortfile|log.LstdFlags,
        )
        m := setupHandlersAndMiddleware(mux, l)

        ts := httptest.NewUnstartedServer(m)
```

```
ts.EnableHTTP2 = true
ts.StartTLS()
defer ts.Close()

client := ts.Client()
_, err := client.Get(ts.URL + "/api")
if err != nil {
        t.Fatal(err)
}

expected := "protocol=HTTP/2.0 path=/api method=GET"
mLogs := buf.String()
if !strings.Contains(mLogs, expected) {
        t.Fatalf(
                "Expected logs to contain %s, Found: %s\n",
                expected, mLogs,
        )
}
}
```

We create a new `bytes.Buffer`, `buf` and specify that as the `io.Writer` when creating a new `log.Logger` object. Then, after obtaining the configured client for the test server, we make an HTTP GET request using the `Get()` method. Since we are testing the middleware functionality, we discard the response. Then we verify whether the logged message in the `buf` object contains the expected string using the `strings.Contains()` function. Save Listing 7.8 as `middleware_test.go` inside the `chap7/tls-server-test` directory and run the test:

```
$ go test -v
=== RUN    TestMiddleware
--- PASS: TestMiddleware (0.01s)
PASS
ok         github.com/practicalgo/code/chap7/tls-server-test    0.557s
```

Great, you have now learned how to set up a TLS-enabled server for your tests as well. In practice, you will not be generating TLS certificates as we did earlier. You will also not be manually configuring each client (such as `curl` or another service) to trust the certificate generated. That is simply not scalable. Instead, do the following:

- For internal domains and services, implement an internal trusted CA using tools such as `cfssl` (`https://github.com/cloudflare/cfssl`) and then have a mechanism for generating certificates and trusting the CA.
- For public-facing domains and services, request certificates from a trusted CA—either manually or in most cases via an automated procedure (for example, `https://github.com/caddyserver/certmagic`).

Summary

You started this chapter by learning how to set up a maximum time limit for your handler function executions. You configured your server to send an HTTP 503 response to the server when a handler function doesn't complete processing a request in a specified interval of time. Then you learned how you can write your handler functions such that they don't continue processing a request if the time-out has already expired or the client disconnected midway. These techniques prevent your server resources from being tied up doing work that is no longer required.

Next you learned how to implement a global read and write time-out for your server applications and how to implement a graceful shutdown for your server applications. Finally, you learned how to implement a secure communication channel between your server and a client using TLS certificates. With these techniques implemented, your HTTP server is closer to being production ready. We will briefly go over some of the remaining tasks in Appendix A, "Making Your Applications Observable," and Appendix B, "Deploying Application."

In the next chapter, you will learn how to build clients and servers using gRPC, a Remote Procedure Call (RPC) framework built on top of HTTP/2.

## CHAPTER 8

Building RPC Applications with gRPC

In this chapter, you will learn to build network applications that use *Remote Procedure Call (RPC)* for communication. Although the standard library supports building such applications, we will do so using gRPC, an open-source *universal* RPC framework. We will start off with a quick background discussion of RPC frameworks, and we will end the chapter having learned to write completely testable gRPC applications. Along the way, you will also learn to use Protocol Buffers, an interface description language and a data interchange format that enables client-server communication over gRPC. Let's jump right in.

gRPC and Protocol Buffers

When you make a function call in your program, the function will usually be one that you have written yourself, or one provided by another package— from either the standard library or a third-party package. When you build the application, the binary contains that function's implementation inside it. Now imagine that you were able to make a function call, but instead of the function defined inside the application binary, the program calls the function defined in another *service* over the *network*. That is what *Remote Procedure Call (RPC)* is in a nutshell. Figure 8.1 illustrates a typical overview of how an RPC client and server communicates. It shows the request flow from the client to the server. The response flow, of course, happens in reverse and traverses through the same layers as the request.

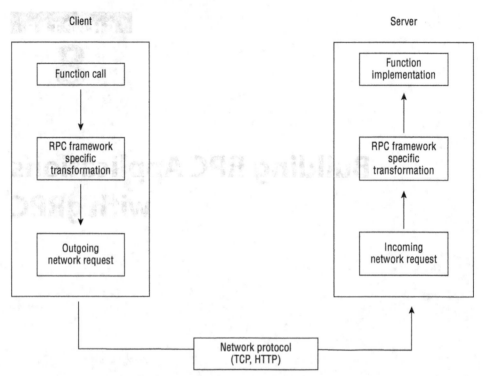

Figure 8.1: Functioning of an RPC-based service architecture

RPC frameworks empower you by taking care of the two important concerns: how does the function call get converted to a network request and how does the request itself get transmitted. In fact, the net/rpc package in the standard library gives you some basic features needed for writing RPC servers and clients. By using it, you can implement an RPC application architecture over HTTP or TCP. Of course, one immediate limitation with using the net/rpc package is that your client and server must both be written in Go. The data interchange happens by default using the Go-specific gob format.

As an improvement over net/rpc, the net/rpc/jsonrpc package allows you instead to use JSON as the data interchange format over HTTP. Thus, the server can now be written in Go, but your client doesn't need to be. This is great if you want to implement an RPC architecture in your application, rather than HTTP. However, JSON has some inherent limitations as a data interchange language; serialization and deserialization costs and the lack of native guarantee around data types are the most important ones.

Hence, when you are looking to design a language-neutral architecture around RPC calls, it is recommended that you select an RPC framework built around more efficient data interchange formats. Examples of such frameworks are *Apache Thrift* and *gRPC*. The key advantage that a universal RPC framework has over the standard library's RPC support is that it enables you to write your server and client applications in different programming languages.

Our focus in this chapter is gRPC, of course. Language-neutral frameworks such as gRPC support clients and servers written in any of the supported languages. It uses a more efficient data interchange format—Protocol Buffers, or *protobuf* for short. Whereas the protobuf data format is only machine readable (unlike JSON), the protocol buffer language is human readable. In fact, the first step in creating an application using gRPC is to define the service interface using the protocol buffer language.

The following code snippet shows the definition of a service in the protocol buffer language. We will call the service, Users, which declares a single *method*, GetUser(). This method takes an *input* message and returns an *output* message as follows:

```
service Users {
  rpc GetUser (UserGetRequest) returns (UserGetReply) {}
}
```

The method GetUser accepts an input message of type UserGetRequest, and it returns a message of type UserGetReply. In gRPC, a function must always have an input message and return an output message. Thus, a client and server application communicate by passing messages.

What is a *message*? It acts as an envelope for the data that needs to be moved between a client and a server. The definition of a message is similar to a struct type. The purpose of the GetUser method is to allow the client to query for a user based on their email or another identifier. Thus, we will define the UserGetRequest message with two fields as follows:

```
message UserGetRequest {
  string email = 1;
  string id = 2;
}
```

Inside the message definition, we define two fields: email (a string) and id (another string). A field definition in a message must specify three things: a type, name, and number. The type of a field can be one of the currently supported integer types (int32, int64, and others), float, double, bool (for Boolean data), string, and bytes (for any arbitrary data).

You can also define a field to be of another message type. The name of a field must all be in lowercase and use the underscore character, _, for separating multiple words, as in, for example, first_name. The field number is a way to express the position of the field within the message. Field numbers can start from 1 and go through 2^29, with certain ranges that are reserved only for usage internally. One recommended strategy is to leave gaps within field numbers. For example, you may number your first field as 1, and then use 10 for the next field. This will mean that you can add any additional fields later on without having to renumber your fields and also have related fields grouped closely to each other.

It's worth pointing out that the field number is an internal detail that your applications won't need to worry about, and hence field numbers should be assigned with care, never changed, and designed with the future revisions in mind. We touch upon this topic later in the chapter in the section on forward and backward compatibility.

Next, we will define the `UserGetReply` message as follows:

```
message UserGetReply {
    User user = 1;
}
```

The above message contains a field, user, of type User. We will define the User message as follows:

```
message User {
    string id = 1;
    string first_name = 2;
    string last_name = 3;
    int32 age = 4;
}
```

Figure 8.2 summarizes the different parts of a protobuf specification for a gRPC service. In a later section, you will learn how to register multiple services in a gRPC server.

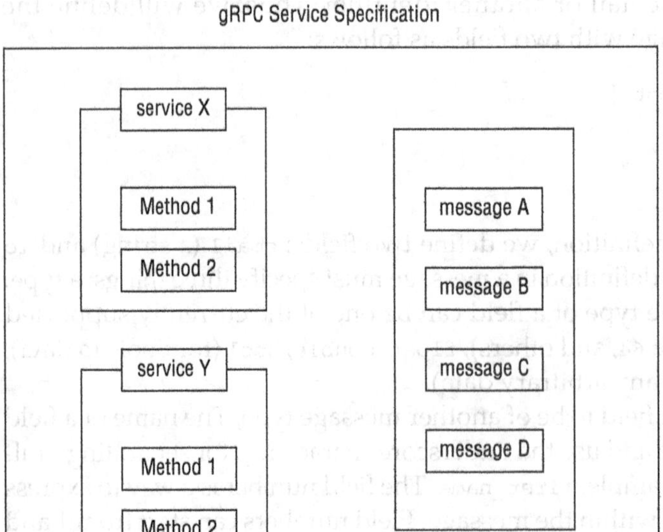

Figure 8.2: Parts of a protobuf language specification

Once you have your *service interface* defined, you will then translate the definition into a format that will be usable from your applications. This translation process will be done using the protobuf compiler, protoc, and a language-specific plugin for the compiler, protoco-gen-go. It's worth mentioning that you will only be interacting directly with the protoc command. If you didn't complete the installation per the instructions in the introduction, this is a good time to do that before you move on to the next section.

Writing Your First Service

The Users service defines one method, GetUser, to get a specific user. Listing 8.1 shows the complete protobuf specification of the service along with the message types.

Listing 8.1: Protobuf specification for Users service

```
// chap8/user-service/service/users.proto

syntax = "proto3";
option go_package = "github.com/username/user-service/service";

service Users {
  rpc GetUser (UserGetRequest) returns (UserGetReply) {}
}

message UserGetRequest {
  string email = 1;
  string id = 2;
}

message User {
  string id = 1;
  string first_name = 2;
  string last_name = 3;
  int32 age = 4;
}

message UserGetReply {
  User user = 1;
}
```

Create a new directory, chap8/user-service. Create a directory service, and initialize a module inside it:

```
$ mkdir -p chap8/user-service/service
$ cd chap8/user-service/service
$ go mod init github.com/username/user-service/service
```

Next, save Listing 8.1 as a new file, users.proto.

The next step is to generate what I refer to as the *magic glue*. This is essentially what ties together the human readable protobuf definition (Listing 8.1), the server and client application implementations (that you will write), and the machine readable protobuf data interchange happening between the two over the network. Referring back to Figure 8.1, the RPC framework specific transformation of a request is performed by this generated code.

Run the following command while you are inside the chap8/user-service/service directory:

```
$ cd chap8/user-service/service
$ protoc --go_out=. --go_opt=paths=source_relative \
  --go-grpc_out=. --go-grpc_opt=paths=source_relative \
  users.proto
```

The --go_out and go-grpc_out options specify the path where these files are generated. Here we specify the current directory. The --go_opt=paths=source_relative and --go-grpc_opt=paths=source_relative specify that the files should be generated with respect to the location of the users.proto file. The result is that when the command completes, you will see two new files created inside the service directory: users.pb.go and users_grpc.pb.go. We will never manually edit these files. They define (at a very high level) the Go language equivalents of the protobuf message types and the interfaces for the service which you, as the application author, will implement. Since we have initialized a module, github.com/username/user-service/service, inside the service directory, you will be importing the various types and calling the functions defined from this module when writing your server and client applications.

Writing the Server

Writing a gRPC server application involves steps similar to writing an HTTP server application: create a server, write service handlers to process requests from a client, and register the handlers with the server. Creating the server involves two steps: creating a network listener and creating a new gRPC server on that listener:

```
lis, err := net.Listen("tcp", ":50051")
s := grpc.NewServer()
log.Fatal(s.Serve(lis))
```

We start a TCP listener using the net.Listen() function defined in the net package. The first argument to the function is the type of listener we want to create, TCP in this case, and the second argument is the network address on which to listen.

Here we set the listener up so that it is listening on all network interfaces on the port 50051. As with 8080 for HTTP servers, 50051 is a conventionally chosen number for gRPC servers. Once we create the listener, we create a `grpc` `.Server` object using the `grpc.NewServer()` function. The `google.golang.org/` `grpc` defines types and functions to enable writing a gRPC applications.

Finally, we call the `Serve()` method defined on this object passing the listener. This method will only return when you terminate the server, or if there is an error. This is a fully functional gRPC server. However, it doesn't yet have any idea of how to accept and process a request for the `Users` service.

The next step is to implement the method `GetUser()`. To define this method, we will import the package we generated earlier:

```
import users "github.com/username/user-service/service"
```

We use an import alias here, `users`, to be able to identify it easily elsewhere in the server code. Then we define a type, `userService`, with a single field: the `users.UnimplementedUsersServer` struct. This is mandatory for any service implementation in gRPC, and this is the first step for implementing the `Users` service:

```go
type userService struct {
        users.UnimplementedUsersServer
}
```

The `userService` type is the *service handler* for the `Users` service. Next, we define the `GetUser()` method as a method of the server struct:

```go
func (s *userService) GetUser(
        ctx context.Context,
        in *users.UserGetRequest,
) (*users.UserGetReply, error) {
        log.Printf(
                "Received request for user with Email: %s Id: %s\n",
                in.Email,
                in.Id,
        )
        components := strings.Split(in.Email, "@")
        if len(components) != 2 {
                return nil, errors.New("invalid email address")
        }
        u := users.User{
                Id:        in.Id,
                FirstName: components[0],
                LastName:  components[1],
                Age:       36,
        }
        return &users.UserGetReply{User: &u}, nil
}
```

The GetUser() method accepts two parameters: a context.Context object and a users.UserGetRequest object. It returns two values: an object of type *users.UserGetReply and an error. Note how the Go equivalent of the RPC method, GetUser(), returns an additional value—an error. For other languages, this might be different.

The struct types corresponding to the messages are defined in the users.pb.go file. Each struct has a few fields internal to protobuf, but you will see that it contains the Go equivalent of the protobuf specification.

First, the UserGetRequest struct:

```
type UserGetRequest struct {
        # other fields
        Email string
        Id    string
}
```

Similarly, the UserGetReply struct will contain a User field:

```
type UserGetReply struct {
        # other fields
        User *User
}
```

The User type will contain the Id, FirstName, LastName, and Age fields:

```
type User struct {
        # Other fields
        Id        string
        FirstName string
        LastName  string
        Age       int32
}
```

The implementation of the method logs the incoming request, extracts the user and domain name from the email address, creates a dummy User object, and sends back a UserGetReply value and a nil error value. If the email address is not well formed, we return an empty UserGetReply value and an error value.

The final step to implementing the gRPC server application is to register the Users service with the gRPC server:

```
lis, err := net.Listen("tcp", listenAddr)
s := grpc.NewServer()
users.RegisterUsersServer(s, &userService{})
log.Fatal(s.Serve(lis))
```

To register the Users service handler with the gRPC server, we call the users.RegisterUsersServer() function that was generated by running the protoc command. This function takes two parameters. The first parameter is a `*grpc.Server` object, and the second parameter is an implementation of the `Users` service, which here is the `userService` type that we defined. Figure 8.3 illustrates graphically the different steps involved.

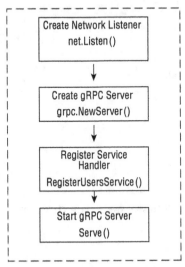

Figure 8.3: Creating the gRPC server with the `Users` service

Listing 8.2 shows the complete listing for the server.

Listing 8.2: gRPC server for the `Users` service

```go
// chap8/user-service/server/sever.go
package main

import (
        "context"
        "log"
        "net"
        "os"

        users "github.com/username/user-service/service"
        "google.golang.org/grpc"
)

type userService struct {
        users.UnimplementedUsersServer
}

// TODO: Insert GetUser() function from above

func registerServices(s *grpc.Server) {
        users.RegisterUsersServer(s, &userService{})
}
```

```
func startServer(s *grpc.Server, l net.Listener) error {
        return s.Serve(l)
}

func main() {
        listenAddr := os.Getenv("LISTEN_ADDR")
        if len(listenAddr) == 0 {
                listenAddr = ":50051"
        }

        lis, err := net.Listen("tcp", listenAddr)
        if err != nil {
                log.Fatal(err)
        }
        s := grpc.NewServer()
        registerServices(s)
        log.Fatal(startServer(s, lis))
}
```

Create a new directory, server, inside the chap8/user-service directory. Initialize a module inside it as follows:

```
$ mkdir -p chap8/user-service/server
$ cd chap8/user-service/server
$ go mod init github.com/username/user-service/server
```

Next, save Listing 8.2 as a new file, server.go, inside it. Run the following command from within the server subdirectory:

```
$ go get google.golang.org/grpc@v1.37.0
```

The above command will fetch the google.golang.org/grpc/ package, update the go.mod file, and create a go.sum file. The final step is manually to add the information for the github.com/username/user-service/service package to the go.mod file. Edit the go.mod file to add the following:

```
require.        v0.0.0
replace github.com/username/user-service/service => ../service
```

The above directives will instruct the go toolchain to look for the github.com/username/user-service/service package in the ../service directory. The final go.mod file is shown in Listing 8.3.

Listing 8.3: go.mod file for the Users gRPC server

```
// chap8/user-service/server/go.mod
module github.com/username/user-service/server

go 1.16
```

```
require (
        github.com/username/user-service/service v0.0.0
        google.golang.org/grpc v1.37.0 // indirect
)

replace github.com/username/user-service/service => ../service
```

Great. Now you are ready to build the server and run it as follows:

```
$ go build -o server
$ ./server
```

The server is now up and running. Leave it like that. Does it work? Let's find out by writing a client to interact with the server.

Writing a Client

There are three steps involved in establishing a client connection. The first step is to establish a connection to the server, referred to as a *channel*. We do that via the `grpc.DialContext()` function defined in the `google.golang.org/grpc` package. Let's write a function to do this:

```
func setupGrpcConnection(addr string) (*grpc.ClientConn, error) {
        return grpc.DialContext(
                context.Background(),
                addr,
                grpc.WithInsecure(),
                grpc.WithBlock(),
        )
}
```

The `setupGrpcConnection()` function is called with a single string value—the address of the server to connect to, for example, `localhost:50051` or `127.0.0.1:50051`. Then, the `grpc.DialContext()` function is called with three parameters.

The first parameter is a `context.Context` object. Here, we create a new one by calling the `context.Background()` function. The second parameter is a string value containing the address of the server or target to connect to. The `grpc.DialContext()` function is *variadic*, and the last parameter is of type `grpc.DialOption`. Thus, you can specify none or any number of values of type `grpc.DialOption`. Here, we specify two such values:

- ■ `grpc.WithInsecure()` to establish a non-TLS (Transport Layer Security) connection with the server. In a later chapter, you will learn how to configure a client and server to communicate over a TLS-encrypted channel for gRPC applications.

- `grpc.WithBlock()` to ensure that the connection is established before returning from the function. This means that if you run the client before the server is up and running, it will wait indefinitely.

The return value from the `grpc.DialContext()` function is an object of type `grpc.ClientConn`, which is then returned.

Once we have created a channel of communication with the server—that is, a valid `grpc.ClientConn` object—we then create a client to communicate with the `Users` service. Let's write a function, `getUsersServiceClient()`, to achieve this for us:

```
import users "github.com/username/user-service/service"
func getUserServiceClient(conn *grpc.ClientConn) users.UsersClient {
        return users.NewUsersClient(conn)
}
```

We call the `getUserServiceClient()` function with the `*grpc.ClientConn` object that we obtained from the `setupGrpcConn()` function. This function then calls the `users.NewUsersClient()` function that was generated as part of the code generation step. The returned value is an object of type `users.UsersClient`, which is returned from this function.

The last step remaining is to call the `GetUser()` method in the `Users` service. Let's write another function to do that for us:

```
func getUser(
        client users.UsersClient,
        u *users.UserGetRequest,
) (*users.UserGetReply, error) {
        return client.GetUser(context.Background(), u)
}
```

The `getUser()` function has two incoming parameters: a client configured to communicate with the Users service and the request to send to the server, a `users.UserGetRequest` object. Inside the function, we call the `GetUser()` function with a context object and the passed-in `users.UserGetRequest` value, u. The returned values are an object of type `users.UserGetReply` and an error value. The `getUser()` function would be called as follows:

```
result, err := getUser(
        c,
        &users.UserGetRequest{Email: "jane@doe.com"},
)
```

Listing 8.4 shows the complete listing for the client.

Listing 8.4: Client for the `Users` service

```go
// chap8/user-service/client/main.go
package main

import (
        "context"
        "fmt"
        "log"
        "os"

        users "github.com/username/user-service/service"
        "google.golang.org/grpc"
)

// TODO: Insert setupGrpcConn() function from above
// TODO: Insert getUsersServiceClient() function from above
// TODO: Insert getUser() function from above

func main() {
        if len(os.Args) != 2 {
                log.Fatal(
                        "Must specify a gRPC server address",
                )
        }
        conn, err := setupGrpcConn(os.Args[1])
        if err != nil {
                log.Fatal(err)
        }
        defer conn.Close()

        c := getUserServiceClient(conn)

        result, err := getUser(
                c,
                &users.UserGetRequest{Email: "jane@doe.com"},
        )
        if err != nil {
                log.Fatal(err)
        }
        fmt.Fprintf(
                os.Stdout, "User: %s %s\n",
                result.User.FirstName,
                result.User.LastName,
        )
}
```

In the `main()` function, we first check if the client has specified an address of the server to connect to as a command-line argument. If one has not been specified, we exit with an error message. Then we call the `setupGrpcConn()` function, passing in the server address. We call the `Close()` method of the connection object in a defer statement so that the client connection is closed before the program exits. Then we call the `getUsersServiceClient()` function to obtain a client to communicate with the `Users` service. Next, we call the `getUser()` function with a value of type `*users.UserGetRequest`. Note that we don't specify the `Id` field in the value, since by default fields in a protobuf message are optional. Thus, we could have as well sent an empty value, in other words, `&users.UserGetRequest{}`. When the call returns from the `getUser()` function, the value in the result is of type `users.UserGetReply`. This value contains a single field of type `users.User`, and here we call the `fmt.Fprintf()` function to display the two string values: `FirstName` and `LastName`.

Create a new directory, `client`, inside the `chap8/user-service` directory. Initialize a module inside it as follows:

```
$ mkdir -p chap8/user-service/client
$ cd chap8/user-service/client
$ go mod init github.com/username/user-service/client
```

Next, save Listing 8.4 as a new file, `main.go`, inside it. Run the following command from within the client subdirectory:

```
$ go get google.golang.org/grpc@v1.37.0
```

The above command will fetch the `google.golang.org/grpc/` package, update the `go.mod` file, and create a `go.sum` file. The final step is manually to add the information for the `github.com/username/user-service/service` package to the `go.mod` file. The final `go.mod` file is shown in Listing 8.5.

Listing 8.5: `go.mod` file for the `Users` service client

```
// chap8/user-service/client/go.mod
module github.com/username/user-service/client

go 1.16

require (
        github.com/username/user-service/service v0.0.0
        google.golang.org/grpc v1.37.0
)

replace github.com/username/user-service/service => ../service
```

The directory chap8/user-service should now appear as shown in Figure 8.4.

```
|
|____server
|   |____go.mod
|   |____server.go
|   |____go.sum
|____service
|   |____go.mod
|   |____users.pb.go
|   |____users_grpc.pb.go
|   |____users.proto
|____client
|   |____go.mod
|   |____go.sum
|   |____main.go
```

Figure 8.4: Directory structure of the Users service

Great. Now you are ready to build the client and run it as follows:

```
$ cd chap8/user-service/client
$ go build -o client
$ ./client localhost:50051
User: Jane Doe
```

On the server side you will see a message that is logged as follows:

```
2021/05/16 08:23:52 Received request for user with Email: jane@doe.com Id:
```

Great. You have written your first server and client application communicating over gRPC. Next, you will learn how to write tests to verify your client and server behavior.

Testing the Server

A key component for testing both the client and the server is the google .golang.org/grpc/test/bufconn (henceforth referred to as the bufconn) package. It allows us to set up a complete in-memory channel of communication between a gRPC client and server. Instead of creating a *real* network listener, we will instead create one using the bufconn package in our tests. This avoids the need to set up real network servers and clients during the testing, while ensuring that the server and client logic we most care about is testable.

Let's write a function to start a test gRPC server for the Users service:

```
func startTestGrpcServer() (*grpc.Server, *bufconn.Listener) {
    l := bufconn.Listen(10)
    s := grpc.NewServer()
    registerServices(s)
    go func() {
```

```
                        err := startServer(s, l)
                        if err != nil {
                                log.Fatal(err)
                        }
                }()
                return s, l
        }
```

First, we create a `*bufconn.Listener` object by calling the `bufconn.Listen()` function. The parameter passed to this function is the size of the listen queue. In this case, it simply means how many connections we can have at any given point of time with the server. For our tests, 10 is a sufficient number.

Next, we create a `*grpc.Server` object by calling the `grpc.NewServer()` function. Then we call the `registerServices()` function defined in the server implementation to register the service handlers with the server and then call the `startServer()` function in a goroutine. Finally, we return the `*grpc.Server` and `*bufconn.Listener` values. To communicate with the test server, we need a specially configured client.

First, we create a *dialer*; that is, a function that satisfies a specific signature, as follows:

```
bufconnDialer := func(
                ctx context.Context, addr string,
        ) (net.Conn, error) {
                return l.Dial()
}
```

The function accepts a `context.Context` object and a string containing the network address to connect to. It returns two values: an object of type `net.Conn` and an `error` value from this function. Here we simply return the values that the `l.Dial()` function returns, where `l` is the `bufconn.Listener` object created via a call to the `bufconn.Listen()` function.

Next, we create the specially configured client as follows:

```
client, err := grpc.DialContext(
                context.Background(),
                "", grpc.WithInsecure(),
                grpc.WithContextDialer(bufconnDialer),
        )
```

Two key observations to note here. First, we specify an empty address string (the second parameter) to the `DialContext()` function call. Second, the final parameter is a call to the `grpc.WithContextDialer()` function passing the `bufConnDialer` function that we created above as a parameter. By doing this, we are asking the `grpc.DialContext()` function to use the dialer that we are specifying via the `grpc.WithContextDialer()` function call. Simplifying it further, we are essentially asking it to use the in-memory *network* connection that the `bufConnDialer` function will set up. Figure 8.5 demonstrates this graphically, comparing the client-server communication over a real network listener with one created via `bufconn`.

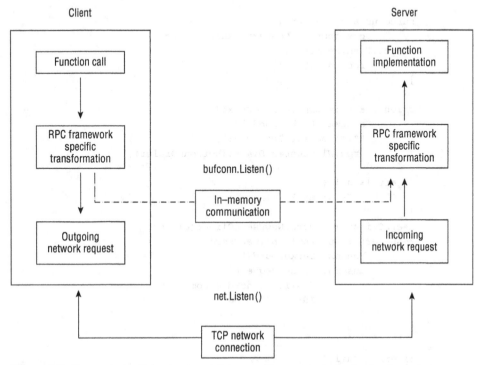

Figure 8.5: Comparison of a real network listener with one created using `bufconn`

Once we have created a `grpc.Client` configured to communicate with the test server, what remains is to make a request to the client and verify the response. Listing 8.6 shows the complete test function.

Listing 8.6: Test for the `Users` service

```go
// chap8/user-service/server/server_test.go
package main

import (
        "context"
        "log"
        "net"
        "testing"

        users "github.com/username/user-service-test/service"
        "google.golang.org/grpc"
        "google.golang.org/grpc/test/bufconn"
)

// TODO Insert definition of startTestGrpcServer() from above
```

```go
func TestUserService(t *testing.T) {

    s, l := startTestGrpcServer()
    defer s.GracefulStop()

    bufconnDialer := func(
            ctx context.Context, addr string,
    ) (net.Conn, error) {
            return l.Dial()
    }

    client, err := grpc.DialContext(
            context.Background(),
            "", grpc.WithInsecure(),
            grpc.WithContextDialer(bufconnDialer),
    )
    if err != nil {
            t.Fatal(err)
    }
    usersClient := users.NewUsersClient(client)
    resp, err := usersClient.GetUser(
            context.Background(),
            &users.UserGetRequest{
                    Email: "jane@doe.com",
                    Id:    "foo-bar",
            },
    )

    if err != nil {
            t.Fatal(err)
    }
    if resp.User.FirstName != "jane" {
            t.Errorf(
                    "Expected FirstName to be: jane, Got: %s",
                    resp.User.FirstName,
            )
    }

}
```

We set up a deferred statement to call the `GracefulStop()` method defined for the `*grpc.Server` object. This is done to ensure that the server is stopped before the test function exits. Save Listing 8.6 as a new file, `server_test.go`, inside the `chap8/user-service/server/` directory and run the test as follows:

```
$ go test
2021/05/28 16:57:42 Received request for user with Email: jane@doe.com
Id: foo-bar
PASS
ok.    github.com/practicalgo/code/chap8/user-service/server    0.133s
```

Testing the Client

When writing a test for the client, we will implement a dummy server for the
Users service:

```
type dummyUserService struct {
        users.UnimplementedUsersServer
}
```

Then we define the dummy GetUser() method for this type:

```
func (s *dummyUserService) GetUser(
        ctx context.Context,
        in *users.UserGetRequest,
) (*users.UserGetReply, error) {
        u := users.User{
                Id: "user-123-a",
                FirstName: "jane",
                LastName: "doe",
                Age: 36,
        }
        return &users.UserGetReply{User: &u}, nil
}
```

Next, we will define a function to create a gRPC server and register the dummy
service implementation:

```
func startTestGrpcServer() (*grpc.Server, *bufconn.Listener) {
        l := bufconn.Listen(10)
        s := grpc.NewServer()
        users.RegisterUsersServer(s, &dummyUserService{})
        go func() {
                err := startServer(s, l)
                if err != nil {
                        log.Fatal(err)
                }
        }()
        return s, l
}
```

The startTestGrpcServer() function is exactly the same as the one we
wrote for the server, except for the registration of the dummy service: users.
RegisterUsersServer(s, &dummyUserService{}). We start the server in a separate goroutine and return the *bufconn.Listener value so that we can create
a dialer for the client, similar to how we did when testing the server. The idea
is that we want the server to run in the background while we make requests to
it in the rest of the test.

The final steps are to make the GetUser() RPC method call and then verify
the results. Listing 8.7 shows the complete test function.

Listing 8.7: Test for the Users service client

```go
// chap8/user-service/client/client_test.go
package main

import (
        "context"
        "log"
        "net"
        "testing"

        users "github.com/username/user-service/service"
        "google.golang.org/grpc"
        "google.golang.org/grpc/test/bufconn"
)

type dummyUserService struct {
        users.UnimplementedUsersServer
}

// TODO Insert definition of GetUser() from above

// TODO Insert definition of startTestGrpcServer() from above
func TestGetUser(t *testing.T) {

        s, l := startTestGrpcServer()
        defer s.GracefulStop()

        bufconnDialer := func(
                ctx context.Context, addr string,
        ) (net.Conn, error) {
                return l.Dial()
        }

        conn, err := grpc.DialContext(
                context.Background(),
                "", grpc.WithInsecure(),
                grpc.WithContextDialer(bufconnDialer),
        )
        if err != nil {
                t.Fatal(err)
        }

        c := getUserServiceClient(conn)
        result, err := getUser(
                c,
                &users.UserGetRequest{Email: "jane@doe.com"},
        )
        if err != nil {
                t.Fatal(err)
        }
```

```
if result.User.FirstName != "jane" ||
        result.User.LastName != "doe" {
        t.Fatalf(
                "Expected: jane doe, Got: %s %s",
                result.User.FirstName,
                result.User.LastName,
        )
    }
}
```

Save Listing 8.7 as a new file, `client_test.go`, inside the `chap8/user-service/` `client` directory. Run the test as follows:

```
$ go test
PASS
ok      github.com/practicalgo/code/chap8/user-service/client 0.128s
```

Before we carry on, let's summarize what you have learned so far. To create a gRPC network application, you must first create your service specification using the protocol buffer language. Then, you use the protobuf compiler (`protoc`) and the go plugin to generate the *magic glue*. This generates code that will take care of the low-level work of serialization and deserialization of the data and communicate it over the network between the client and the server. Using types, implementing interfaces, and calling functions from the generated code, you then write the server and client implementations. Finally, you test your servers and clients.

It's worth briefly comparing this process to writing HTTP servers and clients. First, let's consider a gRPC server and an HTTP server. Both types of server applications set up a network server and the functions to handle network requests. Whereas the HTTP server can define any arbitrary handler functions and register them to handle arbitrary paths, a gRPC server is only able to register functions for handling RPC calls that are defined by the corresponding protobuf specification.

By comparing HTTP clients and gRPC clients, we can see similarities such as creating a client and then sending a request. However, whereas HTTP clients can make arbitrary requests to an HTTP server and perhaps get an error as a response when an invalid request is sent, gRPC clients are confined only to make the RPC calls that have been defined by the protocol buffer specification. Additionally, the client must be aware of the message types defined by the RPC server to be able to send a message to the server that it understands. For HTTP applications, the client doesn't have any such enforced requirement.

Next, let's explore two key topics when working with protocol buffers: marshalling and unmarshalling, and the evolution of the data format over time.

A Detour into Protobuf Messages

Messages form the cornerstone in gRPC applications. When you are interacting with your gRPC application from another application, you will find it necessary to be able to convert bytes of data into protocol buffers and vice versa. We examine this next. After that, you will learn how to design backward- and forward-compatible protobuf messages as your application evolves.

Marshalling and Unmarshalling

Consider the request to the `GetUser()` function for the `Users` service. In the client and the tests, you created a value of type `GetUserRequest` as follows:

```
u := users.UserGetRequest{Email: "jane@doe.com"}
```

Then you called the `GetUser()` function passing this request. Now what if you were calling the `GetUser()` function from a client application where the user is able specify a search query such that it is a JSON-formatted string that maps to the underlying `UserGetRequest` message type? To refresh your memory, the `UserGetRequest` message was defined as follows:

```
message UserGetRequest {
    string email = 1;
    string id = 2;
}
```

A sample JSON-formatted string that will directly map to an object of this message type is `{"email": jane@doe.com, "id": "user-123"}`. Let's see how we can convert this JSON string into a `UserGetRequest` object:

```
u := users.UserGetRequest{}
jsonQuery = `'{"email": jane@doe.com, "id": "user-123"}`
input := []byte(jsonQuery)
err = protojson.Unmarshal(input, &u)
if err != nil {
        log.Fatal(err)
}
```

We make use of the `google.golang.org/protobuf/encoding/protojson` package for unmarshalling a JSON-formatted string into a protocol buffer object. As a result of running the `protojson.Unmarshal()` function, the resultant data in the u object has been populated based on the JSON string in `jsonQuery`. Then we can call the `GetUser()` function passing the object in u. We can use this to update the client for the `Users` service such that it allows the user to specify the search query themselves as a JSON-formatted string via a command-line argument, as shown in Listing 8.8.

Listing 8.8: Client for the `Users` service

```go
// chap8/user-service/client-json/client.go
package main

import (
        "context"
        "fmt"
        "log"
        "os"

        users "github.com/username/user-service/service"
        "google.golang.org/grpc"
        "google.golang.org/protobuf/encoding/protojson"
)

// TODO Insert definition of setupGrpcConn() from Listing 8.4
// TODO Insert definition of getUserServiceClient() from Listing 8.4
// TODO Insert definition of getUser() from Listing 8.4

func createUserRequest(
        jsonQuery string,
) (*users.UserGetRequest, error) {
        u := users.UserGetRequest{}
        input := []byte(jsonQuery)
        return &u, protojson.Unmarshal(input, &u)
}

func main() {
        if len(os.Args) != 3 {
                log.Fatal(
                        "Must specify a gRPC server address and
search query",
                )
        }
        serverAddr := os.Args[1]
        u, err := createUserRequest(os.Args[2])
        if err != nil {
                log.Fatalf("Bad user input: %v", err)
        }

        conn, err := setupGrpcConn(serverAddr)
        if err != nil {
                log.Fatal(err)
        }
        defer conn.Close()

        c := getUserServiceClient(conn)

        result, err := getUser(
                c,
                u,
        )
```

```
            if err != nil {
                    log.Fatal(err)
            }
            fmt.Fprintf(
                    os.Stdout, "User: %s %s\n",
                    result.User.FirstName,
                    result.User.LastName,
            )
    }
```

Create a new directory, `client-json`, inside the `chap8/user-service` directory. Initialize a module inside it as follows:

```
$ mkdir -p chap8/user-service/client-json
$ cd chap8/user-service/client-json
$ go mod init github.com/username/user-service/client-json
```

Next, save Listing 8.8 as a new file, `main.go`, inside it. Run the following command from within the client subdirectory:

```
$ go get google.golang.org/protobuf/encoding/protojson
```

The above command will fetch the `google.golang.org/protobuf/encoding/protojson` package and update the `go.mod` file and create a `go.sum` file. The final step is to add manually the information for the `github.com/username/user-service/service` package to the `go.mod` file. The final `go.mod` file is shown in Listing 8.9.

Listing 8.9: `go.mod` file for the `Users` service client supporting a JSON-formatted query

```
// chap8/user-service/client-json/go.mod
module github.com/username/user-service/client-json

go 1.16

require (
        github.com/username/user-service/service v0.0.0
        google.golang.org/grpc v1.37.0
        google.golang.org/protobuf v1.26.0
)

replace github.com/username/user-service/service => ../service
```

Now, build and run the client specifying a second argument that will be the search query. Let's try out a couple of invalid search queries and see what happens:

```
$ go build
$ ./client-json localhost:50051 '{"Email": "jane@doe.com"}'
2021/05/21 06:53:53 Bad user input: proto: (line 1:2):
unknown field "Email"
```

We specified the email via the incorrect `Email` field (rather than `email`), and we got back an error saying so. If you specify an invalid data for a field, you will get an error as well:

```
$ ./client-json localhost:50051 '{"email": "jane@doe.com", "id": 1}'
2021/05/21 06:56:18 Bad user input: proto: (line 1:33):
invalid value for string type: 1
```

Let's try a valid input now:

```
$ ./client-json localhost:50051 '{"email": "jon@doe.com", "id": "1"}'
User: jon doe.com
```

Next, let's look at how we can present the result back to the user as JSON-formatted data. We will use the `protojson.Marshal()` function from the same package:

```
result, err := client.GetUser(context.Background(), u)
..
data, err := protojson.Marshal(result)
```

If the `Marshal()` function call returned with a `nil` error, the byte slice in the data will contain the result as JSON-formatted bytes. Listing 8.10 shows the updated client code.

Listing 8.10: Client for the `Users` service working with JSON and protobuf

```go
// chap8/user-service/client-json/client.go
package main

import (
        "context"
        "fmt"
        "log"
        "os"

        users "github.com/username/user-service/service"
        "google.golang.org/grpc"
        "google.golang.org/protobuf/encoding/protojson"
)

// TODO Insert definition of setupGrpcConn() from Listing 8.4
// TODO Insert definition of getUserServiceClient() from Listing 8.4
// TODO Insert definition of getUser() from Listing 8.4
// TODO Insert definition of createUserRequest () from Listing 8.9

func getUserResponseJson(result *users.UserGetReply) ([]byte, error) {
        return protojson.Marshal(result)
}
```

```
func main() {
        if len(os.Args) != 3 {
                log.Fatal(
                        "Must specify a gRPC server address and
        search query",
                )
        }
        serverAddr := os.Args[1]
        u, err := createUserRequest(os.Args[2])
        if err != nil {
                log.Fatalf("Bad user input: %v", err)
        }

        conn, err := setupGrpcConn(serverAddr)
        if err != nil {
                log.Fatal(err)
        }
        defer conn.Close()

        c := getUserServiceClient(conn)

        result, err := getUser(
                c,
                u,
        )
        if err != nil {
                log.Fatal(err)
        }
        data, err := getUserResponseJson(result)
        if err != nil {
                log.Fatal(err)
        }
        fmt.Fprint(
                os.Stdout, string(data),
        )
}
```

The key changes are highlighted. We have added a new function, `getUserResponseJson()`, that accepts an object of type `users.UserGetRequest` and returns the equivalent JSON-formatted data as a byte slice. Once you have updated the client code, as shown in Listing 8.10, build and run the client:

```
$ ./client-json localhost:50051 '{"email":"john@doe.com"}'
{"user":{"firstName":"john", "lastName":"doe.com", "age":36}}
```

This brings us nicely to Exercise 8.1, the first exercise of this chapter.

EXERCISE 8.1 IMPLEMENT A COMMAND-LINE CLIENT FOR THE
USERS SERVICE In Chapter 2, you created the skeleton for a gRPC client in
your network client: `mync`. It's now time to implement the functionality. Implement
a new option, `service`, to accept a gRPC service name so that we are able to execute the client to make a gRPC request as follows:

```
$ mync grpc -service Users -method UserGet -request
'{"email":"bill@bryson.com"}' localhost:50051
```

The result should be displayed to the user as a JSON-formatted string. Extra points
for indentation!

Forward and Backward Compatibility

Forward compatibility of software means that older versions will continue to
work with the newer versions. Similarly, the idea of *backward compatibility* is
that newer versions of the software should continue working with the older
versions. We want to evolve our protobuf messages and gRPC methods in a way
that applications that interact with our service via these messages, including the
service itself, are able to do so over time with both its older and newer versions
without surprise breaking changes. When you defined the fields in a message,
you assigned a tag to the fields as follows:

```
message UserGetRequest {
  string email = 1;
  string id = 2;
}
```

For protobuf messages, the key points to remember are as follows:

- *Never change the tag of a field.*
- *You can change the data type of a field only when the old and the new data types
  are compatible with each other.* For example, you can convert between `int32`,
  `uint32`, `int64`, `uint64`, and `bool`. Check the Protocol Buffers 3 specifications about details for other types.
- *Never rename a field.* To rename a field, introduce a new field with an unused
  tag, and then only when all the clients and server have been modified to
  use the new field, remove that field.

For gRPC services, in addition to what you cannot do for protocol buffer
messages, note the following:

- *You cannot rename a service without breaking your existing clients*, unless you
  can absolutely guarantee that both clients and server applications will be
  changed at the same time.

- *You cannot rename a function.* Introduce a new function, switch over all applications using that function to the new one, and then remove the old one.

If you want to change the message type that a function accepts as input and returns as output, you have to consider what kind of change it is. If all of the fields in the message will remain the same, then it's simply a matter of upgrading all of the applications to use the new message name. However, if you are making any changes to the fields—addition/removal/updating—you will have to keep in mind the points mentioned above with respect to protobuf messages.

Exercise 8.2 provides an opportunity to explore one specific scenario where you will need to think about compatibility in gRPC applications.

EXERCISE 8.2 ADD A FIELD TO THE USERREPLY **MESSAGE**

For this exercise, you will create two versions of the protobuf specification, say, Service-v1 and Service-v2. In Service-v2, update the UserReply message to add a new string field location with a new tag. Update your server application to use the Service-v2 version of the service specification and add a Location field to the reply. Update your client application to use the Service-v1 version of the specification.

Make a request from the client to the server. You will see that everything works, but you will not see the Location field in the reply. Updating your client to use the Service-v2 specification will solve this issue.

Multiple Services

A gRPC *server* can serve requests from one or more gRPC *services*. Let's see how we can add a second service, the Repo service, which will be used to query source code repositories for a particular user. First, you will have to create the protobuf specification for the service. Create a directory, chap8/ multiple-services. Copy the service subdirectory from the chap8/user- service inside this directory as follows:

```
$ mkdir -p chap8/multiple-services
$ cp -r chap8/user-service/service chap8/multiple-services/
```

Update the go.mod file to have the following contents:

```
module github.com/username/multiple-services/service
go 1.16
```

Now create a new file, repositories.proto, with the contents shown in Listing 8.11.

Listing 8.11: Protobuf specification for the `Repo` service

```
// chap8/multiple-services/service/repositories.proto

syntax = "proto3";
import "users.proto";

option go_package = "github.com/username/multiple-services/service";

service Repo {
  rpc GetRepos (RepoGetRequest) returns (RepoGetReply) {}
}

message RepoGetRequest {
  string id = 2;
  string creator_id = 1;
}

message Repository {
  string id = 1;
  string name = 2;
  string url = 3;
  User owner = 4;
}

message RepoGetReply {
  repeated Repository repo = 1;
}
```

The `Repository` service defines a single RPC method, `GetRepos`, and two other message types, `RepoGetRequest` and `RepoGetReply`, which correspond to the input and the output for the function. The `RepoGetReply` message type contains a single field, `repo`, of type `Repository`. We have used a new protobuf feature, a `repeated` field. When we declare that a field has `repeated`, the message may contain more than one instance of that field; that is, the `RepoGetReply` message can have zero, one, or more `repo` fields.

A `Repository` has an owner field, which is of type `User`, which is defined in the `users.proto` file. Using the statement import `"users.proto"`, we are able to refer to a message type defined in that file. Next, we will generate the Go code corresponding to both the services as follows:

```
$ protoc --go_out=. --go_opt=paths=source_relative \
    --go-grpc_out=. --go-grpc_opt=paths=source_relative \
  users.proto repositories.proto
```

After you have run the above command, you should see the following files in the `service` directory: `users.pb.go`, `users_grpc.pb.go`, `repositories.pb.go`, and `repositories_grpc.pb.go`.

The go_package option in the .proto files tells the protobuf compiler's go plug-in how the generated package will be imported in your gRPC server or another service. If you look at the package declaration for both the generated users.pb.go and repositories.pb.go files, you will see that both of them declare the package to be a service. Since they are both in the same Go package, the User type is directly usable by the Repository type. If you are curious, examine the definition of the Repository struct in the repositories.pb.go file.

Now we will update the gRPC server code to implement the repositories service. First, create a type to implement the Repo service as follows:

```
import svc "github.com/username/multiple-services/service"
type repoService struct {
        svc.UnimplementedRepoServer
}
```

Then, implement the GetRepos() function:

```
func (s *repoService) GetRepos(
        ctx context.Context,
        in *svc.RepoGetRequest,
) (*svc.RepoGetReply, error) {
        log.Printf(
                "Received request for repo with CreateId: %s Id: %s\n",
                in.CreatorId,
                in.Id,
        )
        repo := svc.Repository{
                Id:    in.Id,
                Name:  "test repo",
                Url:   "https://git.example.com/test/repo",
                Owner: &svc.User{Id: in.CreatorId, FirstName: "Jane"},
        }
        r := svc.RepoGetReply{
                Repo: []*svc.Repository{&repo},
        }
        return &r, nil
}
```

When a field is declared repeated in protobuf, it is generated as a slice in Go. Hence, when constructing the RepoGetReply object, we assign a slice of *Repository objects to the Repo field, as shown in the code highlighted above. Finally, register the service with the gRPC server, s:

```
svc.RegisterRepoServer(s, &repoService{})
```

Listing 8.12 shows the updated server, which registers the Users and Repo services.

Listing 8.12: gRPC Server with both the `Users` and `Repo` services

```go
// chap8/multiple-services/server/server.go
package main

import (
        "context"
        "errors"
        "log"
        "net"
        "os"
        "strings"

        svc "github.com/username/multiple-services/service"
        "google.golang.org/grpc"
        "google.golang.org/grpc/reflection"
)

type userService struct {
        svc.UnimplementedUsersServer
}

type repoService struct {
        svc.UnimplementedRepoServer
}

// TODO Insert definition of getUser() from Listing 8.4
// TODO Insert definition of getRepos() from above

func registerServices(s *grpc.Server) {
        svc.RegisterUsersServer(s, &userService{})
        svc.RegisterRepoServer(s, &repoService{})
        reflection.Register(s)
}

func startServer(s *grpc.Server, l net.Listener) error {
        return s.Serve(l)
}

func main() {
        listenAddr := os.Getenv("LISTEN_ADDR")
        if len(listenAddr) == 0 {
                listenAddr = ":50051"
        }

        lis, err := net.Listen("tcp", listenAddr)
        if err != nil {
                log.Fatal(err)
        }
```

```
s := grpc.NewServer()
registerServices(s)
log.Fatal(startServer(s, lis))
}
```

Create a new directory, server, inside the chap8/multiple-services directory. Initialize a module inside it as follows:

```
$ mkdir -p chap8/multiple-services/server
$ cd chap8/multiple-services/server
$ go mod init github.com/username/multiple-services/server
```

Next, save Listing 8.12 as a new file, server.go, inside it. Run the following command from within the server subdirectory:

```
$ go get google.golang.org/grpc@v1.37.0
```

The above command will fetch the google.golang.org/grpc/ package, update the go.mod file, and create a go.sum file. The final go.mod file is shown in Listing 8.13.

Listing 8.13: go.mod file for gRPC service with the User and Repo services

```
// chap8/multiple-services/server/go.mod
module github.com/username/user-service/server

go 1.16

require (
        github.com/username/multiple-services/service v0.0.0
        google.golang.org/grpc v1.37.0
)

replace github.com/username/multiple-services/service => ../service
```

Next, you will verify if the Repository service is working as expected by writing a test for it as follows:

```
func TestRepoService(t *testing.T) {

        s, l := startTestGrpcServer()
        defer s.GracefulStop()

        bufconnDialer := func(
                ctx context.Context, addr string,
        ) (net.Conn, error) {
                return l.Dial()
        }

        client, err := grpc.DialContext(
                context.Background(),
                "", grpc.WithInsecure(),
```

```
            grpc.WithContextDialer(bufconnDialer),
    )
    if err != nil {
            t.Fatal(err)
    }
    repoClient := svc.NewRepoClient(client)
    resp, err := repoClient.GetRepos(
            context.Background(),
            &svc.RepoGetRequest{
                    CreatorId: "user-123",
                    Id: "repo-123",
            },
    )

    if err != nil {
            t.Fatal(err)
    }
    if len(resp.Repo) != 1 {
            t.Fatalf(
                    "Expected to get back 1 repo,
got back: %d repos", len(resp.Repo),
    )
    }
    gotId := resp.Repo[0].Id
    gotOwnerId := resp.Repo[0].Owner.Id

    if gotId != "repo-123" {
            t.Errorf(
                    "Expected Repo ID to be: repo-123, Got: %s",
                    gotId,
            )
    }
    if gotOwnerId != "user-123" {
            t.Errorf(
                    "Expected Creator ID to be: user-123, Got: %s",
                    gotOwnerId,
            )
    }
}
```

The key statements for testing the Repo service are highlighted. Once we get the response from the call to the GetRepos() function, we check the length of the slice, resp.Repo. We expect that it will only contain one Repository object. If that is not the case, we fail the test. If we find that the slice contains a Repo object, we retrieve its Id and OwnerId by accessing the Repo field, as with any other Go slice. Finally, we verify that the value of these fields matches our expectations.

You can find the complete test in this book's code repository in the file chap8/multiple-services/server/server_test.go file.

In the next exercise, you will extend the `mync grpc` client also to support making requests to the `Repo` service.

EXERCISE 8.3 IMPLEMENT A COMMAND LINE CLIENT FOR THE `REPO` SERVICE In Exercise 8.1, you extended the `mync grpc` subcommand to have an interface like the following:

```
$ mync grpc -service Users -method UserGet -request
'{"email":"bill@bryson.com"}' localhost:50051
```

Now, extend the command to support making requests to the `Repo` service as well, so that the user can specify the repository search criteria as a JSON-formatted string.

The result should be displayed to the user as a JSON-formatted string.

In the final section of this chapter, let's learn about error handling in gRPC applications.

Error Handling

As you have seen so far, in a gRPC method implementation, you return two objects: one is the response and the other is an error value. What happens if we return a non-`nil` error from the method? Let's see what happens if we don't pass a valid email address when calling the `GetUser()` method.

From the terminal, navigate into the `chap8/user-service/server` directory, build the server if necessary, and run it:

```
$ cd chap8/user-service/server
$ go build -o server
$ ./server
```

From a separate terminal session, navigate into the `chap8/user-service/client-json` directory, build the client if necessary, and run it specifying an empty JSON object as follows:

```
$ cd chap8/user-service/client-json
$ go build -o client
$ ./client localhost:50051 '{}'
2021/05/25 21:12:11 rpc error: code = Unknown desc = invalid email
address
```

We get an error message, and the client exits. The text `"invalid email address"` comes from the error value that we returned from the `Users` service's handler:

```
components := strings.Split(in.Email, "@")
if len(components) != 2 {
    return nil, errors.New("invalid email address")
```

The string `"rpc error: code = Unknown desc"` is from the gRPC library, and it's saying that it couldn't find a code in the error response from the server. To fix that, we will need to update our server to return a valid error code, similar to HTTP status codes. gRPC supports a fair number of error codes defined by the `google.golang.org/grpc/codes` package. One of them is `InvalidArgument`, which sounds appropriate here considering that the client didn't specify a valid email address.

Now let's update our server to return an error with this code instead:

```
import (
        "google.golang.org/grpc/codes"
        "google.golang.org/grpc/status"
)
....
components := strings.Split(in.Email, "@")
if len(components) != 2 {
        return nil, status.Error(
                codes.InvalidArgument,
                "Invalid email address specified",
        )
}
```

We make use of another package, `google.golang.org/grpc/status`, to create an error value using the `status.Error()` function. The first argument to the function is the error code and the second is a message describing the error. You can find the updated server code in the `chap8/user-service-error-handling/server` directory of this book's source repository.

Build and run this new version of the server as follows:

```
$ ./server
```

Now, if you make the request again, you will see the code logged as follows:

```
$ ./client-json localhost:50051 '{}'
2021/05/25 21:45:16 rpc error: code = InvalidArgument desc = Invalid email address specified
```

We can improve the client-side error handling slightly by accessing the error code and the error message separately by using the `status.Convert()` function as follows:

```
result, err := getUser(..)
s := status.Convert(err)
if s.Code() != codes.OK {
        log.Fatalf("Request failed: %v - %v\n", s.Code(), s.Message())
}
```

The status.Convert() function returns an object of type *Status. By calling its Code() method, we retrieve the error code, and if it is not codes.OK (that is, an error was returned by the service), we log the error code and the message separately. You can find the updated client code in the chap8/user-service-error-handling/client-json directory.

When you send the same invalid input to the server, you will now see the error logged as follows:

```
2021/05/25 21:59:13 Request failed: InvalidArgument - Invalid email address
specified
```

There are several other error codes defined by the gRPC specification, and you are encouraged to refer to the documentation for the google.golang.org/grpc/codes package to learn about those.

Summary

In this chapter, you learned to write gRPC applications. You became familiar with writing the most basic form of a gRPC application; that is, a request-response server client architecture. You learned to write tests for clients and servers without setting up expensive server processes.

You then learned about protocol buffers and how they are leveraged as the data interchange format for gRPC applications. You also learned how to convert between JSON and protobuf data formats. Then, you learned a bit about maintaining forward and backward compatibility in protobuf specifications. Next, you learned to register multiple services in a gRPC server. Finally, you ended the chapter by learning how to return and handle errors in gRPC applications.

In the next chapter, you will continue your journey by learning advanced gRPC features such as streaming communication patterns, sending binary data, and implementing middleware for your applications.

## CHAPTER 9

Advanced gRPC Applications

In the first half of this chapter, you will learn how to implement streaming communication patterns in gRPC applications. In the latter half, you will learn to implement common server and client functionality as middleware components. Along the way, you will learn how to send and receive binary data and understand more about Protocol Buffers. Let's jump in!

Streaming Communication

As you learned in Chapter 8, data is exchanged between client and server as protobuf messages. You learned to build gRPC applications following the *Unary* RPC pattern. In this pattern, a client sends a request to the server and then waits for the server to send back a response. More specifically, the client application calls an RPC method, sends a request as a protobuf message, and then waits for the response message from the server. There is only *one* message exchange that happens between the client and the server.

Next, we are going to learn three new communication patterns: *server-side streaming*, *client-side streaming*, and a combination of the two, *bidirectional streaming*. In these three patterns, it is possible to exchange more than one request and response message during a single method call. Let's learn about these, starting with server-side streaming.

Server-Side Streaming

In *server-side streaming*, when a client makes a request, the server may send more than one response message. Consider the `GetRepos()` RPC method of the `Repo` service that we implemented in the previous chapter. Instead of sending the list of repositories in a single message, we could respond with multiple `Repo` messages as the response with each message containing the details of a repository. Let's see how we can implement such an application.

First, we will update the protobuf specification for the `Repo` service as follows:

```
service Repo {
  rpc GetRepos (RepoGetRequest) returns (stream RepoGetReply) {}
}
```

The key difference here is the `stream` specification in the return type for the method. This tells the Protocol Buffer compiler and the Go gRPC plugin that the response will contain a *stream* of `RepoGetReply` messages. Listing 9.1 shows the complete protobuf specification for the `Repo` service.

Listing 9.1: Protobuf specification for the `Repo` service

```
// chap9/server-streaming/service/repositories.proto
syntax = "proto3";
import "users.proto";

option go_package = "github.com/username/server-streaming/service";

service Repo {
  rpc GetRepos (RepoGetRequest) returns (stream RepoGetReply) {}
}

message RepoGetRequest {
  string id = 2;
  string creator_id = 1;
}

message Repository {
  string id = 1;
  string name = 2;
  string url = 3;
  User owner = 4;
}

message RepoGetReply {
  Repository repo = 1;
}
```

As compared to the original specification for the service (Chapter 8, Listing 8.11), there are two key changes. The `GetRepos()` method now returns a stream of `RepoGetReply` messages. The `RepoGetReply` message will now have the details of a single repository, hence we have removed the `repeated` declaration from this field.

Create a directory `chap9/server-streaming`. Inside it, create a new subdirectory, `service`, and initialize a module inside it as follows:

```
$ mkdir -p chap9/server-streaming/service
$ go mod init github.com/username/server-streaming/service
```

Next, create a new file inside the `service` directory, `repositories.proto`, with the contents shown in Listing 9.1. Copy the `users.proto` file from `chap8/multiple-services/service/` into this directory. In it, replace `go_package` to read as follows:

```
option go_package = "github.com/username/server-streaming/service";
```

Next, we will generate the Go code corresponding to both of the services:

```
$ protoc --go_out=. --go_opt=paths=source_relative \
    --go-grpc_out=. --go-grpc_opt=paths=source_relative \
    users.proto repositories.proto
```

After you have run the above command, you should see the following files in the `service` directory as earlier: `users.pb.go`, `users_grpc.pb.go`, `repositories.pb.go`, and `repositories_grpc.pb.go`.

Next, we will update the implementation of the `GetRepos()` method to read as follows:

```
func (s *repoService) GetRepos(
        in *svc.RepoGetRequest,
        stream svc.Repo_GetReposServer,
) error {
        log.Printf(
                "Received request for repo with CreateId: %s Id: %s\n",
                in.CreatorId,
                in.Id,
        )
        repo := svc.Repository{
                Id:    in.Id,
                Owner: &svc.User{
                        Id: in.CreatorId,
                        FirstName: "Jane",
                },
        }
        cnt := 1
        for {
                repo.Name = fmt.Sprintf("repo-%d", cnt)
                repo.Url = fmt.Sprintf(
                        "https://git.example.com/test/%s",
                        repo.Name,
```

```
                )
        r := svc.RepoGetReply{
                Repo: &repo,
        }
        if err := stream.Send(&r); err != nil {
                return err
        }
        if cnt >= 5 {
                break
        }
        cnt++
    }
    return nil
}
```

There are a couple of key changes in the above implementation. First, the method implementation now has a different signature. It accepts two parameters: the incoming request, in of type RepoGetRequest, and an object, stream of type Repo_GetReposServer, and it returns an error value. The type, Repo_GetReposServer, is an interface generated by the protobuf compiler:

```
type Repo_GetReposServer interface {
        Send(*RepoGetReply) error
        grpc.ServerStream
}
```

A type that implements this interface must implement the Send() method, which accepts a parameter of type RepoGetReply message—our reply type—and it returns an error value. Of course, as the application author, you don't have to worry about implementing a type that implements this interface, as it's automatically accomplished by the protobuf compiler and the Go grpc plugin. This method is what we use to send back a message of RepoGetReply type as a response to the client. The embedded field grpc.ServerStream is another interface defined in the google.golang.org/grpc package. We will learn more about this in the section "Implementing Middleware Using Interceptors" later in the chapter.

Inside the method body, we first log a message to print the details about the incoming request. Then, we create a Repo object to send back as a response. Inside the for loop, we further customize this object, create a RepoGetReply message, and then send it as a response to the client using the stream.Send() method. We send five such response messages in total, each time changing the Repo object slightly. When we have sent all of the responses, we break out of the loop and return a nil error value.

Listing 9.2 shows the complete listing for the gRPC server with the implementation of the Users and Repo services.

Listing 9.2: gRPC server for `Users` and `Repo` service

```go
// chap9/server-streaming/server/server.go
package main

import (
        "context"
        "errors"
        "fmt"
        "log"
        "net"
        "os"
        "strings"

        svc "github.com/username/server-streaming/service"
        "google.golang.org/grpc"
)

type userService struct {
        svc.UnimplementedUsersServer
}

type repoService struct {
        svc.UnimplementedRepoServer
}

// TODO Insert definition of GetUser() from Chapter 8, Listing 8.2
// TODO Insert definition of GetRepos() as above

func registerServices(s *grpc.Server) {
        svc.RegisterUsersServer(s, &userService{})
        svc.RegisterRepoServer(s, &repoService{})
}

func startServer(s *grpc.Server, l net.Listener) error {
        return s.Serve(l)
}

func main() {
        listenAddr := os.Getenv("LISTEN_ADDR")
        if len(listenAddr) == 0 {
                listenAddr = ":50051"
        }

        lis, err := net.Listen("tcp", listenAddr)
        if err != nil {
                log.Fatal(err)
        }
        s := grpc.NewServer()
        registerServices(s)
        log.Fatal(startServer(s, lis))
}
```

Create a new subdirectory, `server`, inside `chap9/server-streaming`, and initialize a module inside it as follows:

```
$ mkdir -p chap9/server-streaming/server
$ cd chap9/server-streaming/server
$ go mod init github.com/username/server-streaming/server
```

Save Listing 9.2 as `server.go` inside the `server` directory. Next, we will fetch the `google.golang.org/grpc` package (version 1.37.0):

```
$ go get google.golang.org/grpc@v1.37.0
```

Then, update the `go.mod` file to add the dependency on the service package, including the replace directive, so that the final `go.mod` appears as shown in Listing 9.3.

Listing 9.3: `go.mod` file for the server

```
// chap9/server-streaming/server/go.mod

module github.com/username/server-streaming/server
go 1.16

require google.golang.org/grpc v1.37.0
require github.com/username/server-streaming/service v0.0.0

replace github.com/username/server-streaming/service => ../service
```

Make sure that you can now build the server successfully using `go build`. Next, we are going to write a test function to verify the workings of the server. As in Chapter 8, we will be using the `bufconn` package to set up an in-memory communication channel between the test client and the server. Assume that we have an object, `repoClient`, configured to communicate with the `Repo` service in the gRPC test server. We will call the `GetRepos()` method as follows:

```
stream, err := repoClient.GetRepos(
        context.Background(),
        &svc.RepoGetRequest{CreatorId: "user-123", Id: "repo-123"},
)
```

The call to the method returns us two values: `stream`, an object of type `Repo_GetReposClient`, and `err`, an error value. The type, `Repo_GetReposClient`, is the client equivalent of the `Repo_GetReposServer` type, and it is an interface defined as follows:

```
type Repo_GetReposClient interface {
        Recv() (*RepoGetReply, error)
        grpc.ClientStream
}
```

A type that implements this interface must implement the `Recv()` method, which returns a `RepoGetReply` message—the method's reply type—and it returns an error value. The embedded field `grpc.ClientStream` is another interface defined in the `google.golang.org/grpc` package. We will learn more about this in the section "Implementing Middleware Using Interceptors" later in the chapter.

To read the response stream from the server, we will make use of the `Recv()` method:

```
var repos []*svc.Repository
for {
        repo, err := stream.Recv()
        if err == io.EOF {
                break
        }
        if err != nil {
                log.Fatal(err)
        }
        repos = append(repos, repo.Repo)
}
```

Using an infinite for loop, we call the `Recv()` method. If the returned error value is `io.EOF`, there are no more messages to read, and hence we break out of the loop. If we get any other error, we print the error and terminate the execution. Otherwise, we append the repository details in the message to a slice, `repos`. Once we have read the server response, we can verify various details whether they match the expected response or not. Listing 9.4 shows the complete listing for the test function to verify the working of the `GetRepos()` method. (The test function for the `Users` service is not shown here. You can find it in the book's source repository in the directory `chap9/server-streaming/server`.)

Listing 9.4: Test function for the `Repo` service

```
// chap9/server-streaming/server/server_test.go
package main

// TODO: Imports have been omitted for brevity
// TODO: Insert definition of startTestGrpcServer()
// from previous chapter

func TestRepoService(t *testing.T) {

        l := startTestGrpcServer()

        bufconnDialer := func(
                ctx context.Context, addr string,
        ) (net.Conn, error) {
                return l.Dial()
        }
```

```
client, err := grpc.DialContext(
        context.Background(),
        "", grpc.WithInsecure(),
        grpc.WithContextDialer(bufconnDialer),
)
if err != nil {
        t.Fatal(err)
}
repoClient := svc.NewRepoClient(client)
stream, err := repoClient.GetRepos(
        context.Background(),
        &svc.RepoGetRequest{
                CreatorId: "user-123",
                Id: "repo-123",
        },
)
if err != nil {
        t.Fatal(err)
}


// TODO: Insert the for loop to read the streaming response from
// server as earlier illustrated

if len(repos) != 5 {
        t.Fatalf(
                "Expected to get back 5 repos, got back:
%d repos", len(repos))
}

for idx, repo := range repos {
        gotRepoName := repo.Name
        expectedRepoName := fmt.Sprintf("repo-%d", idx+1)

        if gotRepoName != expectedRepoName {
                t.Errorf(
                        "Expected Repo Name to be: %s, Got: %s",
                        expectedRepoName,
                        gotRepoName,
                )
        }
}
}
```

Save Listing 9.4 as `server_test.go` inside the server directory. Verify that you can run the test and that it completes successfully:

```
$ go test -v
=== RUN   TestUserService
2021/06/09 08:43:25 Received request for user with Email:
```

```
jane@doe.com Id: foo-bar
--- PASS: TestUserService (0.00s)
=== RUN   TestRepoService
2021/06/09 08:43:25 Received request for repo with CreateId:
user-123 Id: repo-123
--- PASS: TestRepoService (0.00s)
PASS
Ok.    github.com/practicalgo/code/chap9/server-streaming/server 0.141s
```

Server-side streaming is useful for sending multiple response messages to the client for a single RPC method call. It is likely to be more efficient to stream many objects than to send an array of such objects. Another scenario in which this may be found to be useful is when sending a response whose final value is not yet known, such as streaming the result of another operation.

In the first exercise of the chapter, Exercise 9.1, you will implement a new method in the Repo service that will simulate running a build job for a repository and then streaming the build logs to a client.

EXERCISE 9.1: STREAMING BUILD LOGS FOR A REPOSITORY

In the Repo **service, create a new method,** CreateBuild(), **which accepts a message of type** Repository **and returns a stream of** RepoBuildLog **messages.** RepoBuildLog **is a message type containing two fields: one representing the time stamp when the log line was generated and the other containing a log line. Update the service test (Listing 9.4) to add a test for this method.**

Client-Side Streaming

Similar to server-side streaming, in *client-side streaming* the clients call an RPC method on the server and then send its request as a stream of messages rather than a single message.

Let's add a new method to the Repo service, CreateRepo(), which will now accept a stream of messages as a parameter. Each message will specify the details for creating a new repository. We will define a new message type, RepoCreateRequest, for this method. The protobuf specification for the method will appear as follows:

```
rpc CreateRepo (stream RepoCreateRequest) returns (RepoCreateReply) {}
```

The key here is the stream specification before the message type. The service handler in the server for this method will appear as follows:

```
func (s *repoService) CreateRepo(
        stream svc.Repo_CreateRepoServer,
```

```
) error {
      for {
              data, err := stream.Recv()
              if err == io.EOF {
                      // We have received the complete request
                      // so, we can now process the data
                      r := svc.RepoCreateReply{..}
              }
      }
      return stream.SendAndClose(&r)
}
```

The `CreateRepo()` method implementation accepts a single parameter, `stream`, of type `svc.Repo_CreateRepoServer`, which is an interface type generated by the protobuf compiler, and it is defined as follows:

```
type Repo_CreateRepoServer interface {
      Recv() (*RepoCreateRequest, error)
      SendAndClose(*RepoCreateReply) error
      grpc.ServerStream
}
```

A type implementing this interface will implement two methods, `Recv()` and `SendAndClose()`, and it will embed the `ServerStream` interface. The `Recv()` method is used to receive the incoming messages from the client, and hence it returns a value of `RepoCreateRequest` and an `error` value. The `SendAndClose()` method is used to send back a reply to the client. Hence it accepts a value of type `RepoCreateReply` as a parameter, sends the response back to the client, and closes the connection. Of course, as an application author, you don't have to worry about implementing this type.

Next, let's look at how we can call the `CreateRepo()` method from a client application:

```
repoClient := svc.NewRepoClient(client)
stream, err := repoClient.CreateRepo(
      context.Background(),
)
```

Note that we don't call the `CreateRepo()` method with any request parameters. It only accepts a `context.Context` object. This method returns two values: `stream`, of type `Repo_CreateRepoClient`, and an `error` value. The `Repo_CreateRepoClient` type is an interface defined as follows:

```
type Repo_CreateRepoClient interface {
      Send(*RepoCreateRequest) error
      CloseAndRecv() (*RepoCreateReply, error)
      grpc.ClientStream
}
```

A type implementing this interface will implement two methods, `Send()` and `CloseAndRecv()`, and it will embed the `ClientStream` interface.

To send a message to the server application, we will use the `Send()` method. Hence, it must be called with an object of type `*RepoCreateRequest`.

The `CloseAndRecv()` method is used to receive a response from the server. Hence, it returns a value of type `RepoCreateReply` and an error value.

To send a stream of `RepoCreateRequest` messages to the server, we will call the `Send()` method multiple times in a for loop, for example:

```
for i := 0; i < 5; i++ {
        r := svc.RepoCreateRequest{
                CreatorId: "user-123",
                Name:       "hello-world",
        }
        err := stream.Send(&r)
        if err != nil {
                t.Fatal(err)
        }
}
```

Then, once we have completed streaming our request messages, we will read the response from the server:

```
resp, err := stream.CloseAndRecv()
```

You can find the complete example of the server, as well as a test to verify the functioning, in the `chap9/client-streaming` directory of the book's source repository. Next, you will learn about and implement the streaming pattern that combines both client- and server-side streaming—bidirectional streaming.

Bidirectional Streaming

In *bidirectional streaming*, once a client initiates a connection with the server, each can independently read and write data, in any order. No ordering is imposed and hence no ordering is guaranteed unless your application has enforced it. For example, let's say that we wanted to update the `Users` service to allow a user to get help from the service, similar to asking for help from a website's support via chat. The communication between the client and the server in this case is bidirectional: a user (client) initiates the conversation with the support staff (server), and then an exchange takes place between the two until one of them terminates the connection. We will now create a `Users` service with only one RPC method, `GetHelp()`, as shown in Listing 9.5.

Listing 9.5: Protobuf specification for the `Users` service

```
// chap9/bidi-streaming/service/users.proto
syntax = "proto3";
```

```
option go_package = "github.com/username/bidi-streaming/service";

service Users {
  rpc GetHelp (stream UserHelpRequest) returns (stream UserHelpReply) {}
}

message User {
  string id = 1;
}

message UserHelpRequest {
  User user = 1;
  string request = 2;
}

message UserHelpReply {
  string response = 1;
}
```

The GetHelp() method accepts as a request a stream of UserHelpRequest messages, and it returns a stream of UserHelpReply messages.

Create a directory chap9/bidi-streaming. Inside it, create a new subdirectory, service, and initialize a module inside it:

```
$ mkdir -p chap9/bidi-streaming/service
$ go mod init github.com/username/bidi-streaming/service
```

Save Listing 9.5 as users.proto inside the service directory. Generate the Go code corresponding to both of the services:

```
$ protoc --go_out=. --go_opt=paths=source_relative \
    --go-grpc_out=. --go-grpc_opt=paths=source_relative users.proto
```

After you have run the above command, you should see the following files in the service directory: users.pb.go and users_grpc.pb.go. Now let's implement the GetHelp() method on the server:

```
func (s *userService) GetHelp(
        stream svc.Users_GetHelpServer,
) error {
        log.Println("Client connected")
        for {
                request, err := stream.Recv()
                if err == io.EOF {
                        break
                }
                if err != nil {
                        return err
                }
```

```
        fmt.Printf("Request received: %s\n", request.Request)
        response := svc.UserHelpReply{
                Response: request.Request,
        }
        err = stream.Send(&response)
        if err != nil {
                return err
        }
    }
    log.Println("Client disconnected")
    return nil
}
```

The `GetHelp()` method accepts a parameter of type `Users_GetHelpServer`, which is a generated interface defined as follows:

```
type Users_GetHelpServer interface {
        Send(*UserHelpReply) error
        Recv() (*UserHelpRequest, error)
        grpc.ServerStream
}
```

Since the server will both receive and send a stream of messages, the interface has both the `Send()` and `Recv()` methods, and it embeds the `ServerStream` interface.

The `Send()` method is used to send a reply message of type `UserHelpReply` to the client.

The `Recv()` method is used to receive a request from the client. It returns a value of type `UserHelpRequest` and an `error` value.

Then, we create a for loop where we continuously attempt to read a value from the client's stream, breaking out of the loop if we get an `io.EOF` error and returning an error value if we get any other error. If we get a valid request from the client, we construct a `UserHelpReply` message that echoes the help request message back to the client using the `Send()` method. Listing 9.6 shows the gRPC server application implementing the `Users` service.

Listing 9.6: Server for the `Users` service

```
// chap9/bidi-streaming/server/server.go
package main

import (
        "fmt"
        "io"
        "log"
        "net"
        "os"
```

```
        svc "github.com/username/bidi-streaming/service"
        "google.golang.org/grpc"
)

type userService struct {
        svc.UnimplementedUsersServer
}

// TODO: Insert definition of GetHelp() method from above

func registerServices(s *grpc.Server) {
        svc.RegisterUsersServer(s, &userService{})
}

func startServer(s *grpc.Server, l net.Listener) error {
        return s.Serve(l)
}

func main() {
        listenAddr := os.Getenv("LISTEN_ADDR")
        if len(listenAddr) == 0 {
                listenAddr = ":50051"
        }

        lis, err := net.Listen("tcp", listenAddr)
        if err != nil {
                log.Fatal(err)
        }
        s := grpc.NewServer()
        registerServices(s)
        log.Fatal(startServer(s, lis))
}
```

Inside the chap9/bidi-streaming directory, create a new subdirectory, server.
Initialize a module inside it as follows:

```
$ mkdir -p chap9/bidi-streaming/server
$ cd chap9/bidi-streaming/server
$ go mod init github.com/username/bidi-streaming/server
```

Save Listing 9.6 as server.go inside the server directory. Next, we will fetch
the google.golang.org/grpc package (version 1.37.0) as follows:

```
$ go get google.golang.org/grpc@v1.37.0
```

Then, update the go.mod file to add the dependency on the service package,
including the replace directive, so that the final go.mod appears as shown in
Listing 9.7.

Listing 9.7: `go.mod` file for the server

```
// chap9/bidi-streaming/server/go.mod

module github.com/username/bidi-streaming/server
go 1.16

require google.golang.org/grpc v1.37.0
require github.com/username/bidi-streaming/service v0.0.0

replace github.com/username/bidi-streaming/service => ../service
```

Make sure that you can now build the server successfully using `go build`. Next, let's see how we can set up a client. Consider a function `setupChat()` that accepts an `io.Reader` from which it will read a user's help request, a configured `UsersClient` object, to communicate with the `Users` service, and an `io.Writer` to write the server response to.

```go
func setupChat(r io.Reader, w io.Writer, c svc.UsersClient) error {
        stream, err := c.GetHelp(context.Background())
        if err != nil {
                return err
        }
        for {
                scanner := bufio.NewScanner(r)
                prompt := "Request: "
                fmt.Fprint(w, prompt)

                scanner.Scan()
                if err := scanner.Err(); err != nil {
                        return err
                }
                msg := scanner.Text()
                if msg == "quit" {
                        break
                }
                request := svc.UserHelpRequest{
                        Request: msg,
                }
                err := stream.Send(&request)
                if err != nil {
                        return err
                }
                resp, err := stream.Recv()
                if err != nil {
                        return err
                }
                fmt.Printf("Response: %s\n", resp.Response)
        }
        return stream.CloseSend()
}
```

First, we call the `GetHelp()` RPC method, which returns a value of type `Users_GetHelpClient`, a generated interface defined as follows:

```
type Users_GetHelpClient interface {
        Send(*UserHelpRequest) error
        Recv() (*UserHelpReply, error)
        grpc.ClientStream
}
```

Similar to the `Users_GetHelpServer` type, the `Users_GetHelpClient` type defines methods for both sending and receiving messages, and it embeds the `ClientStream` interface.

Once we have obtained the stream, we set up a for loop that interactively reads user input and then sends it off to the server as a `UserHelpRequest` message. If the user types in **quit**, the connection is closed.

Listing 9.8 shows the listing for the client application.

Listing 9.8: Client for the `Users` service

```
// chap9/bidi-streaming/client/main.go
package main

import (
        "bufio"
        "context"
        "fmt"
        "io"
        "log"
        "os"

        svc "github.com/username/bidi-streaming/service"
        "google.golang.org/grpc"
)

func setupGrpcConn(addr string) (*grpc.ClientConn, error) {
        return grpc.DialContext(
                context.Background(),
                addr,
                grpc.WithInsecure(),
                grpc.WithBlock(),
        )
}

func getUserServiceClient(conn *grpc.ClientConn) svc.UsersClient {
        return svc.NewUsersClient(conn)
}

// TODO Insert definition of setupChat() from earlier
```

```go
func main() {
        if len(os.Args) != 2 {
                log.Fatal(
                        "Must specify a gRPC server address",
                )
        }
        conn, err := setupGrpcConn(os.Args[1])
        if err != nil {
                log.Fatal(err)
        }
        defer conn.Close()

        c := getUserServiceClient(conn)
        err = setupChat(os.Stdin, os.Stdout, c)
        if err != nil {
                log.Fatal(err)
        }
}
```

Inside the directory chap9/bidi-streaming, create a new subdirectory, client, and initialize a module inside it as follows:

```
$ mkdir -p chap9/bidi-streaming/client
$ cd chap9/bidi-streaming/client
$ go mod init github.com/username/bidi-streaming/client
```

Save Listing 9.8 as client.go inside the client directory. Next, we will fetch the google.golang.org/grpc package (version 1.37.0):

```
$ go get google.golang.org/grpc@v1.37.0
```

Then, update the go.mod file to add the dependency on the service package, including the replace directive, so that the final go.mod appears as shown in Listing 9.9.

Listing 9.9: go.mod file for the client

```
// chap9/bidi-streaming/client/go.mod

module github.com/username/bidi-streaming/client
go 1.16

require google.golang.org/grpc v1.37.0
require github.com/username/bidi-streaming/service v0.0.0

replace github.com/username/bidi-streaming/service => ../service
```

Build the client.
Now, in one terminal session, run the server:

```
$ cd chap9/bidi-streaming/server
$ go build
$ ./server
```

In a separate terminal session, run the client:

```
$ ./client localhost:50051
Request: Hello there
Response: Hello there
Request: I need some help
Response: I need some help
Request: quit
```

On the server side, you will see the following messages:

```
2021/06/24 20:46:56 Client connected
Request received: Hello there
Request received: I need some help
2021/06/24 20:47:29 Client disconnected
```

When you typed in **quit** from the client terminal session, the client called the
CloseSend() method, which in turn closed the client connection on the server
returning an io.EOF error value.

You have now studied the three categories of streaming communication
possible in gRPC. As compared to Unary RPC method calls, where there was
only a request and response message exchanged, in streaming communication,
multiple such messages are exchanged, which is summarized in Figure 9.1.

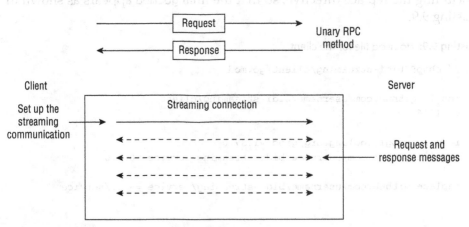

Figure 9.1: Streaming communication pattern

Next, you will learn how to leverage streaming when it comes to transmitting

Receiving and Sending Arbitrary Bytes

So far, we have only focused on transmission of strings and integers between a gRPC server application and client. How do you send and process any arbitrary data, such as data you would store in a repository, say a `.tar.gz` file? That's where the `bytes` type comes in. Let's update the `RepoCreateRequest` data type to add a field, `data`, that will contain arbitrary bytes such as the contents of a file to be stored in the repository:

```
message RepoCreateRequest {
  string creator_id = 1;
  string name = 2;
  bytes data = 3;
}
```

Anything that you can store as a byte slice in Go, you can store in the data field. To ask the server to create a repository, the client would make a request as follows:

```
repoData := []byte("Arbitrary data")
resp, err := repoClient.CreateRepo(
            context.Background(),
            &svc.RepoCreateRequest{
                  CreatorId: "user-123",
                  Name:      "test-repo",
                  Data:      repoData,
            },
  )
```

On the server side, the method would then process the request including the data as follows:

```
func (s *repoService) CreateRepo(
        ctx context.Context,
        in *svc.RepoCreateRequest,
) (*svc.RepoCreateReply, error) {
        repoId := fmt.Sprintf("%s-%s", in.Name, in.CreatorId)
        repoURL := fmt.Sprintf("https://git.example.com/%s/%s",
in.CreatorId, in.Name)
        data := in.Data
        repo := svc.Repository{
                Id:   repoId,
                Name: in.Name,
                Url:  repoURL,
        }
```

```
r := svc.RepoCreateReply{
        Repo: &repo,
        Size: int32(len(data)),
    }
    return &r, nil
}
```

You can find the code for the example in the `chap9/binary-data` directory of this book's source repository. This mechanism of sending any arbitrary bytes is straightforward, and it works perfectly when the size of the data transmitted is limited to a few bytes. For larger data transmissions, it is instead recommended that you use streaming communication patterns.

In the example scenario above, client-side streaming would be perfectly suitable. Read bytes of data incrementally from a source, such as a file, and then send a message containing the data to the server. Keep doing this until all of the data has been read.

In streaming, the client or the server sends multiple messages for a request or a response, respectively. We only want the data to be streamed, hence we could design our protobuf message to contain a single data field:

```
message RepoData {
  bytes data = 1;
}
```

Rarely, though, you will transmit arbitrary bytes without any contextual information. For example, the `RepoCreateRequest` message discussed earlier included a `creator_id`, `name`, and the `data`. If we use this message type for streaming, we will have to send the same `creator_id` and `name` across all of the messages. It is thus recommended that you instead send the `creator_id` and `name` fields in the first message of the stream, and then all subsequent messages in the stream should contain only the `data` bytes.

Luckily, we can use a Protocol Buffer feature called `oneof` when defining the message to do this rather elegantly. This keyword allows us to define a message where only one field among a group of fields can be set at any given point of time. Let's redefine the `RepoCreateRequest` message using the `oneof` keyword as follows:

```
message RepoCreateRequest {
  oneof body {
    RepoContext context = 1;
    bytes data = 2;
  }
}
```

We define the `RepoCreateRequest` to have a `oneof` field with the name `body`. This field will only ever have either `context` (of type `RepoContext`) or `data` (of type `bytes`) set in a message, but not both. The new message type, `RepoContext`, will contain the contextual information for the repository being created, and it is defined as follows:

```
message RepoContext {
  string creator_id = 1;
  string name = 2;
}
```

Listing 9.10 shows the updated protobuf specification for the `Repo` service.

Listing 9.10: Protobuf specification for the Repo service

```
// chap9/bindata-client-streaming/service/repositories.proto

syntax = "proto3";

option go_package = "github.com/username/bindata-client-streaming
/service";

service Repo {
  rpc CreateRepo (stream RepoCreateRequest) returns (RepoCreateReply){}
}

message RepoCreateRequest {
  oneof body {
    RepoContext context = 1;
    bytes data = 2;
  }
}

message RepoContext {
  string creator_id = 1;
  string name = 2;
}

message Repository {
  string id = 1;
  string name = 2;
  string url = 3;
}

message RepoCreateReply {
  Repository repo = 1;
  int32 size = 2;
}
```

The `CreateRepo()` method is now specified to accept a stream of `RepoCreateRequest` messages and return a `RepoCreateReply` message. Create a directory `chap9/bindata-client-streaming`. Inside it, create a new subdirectory, `service`, and initialize a module inside it:

```
$ mkdir -p chap9/bindata-client-streaming/service
$ go mod init github.com/username/bindata-client-streaming/service
```

Next, create a new file inside the `service` directory, `repositories.proto`, with the contents shown in Listing 9.10.

Next, we will generate the Go code corresponding to the service:

```
$ protoc --go_out=. --go_opt=paths=source_relative \
    --go-grpc_out=. --go-grpc_opt=paths=source_relative \
  repositories.proto
```

As in previous cases, you should see two files generated: `repositories` `.pb.go` and `repositories_grpc.pb.go`.

Next, let's write the implementation for the `CreateRepo()` method in the server:

```go
func (s *repoService) CreateRepo(
        stream svc.Repo_CreateRepoServer,
) error {
        var repoContext *svc.RepoContext
        var data []byte
        for {
                r, err := stream.Recv()
                if err == io.EOF {
                        break
                }
                switch t := r.Body.(type) {
                case *svc.RepoCreateRequest_Context:
                        repoContext = r.GetContext()
                case *svc.RepoCreateRequest_Data:
                        b := r.GetData()
                        data = append(data, b...)
                case nil:
                        return status.Error(
                                codes.InvalidArgument,
                                "Message doesn't contain context or data",
                        )
                default:
                        return status.Errorf(
                                codes.FailedPrecondition,
                                "Unexpected message type: %s",
                                t,
                        )
                }
        }
        // TODO: Create the response message
}
```

The method accepts a single parameter, stream, of type Repo_Create RepoServer, and it returns an error value. Repo_CreateRepoServer is a generated interface defined as follows:

```
type Repo_CreateRepoServer interface {
        SendAndClose(*RepoCreateReply) error
        Recv() (*RepoCreateRequest, error)
        grpc.ServerStream
}
```

Thus, we will use stream to read the incoming stream from the client and then write the response back.

Inside the method body, we declare an object, repoContext, of type RepoContext, and a byte slice, data. We will store the incoming contextual information related to the repo in repoContext object and the repository contents in data.

Next, we define a for loop to read from the stream continuously using stream .Recv() until we encounter an io.EOF error. Now when we read an object using the Recv() method, it is of type RepoCreateRequest. However, we know that only one of the fields—context or data—will be set. To figure out which one is set, we look at the type of r.Body, where Body is the oneof field (body in protobuf):

1. If the type is RepoCreateRequest_Context, the context field was set, which we retrieve by calling the GetContext() method. We assign the retrieved value to the repoContext object.

2. If the type is RepoCreateRequest_Data, we retrieve the bytes by calling the GetData() method and append it to the data slice.

3. If the type is nil or neither of the two above, we return an error back to the client.

We use a switch..case statement to accomplish the above logic. Figure 9.2 summarizes the mapping between the protobuf specification and the generated Go type for the Body field.

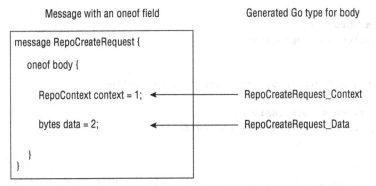

Figure 9.2: Protobuf oneof field and the equivalent generated Go type

Once we have finished reading the complete request, we construct a response message and send it to the client using the `SendAndClose()` method defined for the stream object:

```
repo := svc.Repository{
            Name: repoContext.Name,
            Url: fmt.Sprintf(
                    "https://git.example.com/%s/%s",
                    repoContext.CreatorId,
                    repoContext.Name,
            ),
        }
        r := svc.RepoCreateReply{
                Repo: &repo,
                Size: int32(len(data)),
        }
        return stream.SendAndClose(&r)
```

Listing 9.11 shows the implementation of the server for the Repo service.

Listing 9.11: Server for the Repo service

```
// chap9/bindata-client-streaming/server/server.go
package main

import (
        "fmt"
        "io"
        "log"
        "net"
        "os"

        svc "github.com/username/bindata-client-streaming/service"
        "google.golang.org/grpc"
        "google.golang.org/grpc/codes"
        "google.golang.org/grpc/status"
)

type repoService struct {
        svc.UnimplementedRepoServer
}

// TODO Insert the definition of CreateRepo() from earlier

func registerServices(s *grpc.Server) {
        svc.RegisterRepoServer(s, &repoService{})
}
```

```
func startServer(s *grpc.Server, l net.Listener) error {
     return s.Serve(l)
}

func main() {
        listenAddr := os.Getenv("LISTEN_ADDR")
        if len(listenAddr) == 0 {
               listenAddr = ":50051"
        }

        lis, err := net.Listen("tcp", listenAddr)
        if err != nil {
              log.Fatal(err)
        }
        s := grpc.NewServer()
        registerServices(s)
        log.Fatal(startServer(s, lis))
}
```

Create a directory, `server`, inside `chap9/bindata-client-streaming`, and initialize a module inside it as follows:

```
$ mkdir -p chap9/bindata-client-streaming/server
$ cd chap9/bindata-client-streaming/server
$ go mod init github.com/username/bindata-client-streaming/server
```

Save Listing 9.11 as `server.go` inside it. Fetch the `google.golang.org/grpc` package as follows:

```
$ go get google.golang.org/grpc@v1.37.0
```

Set up `replace` directives in the `go.mod` file so that it adds the reference to the `github.com/username/bindata-client-streaming/service` package to the `../service` directory. The final `go.mod` file is shown in Listing 9.12.

Listing 9.12: `go.mod` file for the `Repo` service server implementation

```
// chap9/bindata-client-streaming/server/go.mod
module github.com/username/bindata-client-streaming/server

go 1.16

require google.golang.org/grpc v1.37.0

require github.com/username/bindata-client-streaming/service v0.0.0

replace github.com/username/bindata-client-streaming/
service v0.0.0 => ../service
```

Make sure that you can build the server before moving on.

Calling the `CreateRepo()` method to create a repository from a test function or a client application involves two key steps:

1. The first message will send a `RepoCreateContext` object containing only the `context` field set. This message will be used to communicate the repository name and owner to the server.

2. The second and subsequent messages, if any, will send a `RepoCreateContext` object containing only the `data` field set. These messages will be used to transmit the data to be created in the repository.

The following code snippet will implement the first step (with error handling omitted):

```
stream, err := repoClient.CreateRepo(context.Background())
c := svc.RepoCreateRequest_Context{
        Context: &svc.RepoContext{
                CreatorId: "user-123",
                Name:      "test-repo",
        },
}
r := svc.RepoCreateRequest{
        Body: &c,
}
err = stream.Send(&r)
```

We create a `RepoCreateRequest_Context` object, c, containing the `Context` field, which is an object of type `RepoContext` containing the `CreatorId` and `Name` of the repository that we want to create. Then, we create an object of type `RepoCreateRequest` and specify the value of `Body` as a pointer to the object, c. Finally, we call the `Send()` method of the stream object sending the `RepoCreateRequest` object as the first message.

To implement the second step, we will first set up a source from which to read the data:

```
data := "Arbitrary Data Bytes"
repoData := strings.NewReader(data)
```

The `strings.NewReader()` function returns an object satisfying the `io.Reader` interface, and thus we can use any compatible function to read the bytes and send it to the server:

```
for {
        b, err := repoData.ReadByte()
        if err == io.EOF {
                break
        }
}
```

```
bData := svc.RepoCreateRequest_Data{
        Data: []byte{b},
    }
r := svc.RepoCreateRequest{
        Body: &bData,
    }
err = stream.Send(&r)
if err != nil {
        t.Fatal(err)
    }
}
```

We read one byte at a time from repoData. The byte read is stored in b. Then we create an object of type RepoCreateRequest_Data with the Data field containing a byte slice containing the read byte in b. Next, we create a RepoCreateRequest object with the Body field now pointing to the RepoCreateRequest_Data object. Finally, we call the Send() method to send this message. We continue this until we have read all the bytes from repoData. After that, we will read the response from the server and verify that the response contains the expected data:

```
resp, err := stream.CloseAndRecv()
        if err != nil {
                t.Fatal(err)
        }
        expectedSize := int32(len(data))
        if resp.Size != expectedSize {
                t.Errorf(
                        "Expected Repo Created to be: %d bytes
Got back: %d",
                        expectedSize,
                        resp.Size,
                )
        }
        expectedRepoUrl := "https://git.example.com/user-123/test-repo"
        if resp.Repo.Url != expectedRepoUrl {
                t.Errorf(
                        "Expected Repo URL to be: %s, Got: %s",
                        expectedRepoUrl,
                        resp.Repo.Url,
                )
        }
```

You can find the complete test function in the file server_test.go in this book's source repository in the directory chap9/bindata-client-streaming/server/.

Next, you will learn to implement common functionalities in gRPC client and server applications using *interceptors*. Before we move on, though, you have an exercise to attempt (Exercise 9.2).

EXERCISE 9.2: CREATE REPOSITORY CONTENTS FROM A FILE

Create a client application for the `Repo` service that uses client-side streaming to create a repository where it allows the user to specify the contents of the repository as a `.tar.gz` file. The client application will expect the user to specify the path to the file as a flag.

Implementing Middleware Using Interceptors

Middleware plays the same role in gRPC clients and servers that it does for HTTP clients and servers. It allows you to implement common functionality in your applications, such as emitting logs, publishing metrics, attaching metadata such as a request identifier, and adding authentication information.

Implementing middleware logic in gRPC applications is achieved via writing components known as *interceptors*. Depending on the communication pattern you are using — unary RPC or one of the streaming patterns — your interceptor implementation details will vary. First, let's learn how to implement client-side interceptors.

We will implement interceptors for the `Users` service created in Chapter 8. Make a directory `chap9/interceptors`, and copy the Chapter 8 `service`, `client`, and `server` directories inside it:

```
$ mkdir -p chap9/interceptors/
$ cd chap9/interceptors
$ cp -r ../../chap8/user-service/{service,client,server} .
```

Now, update the `go.mod` file inside the `service` directory to read as shown in Listing 9.13.

Listing 9.13: `go.mod` file for the `Users` service

```
// chap9/interceptors/service/go.mod
module github.com/username/interceptors/service

go 1.16
```

Generate the Go code corresponding to protobuf specification:

```
$ cd service
$ protoc --go_out=. --go_opt=paths=source_relative \
    --go-grpc_out=. --go-grpc_opt=paths=source_relative \
  users.proto
```

Now, update the `go.mod` file inside the `server` directory to read as shown in Listing 9.14.

Listing 9.14: `go.mod` file for the `Users` server

```
// chap9/interceptors/server/go.mod
module github.com/username/interceptors/server

go 1.16
require google.golang.org/grpc v1.37.0
require github.com/username/interceptors/service v0.0.0
replace github.com/username/interceptors/service => ../service
```

Make sure that the import path for the service package has been updated in `server.go` as follows:

```
users "github.com/username/interceptors/service"
```

Do the same for the import in the `server_test.go` file. Make sure that your tests pass before moving on.

Now, update the `go.mod` file inside the `client` directory to read as shown in Listing 9.15.

Listing 9.15: `go.mod` file for the `Users` client

```
// chap9/interceptors/client/go.mod
module github.com/username/interceptors/client

go 1.16

require (
        github.com/usernameinterceptors/service v0.0.0
        google.golang.org/grpc v1.37.0
)

replace github.com/interceptors/service => ../service
```

Make sure that the import path for the service package has been updated in `client.go` as follows:

```
users "github.com/username/interceptors/service"
```

Do the same for the import in the `client_test.go` file. Make sure that your tests pass before moving on.

Client-Side Interceptors

There are two kinds of *client-side interceptors:*

Unary Client Interceptor: Interceptors of this category will intercept only unary RPC method calls.

Stream Client Interceptor: Interceptors of this category will intercept only streaming RPC method calls.

A client-side unary interceptor is a function of type `grpc.UnaryClient Interceptor` declared as follows:

```
type UnaryClientInterceptor func(
        ctx context.Context, method string,
        req, reply interface{}, cc *ClientConn,
        invoker UnaryInvoker,
        opts ...CallOption,
) error
```

The various parameters to the function are as follows:

ctx is the context associated with the RPC method call.

method is the RPC method name.

req and **reply** are the request and response messages, respectively.

cc is the underlying `grpc.ClientConn` object.

invoker is either the originally intercepted RPC method call or another interceptor.

Interceptors can be chained as you will learn shortly.

opts are any values of type `grpc.CallOption` that the original RPC method was invoked with.

As you will see, most of these parameters are passed as is to the original RPC method call. Let's write our first interceptor, which will add a unique identifier for a request to any outgoing unary RPC call to the Users service:

```
func metadataUnaryInterceptor(
        ctx context.Context,
        method string,
        req, reply interface{},
        cc *grpc.ClientConn,
        invoker grpc.UnaryInvoker,
        opts ...grpc.CallOption,
) error {
        ctxWithMetadata := metadata.AppendToOutgoingContext(
                ctx,
                "Request-Id",
                "request-123",
        )
        return invoker(
                ctxWithMetadata,
                method,
                req,
                reply,
                cc,
                opts...,
        )
}
```

We add the request identifier to the outgoing method call's context. In gRPC, this is done using the `google.golang.org/grpc/metadata` package that provides functions to store and retrieve metadata for RPC method calls. The `AppendToOutgoingContext()` function is called with the original context, `ctx`, and a key-value pair to add as metadata, and it returns a new context that will then be used to invoke the RPC method instead of the original context. Thus, here we add the key `Request-Id` for the request identifier, and a dummy value, `request-123`, as metadata. The newly created context, `ctxWithMetadata`, is then used to invoke the original RPC method. The error value obtained from the call to `invoker()` is returned.

To register the `metadataUnaryInterceptor` as a client-side interceptor, we specify a new `grpc.DialOption` obtained via calling the `grpc.WithUnaryInterceptor()` function, passing it the `metadataUnaryInterceptor` function as a parameter. The final `setupGrpcConn()` function will read as follows:

```
func setupGrpcConn(addr string) (*grpc.ClientConn, error) {
        return grpc.DialContext(
                context.Background(),
                addr,
                grpc.WithInsecure(),
                grpc.WithBlock(),
                grpc.WithUnaryInterceptor(metadataUnaryInterceptor),
        )
}
```

Update the `client.go` file to add the `metadataUnaryInterceptor()` function definition and update the `setupGrpcConn()` function to add the above `DialOption`. Make sure that you can build the client before you move on.

Let's now move on to writing an interceptor to attach a request identifier for streaming RPC method calls. Update the protobuf specification in `chap9/interceptors/service/users.proto` to add `GetHelp()` to the `Users` service, as shown in Listing 9.16.

Listing 9.16: Updated protobuf specification for the `Users` service

```
//chap9/interceptors/service/users.proto
syntax = "proto3";

option go_package = "github.com/username/interceptors/service/users";

service Users {
  rpc GetUser (UserGetRequest) returns (UserGetReply) {}
  rpc GetHelp (stream UserHelpRequest) returns (stream UserHelpReply) {}
}

message UserGetRequest {
  string email = 1;
```

```
      string id = 2;
}

message User {
   string id = 1;
   string first_name = 2;
   string last_name = 3;
   int32 age = 4;
}

message UserGetReply {
   User user = 1;
}

message UserHelpRequest {
   User user = 1;
   string request = 2;
}

message UserHelpReply {
   string response = 1;
}
```

Regenerate the Go code corresponding to protobuf specification as follows:

```
$ cd chap9/intereceptors/service
$ protoc --go_out=. --go_opt=paths=source_relative \
    --go-grpc_out=. --go-grpc_opt=paths=source_relative \
    users.proto
```

Next, update the client by inserting the definition of the `setupChat()` method in `chap9/intereceptors/client/main.go` from Listing 9.8.

Now, we will write the interceptor to intercept streaming RPC method calls. A client-side stream interceptor is a function of type `grpc.StreamClientInterceptor`, which is declared as follows:

```
type StreamClientInterceptor func(
        ctx context.Context,
        desc *StreamDesc,
        cc *ClientConn,
        method string,
        streamer Streamer,
        opts ...CallOption,
) (ClientStream, error)
```

The various parameters to the function are as follows:

ctx is the context associated with the RPC method call.

desc is an object of type `*grpc.StreamDesc` that contains various properties

related to the stream itself, such as the RPC method name, the service
handler for the method, and whether the stream supports sending and
receiving operations.

cc is the underlying `grpc.ClientConn` object.

method is the RPC method name.

streamer is either the originally intercepted RPC streaming method call
or another streaming interceptor when you have a chain of streaming
interceptors.

opts are any values of type `grpc.CallOption` that the original RPC method
was invoked with.

The metadata interceptor for the streaming RPC method calls will then be
written as follows:

```
func metadataStreamInterceptor(
        ctx context.Context,
        desc *grpc.StreamDesc,
        cc *grpc.ClientConn,
        method string,
        streamer grpc.Streamer,
        opts ...grpc.CallOption,
) (grpc.ClientStream, error) {
        ctxWithMetadata := metadata.AppendToOutgoingContext(
                ctx,
                "Request-Id",
                "request-123",
        )
        clientStream, err := streamer(
                ctxWithMetadata,
                desc,
                cc,
                method,
                opts...,
        )
        return clientStream, err
}
```

Like the unary interceptor, we add the request identifier to the incoming
request context by using the `AppendToOutgoingContext()` function and the created context to set up the streaming communication. To register the interceptor,
we will create a new `DialOption` with the `grpc.WithStreamInterceptor(met
adataStreamInterceptor)` and then specify that to the `grpc.DialContext()`
function. The updated `setupGrpcConn()` function will appear as follows:

```
func setupGrpcConn(addr string) (*grpc.ClientConn, error) {
        return grpc.DialContext(
```

```
            context.Background(),
            addr,
            grpc.WithInsecure(),
            grpc.WithBlock(),
            grpc.WithUnaryInterceptor(metadataUnaryInterceptor),
            grpc.WithStreamInterceptor(metadataStreamInterceptor),
    )
}
```

Listing 9.17 shows the complete client application.

Listing 9.17: Client application for the `Users` service with interceptors

```go
// chap9/interceptors/client/main.go
package main

import (
        "bufio"
        "context"
        "fmt"
        "io"
        "log"
        "os"

        svc "github.com/username/interceptors/service"
        "google.golang.org/grpc"
        "google.golang.org/grpc/metadata"
)

// TODO Insert definition of metadataUnaryInterceptor() from earlier
// TODO Insert definition of metadataStreamInterceptor() from earlier
// TODO Insert definition of setupGrpcConn() function from earlier

func getUserServiceClient(conn *grpc.ClientConn) svc.UsersClient {
        return svc.NewUsersClient(conn)
}

// TODO Insert definition of GetUser() from Chapter 8, Listing 8.2
// TODO Insert definition of setupChat() from Listing 9.8

func main() {
        if len(os.Args) != 3 {
                log.Fatal(
                        "Specify a gRPC server and method to call",
                )
        }
        serverAddr := os.Args[1]
        methodName := os.Args[2]

        conn, err := setupGrpcConn(serverAddr)
        if err != nil {
```

```
                log.Fatal(err)
        }
        defer conn.Close()

        c := getUserServiceClient(conn)

        switch methodName {
        case "GetUser":
                result, err := getUser(
                        c,
                        &svc.UserGetRequest{Email: "jane@doe.com"},
                )
                if err != nil {
                        log.Fatal(err)
                }
                fmt.Fprintf(
                        os.Stdout, "User: %s %s\n",
                        result.User.FirstName,
                        result.User.LastName,
                )
        case "GetHelp":
                err = setupChat(os.Stdin, os.Stdout, c)
                if err != nil {
                        log.Fatal(err)
                }
        default:
                log.Fatal("Unrecognized method name")
        }
}
```

We have written the `main()` function such that the client application for the `Users` service can be asked to call either the `GetUser()` or `GetHelp()` method. The first command-line argument to be specified is the gRPC server address and the second argument is the RPC method to call. Make sure that you can build the client before moving on to implementing the server-side interceptors.

Server-Side Interceptors

Similar to client-side interceptors, there are two kinds of *server-side interceptors*:

Unary Server Interceptor: Interceptors of this category will intercept only incoming unary RPC method calls.

Stream Server Interceptor: Interceptors of this category will intercept only incoming streaming RPC method calls.

Let's first implement a server interceptor to log the request details for Unary RPC method calls including the request identifier that we set in the client in the previous section, the method name, and others. A server-side unary interceptor is a function of type `grpc.UnaryServerInterceptor` declared as follows:

```
type UnaryServerInterceptor func(
        ctx context.Context,
        req interface{},
        info *UnaryServerInfo,
        handler UnaryHandler,
) (resp interface{}, err error)
```

The various parameters for the function are as follows:

ctx is the context associated with the RPC method call.

req is the incoming request.

info is an object of type `*UnaryServerInfo`, which contains data related to the implementation of the service as well as the RPC method that it has intercepted.

handler is the function implementing the RPC method: `GetHelp()` or `GetUser()`, for example.

The logging server interceptor for the unary RPC method calls will hence be defined as follows:

```
func loggingUnaryInterceptor(
        ctx context.Context,
        req interface{},
        info *grpc.UnaryServerInfo,
        handler grpc.UnaryHandler,
) (interface{}, error) {
        start := time.Now()
        resp, err := handler(ctx, req)
        logMessage(ctx, info.FullMethod, time.Since(start), err)
        return resp, err
}
```

We store the current time in start and call the `handler()` function, passing it the context and the request itself. Once the RPC method finishes execution, we call the `logMessage()` function (the implementation of which will be discussed shortly) to log the various call data along with the latency for the call. The `FullMethod` attribute of the `*UnaryServerInfo` object, `info`, contains the name of the RPC method that's called along with the service name. Finally, we return the response and the error value from this interceptor.

The *stream server interceptor* is defined as a function of type `grpc.StreamServerInterceptor`, which is declared as follows:

```
type StreamServerInterceptor func(srv interface{}, ss ServerStream, info
*StreamServerInfo, handler StreamHandler) error
```

The various parameters for the function are as follows:

srv is the implementation of the gRPC server that is passed when the interceptor is invoked. It will be passed through as is to the next interceptor or the actual method call.

ss is an object of type grpc.ServerStream, which contains fields describing the server-side behavior of the streaming connection.

info is an object of type *grpc.StreamServerInfo, which contains the name of the RPC method and whether the stream is a client-side or a server-side stream.

handler is the function implementing the streaming RPC method, GetHelp() in this case.

The logging interceptor for streaming RPC calls will hence be implemented as follows:

```
func loggingStreamInterceptor(
        srv interface{},
        stream grpc.ServerStream,
        info *grpc.StreamServerInfo,
        handler grpc.StreamHandler,
) error {

        start := time.Now()
        err := handler(srv, stream)
        ctx := stream.Context()
        logMessage(ctx, info.FullMethod, time.Since(start), err)
        return err

}
```

We store the current time and then call the handler function to start the streaming communication. Next, we retrieve the context associated with the call by calling the Context() method. Then we call the logMessage() function to log the RPC method call details. Finally, we return the error value obtained from the handler function call.

Now let's look at the definition of the logMessage() function:

```
func logMessage(
        ctx context.Context,
        method string,
        latency time.Duration,
        err error,
) {

        var requestId string
        md, ok := metadata.FromIncomingContext(ctx)
        if !ok {
                log.Print("No metadata")
```

```
        } else {
            if len(md.Get("Request-Id")) != 0 {
                requestId = md.Get("Request-Id")[0]
            }
        }
        log.Printf("Method:%s, Duration:%s, Error:%v, Request-Id:%s",
            method,
            latency,
            err,
            requestId,
        )
    }
```

The key statements in the function are highlighted above. We first attempt to retrieve the metadata from the call context using the `FromIncomingContext()` function from the metadata package. This function returns two values: one of type `metadata.MD` (which is a map defined as type `MD map[string][]string`) and a Boolean value, `ok`. If metadata was found in the context, `ok` is set to `true`, and `false` otherwise. Thus, in the function, we check if the value was true and then attempt to get the value (a slice of strings) corresponding to the `Request-Id` key. If one is found, we set the value of `requestId` to the first element of the slice, and then it is logged using a call to the `log.Printf()` function. Listing 9.18 shows the complete client application.

Listing 9.18: Server application for the `Users` service with interceptors

```go
// chap9/interceptors/server/server.go

package main

import (
    "context"
    "errors"
    "fmt"
    "io"
    "log"
    "net"
    "os"
    "strings"
    "time"

    svc "github.com/username/interceptors/service"
    "google.golang.org/grpc"
    "google.golang.org/grpc/metadata"
)

type userService struct {
    svc.UnimplementedUsersServer
}
```

```
// TODO Insert definition of logMessage() from earlier
// TODO Insert definition of loggingUnaryInterceptor() from earlier
// TODO Insert definition of loggingStreamInterceptor() from earlier
// TODO Insert definition of GetUser() from Chapter 8, Listing 8.2
// TODO Insert definition of GetHelp() from Listing 9.6

func registerServices(s *grpc.Server) {
        svc.RegisterUsersServer(s, &userService{})
}

func startServer(s *grpc.Server, l net.Listener) error {
        return s.Serve(l)
}

func main() {
        listenAddr := os.Getenv("LISTEN_ADDR")
        if len(listenAddr) == 0 {
                listenAddr = ":50051"
        }

        lis, err := net.Listen("tcp", listenAddr)
        if err != nil {
                log.Fatal(err)
        }
        s := grpc.NewServer(
                grpc.UnaryInterceptor(loggingUnaryInterceptor),
                grpc.StreamInterceptor(loggingStreamInterceptor),
        )
        registerServices(s)
        log.Fatal(startServer(s, lis))
}
```

To register the interceptors with the gRPC server, we call the grpc.NewServer()
function with two values, both of type grpc.ServerOption (similar to grpc
.DialOption for client applications). These two values are obtained by calling
the grpc.UnaryInterceptor() and grpc.StreamInterceptor() functions with
the values loggingUnaryInterceptor and logginStreamInterceptor, respectively. Build the server and run it:

```
$ cd chap9/interceptors/server
$ go build
$ ./server
```

Now, from a new terminal session, run the client application to invoke the
GetUser method first:

```
$ cd chap9/interceptors/client
$ go build
$ ./client localhost:50051 GetUser
User: jane doe.com
```

On the terminal session where the server was running, you will see logs as follows:

```
2021/06/26 22:14:04 Received request for user with Email: jane@doe.com Id:
2021/06/26 22:14:04 Method:/Users/GetUser, Duration:214.333µs, Error:<nil>,
Request-Id:request-123
```

The RPC method name is logged along with the service name, the duration it took for the method call to complete, and the value of `Request-Id` that was specified in the client.

Next, let's invoke the `GetHelp` method from the client:

```
Request: Hello there
Response: Hello there
Request: how are you
Response: how are you
Request: quit
```

On the server side, you will see the following logs:

```
2021/06/26 22:24:40 Client connected
Request received: Hello there
Request received: how are you
2021/06/26 22:24:46 Client disconnected
2021/06/26 22:24:46 Method:/Users/GetHelp, Duration:6.186660625s,
Error:<nil>, Request-Id:request-123
```

As you will see, the duration reported is for the entire time the RPC streaming connection was active, in other words, as long as you were continuing the communication from the client.

The client and server interceptors that we have written so far allow us to intercept the *beginning* and *end* of the RPC method calls. For Unary RPC method calls, that is exactly what we want. However, for streaming method calls, a client-side interceptor doesn't wait for the entire streaming communication to complete but returns immediately after *setting up* the streaming communication channel (see Figure 9.3). So, if you wanted to log the duration of the entire streaming communication, you will need to implement the client interceptor differently. Similarly, for server-side interceptors, what if you wanted to implement an interceptor to run custom code during each *message* exchange? The solution to both use cases is to create your own custom stream to wrap the original client or server stream.

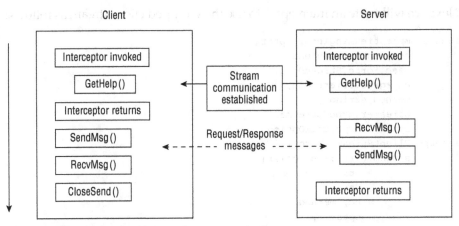

Figure 9.3: Interceptors and streaming communication

Wrapping Streams

First, let's see an example that wraps a client stream:

```
type wrappedClientStream struct {
        grpc.ClientStream
}
```

Then, we add our custom implementations for the three methods: SendMsg(), RecvMsg(), and CloseSend(). First, let's look at the SendMsg() method implementation:

```
func (s wrappedClientStream) SendMsg(m interface{}) error {
        log.Printf("Send msg called: %T", m)
        return s.Stream.SendMsg(m)
}
```

Every time that the client sends a message to the server, the above method will be called. A message will be logged and then the underlying stream's SendMsg() is called. Similarly, the custom RecvMsg() is implemented as follows:

```
func (s wrappedClientStream) RecvMsg(m interface{}) error {
        log.Printf("Recv msg called: %T", m)
        return s.Stream.RecvMsg(m)
}
```

Finally, we will implement the custom CloseSend() method as follows:

```
func (s wrappedClientStream) CloseSend() error {
        log.Println("CloseSend() called")
        return s.ClientStream.CloseSend()
}
```

Next, we will write an interceptor to use the wrapped client stream as follows:

```
func exampleStreamingInterceptor(
        ctx context.Context,
        desc *grpc.StreamDesc,
        cc *grpc.ClientConn,
        method string,
        streamer grpc.Streamer,
        opts ...grpc.CallOption,
) (grpc.ClientStream, error) {
        stream, err := streamer(
                ctx,
                desc,
                cc, method,
                opts...,
        )
        clientStream := wrappedClientStream{
                ClientStream: stream,
        }
        return clientStream, err
}
```

To create a wrapped server stream, we will create a struct wrapping `grpc` `.ServerStream`:

```
type wrappedServerStream struct {
        grpc.ServerStream
}
```

Then, we will implement the methods within which we want to run our custom code. The key operations are message sending and receiving; thus, we will override the `SendMsg()` and `RecvMsg()` methods:

```
func (s wrappedServerStream) SendMsg(m interface{}) error {
        log.Printf("Send msg called: %T", m)
        return s.ServerStream.SendMsg(m)
}
func (s wrappedServerStream) RecvMsg(m interface{}) error {
        log.Printf("Waiting to receive a message: %T", m)
        return s.ServerStream.RecvMsg(m)
}
```

Once we have created a wrapped server stream and implemented the custom methods, we will then update the logging interceptor that we wrote earlier as follows:

```
func loggingStreamInterceptor(
        srv interface{},
        stream grpc.ServerStream,
```

```
        info *grpc.StreamServerInfo,
        handler grpc.StreamHandler,
) error {
        serverStream := wrappedServerStream{
                ServerStream: stream,
        }
        err := handler(srv, serverStream)
        // Everything else remains the same
        // ...
        return err
}
```

Wrapping client and server streams allows your interceptors to run custom code during every message exchange over a streaming connection. This enables writing interceptors that require knowledge of the messages being exchanged, such as storing or retrieving data from a caching store or implementing a rate limiting mechanism. Next, we are going to learn how to create a chain of interceptors.

Chaining Interceptors

Since interceptors are used to implement common functionality in your applications, chaining interceptors together allows you to integrate more than one interceptor for your application. Let's try an example for a client application first. We will set up the chain when creating the DialContext. Here's an updated setupGrpcConn() function:

```
func setupGrpcConn(addr string) (*grpc.ClientConn, error) {
        return grpc.DialContext(
                context.Background(),
                addr,
                grpc.WithInsecure(),
                grpc.WithBlock(),
                grpc.WithChainUnaryInterceptor(
                        loggingUnaryInterceptor,
                        metadataUnaryInterceptor,
                ),
                grpc.WithChainStreamInterceptor(
                        loggingStreamingInterceptor,
                        metadataStreamingInterceptor,
                ),
        )
}
```

The WithChainUnaryInterceptor() function defined in the google .golang.org/grpc package is used to register multiple interceptors. Here, loggingUnaryIntereceptor and metadataUnaryInterceptor are two such interceptors. The `WithChainStreamInterceptor()` function in the same package is used to register multiple stream interceptors: `loggingStreamingInterceptor` and `metadataStreamingInterceptor` in this case. In both cases, the innermost interceptor is executed first.

You can find a complete client application in `chap9/interceptor-chain/client` in this book's source repository, which shows how you can set up a chain of client interceptors. The implementation of `logStreamingInterceptor` also demonstrates wrapping the client stream.

To set up a chain of interceptors on the server side, you will register the interceptors when creating the `grpc.Server` object:

```
s := grpc.NewServer(
    grpc.ChainUnaryInterceptor(
        metricUnaryInterceptor,
        loggingUnaryInterceptor,
    ),
    grpc.ChainStreamInterceptor(
        metricStreamInterceptor,
        loggingStreamInterceptor,
    ),
)
```

The `ChainUnaryInterceptor()` and `ChainStreamInterceptor()` functions are used to register multiple interceptors with the innermost interceptor executed first. You can find a complete server application in `chap9/interceptor-chain/server` of this book's source repository, which shows how you can set up a chain of server interceptors. The implementation of `logStreamingInterceptor` also demonstrates wrapping the server stream.

In these sections, you have learned about writing interceptors in gRPC applications. You learned how to write interceptors for both unary and streaming RPC communication between the client and server applications. Next, you have a final exercise to attempt to apply your understanding (Exercise 9.3).

> **EXERCISE 9.3: LOG THE NUMBER OF MESSAGES EXCHANGED IN A STREAM**   Implement a client-side interceptor and a server-side interceptor to log the number of messages exchanged over a `GetHelp()` method call in the `Repository` service. Use the code in `chap9/intereceptor-chain` in this book's source repository as a starting point.

Summary

In this chapter, you learned how to build gRPC applications that go beyond unary RPC methods. You learned to implement various streaming communication patterns, starting off with client-side streaming, moving on to server-side streaming, and finishing off with bidirectional streaming. These techniques allow you to transmit data efficiently between the client and server applications.

You then learned how to exchange arbitrary data between client and server applications going beyond numbers and strings. You also learned how to leverage streaming to transmit data more efficiently.

Next, you learned to implement middleware for your gRPC applications using interceptors. You learned how to implement both client-side and server-side interceptors for both unary and streaming communication patterns. You also learned how to attach metadata to your requests.

In the next chapter, you will learn how to implement various techniques in your gRPC applications to make them scalable and secure.

Production-Ready gRPC Applications

In this chapter, you will start by learning how to implement TLS-enabled secure gRPC applications. Then you will study techniques to implement health checks, handle runtime errors, and cancel processing in your server applications. After that, you will learn about techniques to improve the robustness of your client applications, such as configuring time-outs for various operations and handling transient failures. In the final section, you will learn how connections between clients and servers are internally managed by the gRPC library. Let's dive in!

Securing Communication with TLS

The client and server applications that we have written so far communicate over an *insecure* channel—this is the setupGrpcCommunication() function that we have been using in our clients to set up communication with a server:

```
func setupGrpcConnection(addr string) (*grpc.ClientConn, error) {
        return grpc.DialContext(
                context.Background(),
                addr,
                grpc.WithInsecure(),
                grpc.WithBlock(),
        )
}
```

The grpc.WithInsecure() DialOption explicitly states that the client must communicate with the server over an insecure channel. Of course, this only works because our server applications were not configured to communicate over one. You will recall that we used Transport Layer Security (TLS) to secure the communication between HTTP client and server applications in Chapter 7, "Production-Ready HTTP Servers." We can use the same technique to set up a secure a communication channel between gRPC applications.

First, let's configure a gRPC server only to allow communication over TLS (ignoring error handling):

```
tlsCertFile := os.Getenv("TLS_CERT_FILE_PATH")
tlsKeyFile := os.Getenv("TLS_KEY_FILE_PATH")
creds, err := credentials.NewServerTLSFromFile(
        tlsCertFile,
        tlsKeyFile,
)
credsOption := grpc.Creds(creds)
s := grpc.NewServer(credsOption)
```

First, we call the credentials.NewServerTLSFromFile() function from the google.golang.org/grpc/credentials package, passing its path to a TLS certificate and the corresponding private key. This function returns an object, creds, of type credentials.TransportCredentials, and an error value. We then call the grpc.Creds() function with creds as a parameter. This function returns a value, credsOption, of type grpc.ServerOption. Finally, we call the grpc.NewServer() function with this value. That's it.

Unlike HTTP over TLS servers, where it is conventional to use a different port number for TLS-enabled servers, we will use the same port number, 50051, for TLS-enabled gRPC servers as well.

Next, you will need to configure the client application to communicate with the server over TLS:

```
func setupGrpcConn(
        addr string,
        tlsCertFile string,
) (*grpc.ClientConn, error) {
        creds, err := credentials.NewClientTLSFromFile(tlsCertFile, "")
        if err != nil {
                return nil, err
        }
        credsOption := grpc.WithTransportCredentials(creds)
        return grpc.DialContext(
                context.Background(),
                addr,
                credsOption,
                grpc.WithBlock(),
        )
}
```

We have updated the `setupGrpcConn()` to return a `*grpc.ClientConn` object, which is configured to communicate with a server over TLS. It now takes an additional argument, `tlsCertFile`, a string containing the path to the TLS certificate that the client should trust. We call the `NewClientTLSFromFile()` function, defined by the `google.golang.org/grpc/credentials` package, with the path to a TLS certificate. The second argument, if non-empty, will override the hostname found in the certificate, and that hostname will be trusted instead. We will generate our TLS certificates for the `localhost` hostname, which is the hostname that we want our client to trust. Hence, we specify an empty string. The function returns a value, `creds`, of type `credentials.TransportCredentials`, and an error value. We then create a `ClientOption` value, `credsOption`, corresponding to the credentials, by calling the `grpc.WithTransportCredentials()` function, passing `creds` as a parameter. Finally, we call the `DialContext()`, passing `credsOption` as a `ClientOption`. The path to the certificate in `tlsCertFile` must point to the same certificate as the one used by the server.

The final step is to generate the self-signed TLS certificates. As in Chapter 7, we will use the `openssl` command to do so with a slightly different set of arguments in order to comply with the underlying Go library's client-side TLS verification requirements:

```
$ openssl req -x509 -newkey rsa:4096 -keyout server.key -out server.crt \
   -days 365 \
   -subj "/C=AU/ST=NSW/L=Sydney/O=Echorand/OU=Org/CN=localhost" \
   -extensions san \
   -config <(echo '[req]'; echo 'distinguished_name=req';
           echo '[san]'; echo 'subjectAltName=DNS:localhost') \
   -nodes
```

This will create two files, `server.key` and `server.crt`, corresponding to the TLS key and the certificate, respectively. You can now point these files to the server and the certificate to the client.

You can find the code for the server and client applications in the `chap10/user-service-tls` directory of the book's code repository. The server implements the `Users` service that we first implemented in Chapter 8, "Building RPC Applications with gRPC," with the communication with the client now occurring over a TLS-encrypted channel. You will also find the server and client tests updated to communicate over TLS instead.

Let's see a quick demonstration of how we will run the applications. First, the server:

```
$ cd chap10/user-service-tls/server
$ go build
$ TLS_KEY_FILE_PATH=../tls/server.key \
  TLS_CERT_FILE_PATH=../tls/server.crt \
  ./server
```

In a separate terminal, we will run the client:

```
$ cd chap10/user-service-tls/client
$ go build
$ TLS_CERT_FILE_PATH=../tls/server.crt \
  ./client localhost:50051
User: jane doe.com
```

As we discussed in Chapter 7, generating and distributing certificates manually isn't scalable. If your services are internal, implement an internal trusted CA using tools such as `cfssl` (`https://github.com/cloudflare/cfssl`) and then have a mechanism for generating certificates and trusting the CA.

For public-facing services, you will likely find autocert (`https://pkg.go.dev/golang.org/x/crypto/acme/autocert`) useful for obtaining certificates from Let's Encrypt, a free and open certificate authority.

Next, you are going to study various techniques to make your server applications robust.

Robustness in Servers

In the following sections, you will first learn how to implement health checks in your server application. Then you will learn how to make your applications immune to unhandled runtime errors. After that, you will learn how to use interceptors to abort request processing to prevent resource exhaustion.

Implementing Health Checks

When a server starts up, it may need a few seconds for the network listener to be created, register the gRPC services, and establish connections to data stores or other services. Hence, it is likely not *immediately* ready to process client requests. On top of that, the server may become so overloaded with requests during its operation that it shouldn't really accept any new ones. In both scenarios, it is recommended to add an RPC method in your service that can be used to probe whether the server is *healthy* or not. Usually, this probe would be performed by another application, such as a load balancer or a proxy service, which forwards the requests to your server based on whether the health probe is successful or not.

The gRPC health checking protocol defines the specification for a dedicated `Health` gRPC service. It defines a protobuf specification that such a service must follow:

```
syntax = "proto3";
package grpc.health.v1;
```

```
message HealthCheckRequest {
  string service = 1;
}

message HealthCheckResponse {
  enum ServingStatus {
    UNKNOWN = 0;
    SERVING = 1;
    NOT_SERVING = 2;
    SERVICE_UNKNOWN = 3;  // Used only by the Watch method.
  }
  ServingStatus status = 1;
}

service Health {
  rpc Check(HealthCheckRequest) returns (HealthCheckResponse);
  rpc Watch(HealthCheckRequest) returns (stream HealthCheckResponse);
}
```

The `HealthCheckRequest` message is used by another application, such as a load balancer, to request the health of the server. It contains one `string` field, `service`, indicating the service name for which the client is querying its health. As you will see, you can configure the health of individual services.

The `HealthCheckResponse` message is used to send the result of a health check request. It contains a single field, `status`, of type `ServingStatus`, an enum. The value of `status` will be one of the following four values:

UNKNOWN

SERVING

NOT_SERVING

SERVICE_UNKNOWN

The `google.golang.org/grpc/health/grpc_health_v1` package contains the generated Go code for the `Health` service based on the above protobuf specification. The `google.golang.org/grpc/health/` package contains an implementation of the `Health` service. Thus, to register the `Health` service with a gRPC server, we will update the code where we register other services as follows:

```
import (
        healthsvc "google.golang.org/grpc/health"
        healthz "google.golang.org/grpc/health/grpc_health_v1"
)

func registerServices(s *grpc.Server, h *healthz.Server) {
        svc.RegisterUsersServer(s, &userService{})
        healthsvc.RegisterHealthServer(s, h)
}
```

The `registerServices()` function takes an additional argument—a value of type `health.Server`, which is defined in the `google.golang.org/grpc/health` package, pointing to the `Health` service implementation. To register the `Health` service, we call the `RegisterHealthServer()` function defined in the `grpc_health_v1` package.

We will call the `registerServices()` function as follows:

```
s := grpc.NewServer()
h := healthz.NewServer()
registerServices(s, h)
```

We call the `NewServer()` function defined in the `grpc_health_v1` package, which initializes the health service's internal data structures. This returns an object of type `*healthz.Server`—the implementation of the `Health` service. We then call the `registerServices()` function with the `*grpc.Server` and the `*healthz.Server` values. In addition to the `Users` service, the gRPC server is now configured to handle requests to the `Health` service.

Next, we will configure the health status for individual services. The `SetServingStatus()` method of the `healthz.Server` object is used to set the status of a service. It accepts two parameters—a string, `service`, containing the service name, and a value of type `ServiceStatus` (an `enum` defined as part of the `HealthCheckResponse` message). We will define a helper function to wrap this logic as follows:

```
func updateServiceHealth(
        h *healthz.Server,
        service string,
        status healthsvc.HealthCheckResponse_ServingStatus,
) {
        h.SetServingStatus(
                service,
                status,
        )
}
```

In the server, after calling the `registerServices()` function, we will set the health status of the `Users` service as follows:

```
s := grpc.NewServer()
h := healthz.NewServer()
registerServices(s, h)
updateServiceHealth(
        h,
        svc.Users_ServiceDesc.ServiceName,
        healthsvc.HealthCheckResponse_SERVING,
)
```

We obtain the service name for the Users service using the Users_ServiceDesc .ServiceName attribute and then set the health status of the service as HealthCheckResponse_SERVING by calling the SetServingStatus() method. You can find the code for a gRPC server, which registers the Users service, as described in Chapter 9, "Advanced gRPC Applications," and the Health service in the chap10/server-healthcheck/server directory of the book's code repository.

Now let's write a few tests to verify the behavior of the Health service. In all the tests, we will first need to create a client to communicate with the Health service. We will do so by defining the following function:

```
package main

import (
        // Other imports
        healthsvc "google.golang.org/grpc/health/grpc_health_v1"
)

func getHealthSvcClient(
        l *bufconn.Listener,
) (healthsvc.HealthClient, error) {

        bufconnDialer := func(
                ctx context.Context, addr string,
        ) (net.Conn, error) {
                return l.Dial()
        }

        client, err := grpc.DialContext(
                context.Background(),
                "", grpc.WithInsecure(),
                grpc.WithContextDialer(bufconnDialer),
        )
        if err != nil {
                return nil, err
        }
        return healthsvc.NewHealthClient(client), nil
}
```

The getHealthSvcClient() is called with an object, l, of type bufconn.Listener, and it returns a value of type healthsvc.HealthClient and an error. Inside the function, we create a *dialer*, bufconnDialer, which is then used to create a *grpc. ClientConn object, client. Then, we call the NewHealthClient() function defined in the grpc_health_v1 package to create the healthsvc.HealthClient object.

The first test function we will write will call the Check() method of the Health service with an empty HealthCheckRequest object:

```
func TestHealthService(t *testing.T) {

        l := startTestGrpcServer()
        healthClient, err := getHealthSvcClient(l)
        if err != nil {
                t.Fatal(err)
        }

        resp, err := healthClient.Check(
                context.Background(),
                &healthsvc.HealthCheckRequest{},
        )
        if err != nil {
                t.Fatal(err)
        }
        serviceHealthStatus := resp.Status.String()
        if serviceHealthStatus != "SERVING" {
                t.Fatalf(
                        "Expected health: SERVING, Got: %s",
                        serviceHealthStatus,
                )
        }
}
```

We create a test server using the startTestGrpcServer() function (as we have defined in Chapter 8 and Chapter 9). The returned *bufconn.Listener object is then passed as a parameter to the getHealthSvcClient() function defined earlier to obtain a client configured to communicate with the Health service.

Then, we call the Check() method with an empty HealthCheckRequest value. The returned value, of type HealthCheckResponse, is then examined to ensure that the value of the Status field matches the one we expect. When the service name is not specified, and the server is able to reply to the request successfully, the response status is set to 1 (or SERVING). Since the status field is an enum, we call the defined String() method to obtain the corresponding string value, irrespective of whether you have set the health status of the registered services and whether they are healthy or not.

To check the health status of the Users service, we would call the Check() method as follows:

```
resp, err := healthClient.Check(
        context.Background(),
                &healthsvc.HealthCheckRequest{
                        Service: "Users",
                },
    )
```

If we specified a service for which we haven't set the health status, we will get a non-`nil` error response and the value of response, `resp`, will be `nil`. The error response code will be set to `codes.NotFound`, as defined in the `google.golang.org/grpc/codes` package. The following test will verify that behavior:

```go
func TestHealthServiceUnknown(t *testing.T) {

        l := startTestGrpcServer()
        healthClient, err := getHealthSvcClient(l)
        if err != nil {
                t.Fatal(err)
        }

        _, err = healthClient.Check(
                context.Background(),
                &healthsvc.HealthCheckRequest{
                        Service: "Repo",
                },
        )
        if err == nil {
                t.Fatalf("Expected non-nil error, Got nil error")
        }
        expectedError := status.Errorf(
                codes.NotFound, "unknown service",
        )
        if !errors.Is(err, expectedError) {
                t.Fatalf(
                        "Expected error %v, Got; %v",
                        err,
                        expectedError,
                )
        }
}
```

The key statements are highlighted above. We construct an error value using the `google.golang.org/grpc/status` package's `Errorf()` function, and then we use the `errors.Is()` function from the `errors` package to check if the returned and expected errors match.

Next, let's look at `Watch()`, the second method defined in the `Health` service. This is a server-side streaming RPC method, and it is useful when the health checking client wants to be *notified* of any health state changes in the service. Let's see how it works.

We call the method with two arguments—a `context.Context` object and a `HealthCheckRequest` object specifying that we want to watch the health status of the `Users` service:

```go
client, err := healthClient.Watch(
        context.Background(),
```

```
        &healthsvc.HealthCheckRequest{
                Service: "Users",
        },
)
```

The `Watch()` method returns two values: `client`, of type `Health_WatchClient`, and an error value. `Health_WatchClient` is an interface defined in the `grpc_health_v1` package as follows:

```
type Health_WatchClient interface {
        Recv() (*HealthCheckResponse, error)
        grpc.ClientStream
}
```

The `Recv()` method will return an object of type `HealthCheckResponse` and error value. Then we write an unconditional for loop, where we will call the `Recv()` method to obtain a response from the server when one is available:

```
for {
        resp, err := client.Recv()
        if err == io.EOF {
                break
        }
        if err != nil {
                log.Printf("Error in Watch: %#v\n", err)

        }
        log.Printf("Health Status: %#v", resp)
        if resp.Status != healthsvc.HealthCheckResponse_SERVING {
                log.Printf("Unhealthy: %#v", resp)
        }
}
```

When we call `Recv()` for the first time, we will receive a response containing the health status of the `Users` service. After that, we will only get a response when there is a change in the health status of the service.

The following test function verifies the behavior:

```
func TestHealthServiceWatch(t *testing.T) {

        // TODO setup and obtain healthClient

        client, err := healthClient.Watch(
                context.Background(),
                &healthsvc.HealthCheckRequest{
                        Service: "Users",
                },
        )
```

```
        if err != nil {
                t.Fatal(err)
        }

        resp, err := client.Recv()
        if err != nil {
                t.Fatalf("Error in Watch: %#v\n", err)
        }
        if resp.Status != healthsvc.HealthCheckResponse_SERVING {
                t.Errorf(
                        "Expected SERVING, Got: %#v",
                        resp.Status.String(),
                )
        }

        updateServiceHealth(
                h,
                "Users",
                healthsvc.HealthCheckResponse_NOT_SERVING,
        )

        resp, err = client.Recv()
        if err != nil {
                t.Fatalf("Error in Watch: %#v\n", err)
        }
        if resp.Status != healthsvc.HealthCheckResponse_NOT_SERVING {
                t.Errorf(
                        "Expected NOT_SERVING, Got: %#v",
                        resp.Status.String(),
                )
        }
}
```

We call the `Watch()` method and then call the `Recv()` method—*once*. We verify that the health status is reported as SERVING. Then, we call the `updateServiceHealth()` to change the health status of the service to NOT_SERVING. We call the `Recv()` method again. This time, we verify that the response has the status field's value as NOT_SERVING. Thus, whereas a client will have to call the `Check()` method periodically to become aware of any health state changes in the server, the `Watch()` method instead *notifies* the client, which can then react appropriately.

You can find the source for all of the test functions in the file `health_test.go` in the `chap10/server-healthcheck/server` directory of the book's code repository.

In the next section, you will learn how to implement an interceptor to set up a recovery mechanism to stop the server from termination in the event of a runtime error. Before doing that, though, you will implement a client for the `Health` service in the first exercise of this chapter, Exercise 10.1.

EXERCISE 10.1: A HEALTH CHECK CLIENT Implement a command-
line client for the `Health` service. The client should support both the `Check` and
`Watch` methods. If the health status is unsuccessful, the client should exit with a
non-zero exit code.

Your application should allow the client to set up an insecure or a TLS-encrypted communication channel with the server. Your application should also support accepting
a specific service name for which it should check its health.

Handling Runtime Errors

When a client application makes a request to a gRPC server, the request is
handled in a separate goroutine—like what you learned about HTTP servers.
However, unlike HTTP servers, if an unhandled runtime error (such as one
caused by a call to the `panic()` function) occurs during the request processing,
it will terminate the entire server process, which will also terminate any other
request currently being processed. Whether this is desirable or not will depend
mostly on your specific application behavior. Let's say that we don't find this
desirable, and we want to implement a mechanism in server applications so that
the existing requests as well as new requests continue to be processed, even if
there is an unhandled error when handling another request. The conventional
approach to implement this mechanism is to define a server-side interceptor. In
this interceptor, we will set up a deferred call to another function, where we call
the `recover()` function and log the error, if any. When a runtime error occurs,
this deferred function gets called instead of the application being terminated.

First, let's look at the unary interceptor:

```
func panicUnaryInterceptor(
        ctx context.Context,
        req interface{},
        info *grpc.UnaryServerInfo,
        handler grpc.UnaryHandler,
) (resp interface{}, err error) {
        defer func() {
                if r := recover(); r != nil {
                        log.Printf("Panic recovered: %v", r)
                        err = status.Error(
                                codes.Internal,
                                "Unexpected error happened",
                        )
                }
        }()
        resp, err = handler(ctx, req)
        return
}
```

We have defined the interceptor to make use of *named* return values: `resp` and `err`. This allows us to set the values that are returned when there is a runtime error. When a runtime error occurs, the `recover()` function returns a non-nil value. We log this value and assign `err` to a new error value created using `status .Error()` function. We set the response code to `codes.Internal` and configure the error to have a custom error message. This way, we will log the actual error on the server side but send only a brief error message to the client. Depending on your application, this is the opportunity to run any other operation in the event of an unexpected runtime error. The default value of `resp` (that is, `nil`) will be returned as the response for the RPC request.

The server-side stream interceptor would be configured similarly. An interesting aspect of the stream interceptor is that it works equally well whether the runtime error is caused during the initial stream setup or during one of the subsequent message exchanges.

The directory `chap10/svc-panic-handling` of the book's code repository contains a modified version of the gRPC application from Chapter 9—Chaining Interceptors (`chap9/interceptor-chain`). The server has been updated to register panic handling interceptors to be the innermost interceptor for unary and streaming RPC method calls:

```
s := grpc.NewServer(
        grpc.ChainUnaryInterceptor(
                metricUnaryInterceptor,
                loggingUnaryInterceptor,
                panicUnaryInterceptor,
        ),
        grpc.ChainStreamInterceptor(
                metricStreamInterceptor,
                loggingStreamInterceptor,
                panicStreamInterceptor,
        ),
)
```

Registering the panic handling interceptor as the innermost interceptor means that a runtime error in a service handler doesn't hamper the functioning of the other interceptors. This, of course, assumes that there will be no runtime error in any of the outer interceptors, which may or may not hold. Of course, we could attach the panic handling interceptor twice as the outermost and the innermost interceptor enclosing all other interceptors.

To illustrate the working of the interceptor, the server and client applications have been modified as described next.

The `Users` service's `GetUser()` method is modified to call the `panic()` function if the user's email address has the form `panic@example.com`:

```
components := strings.Split(in.Email, "@")
if len(components) != 2 {
```

```
            return nil, errors.New("invalid email address")
}
if components[0] == "panic" {
        panic("I was asked to panic")
}
```

The client application is modified to accept a third argument corresponding to the email address for the user, which is then specified in the request to the `GetUser()` method.

The `GetHelp()` method is modified to call `panic()` if the incoming request message is `panic`:

```
fmt.Printf("Request receieved: %s\n", request.Request)
if request.Request == "panic" {
        panic("I was asked to panic")
}
```

Let's now build and run the server from a terminal session:

```
$ cd chap10/svc-panic-handling/server
$ go build
$ ./server
```

In a separate terminal session, build and run the client:

```
$ cd chap10/svc-panic-handling/client
$ go build
```

Then, let's call the `GetUser()` method:

```
$ ./client localhost:50051 GetUser panic@example.com
2021/07/05 21:02:25 Method:/Users/GetUser, Duration:1.494875ms,
Error:rpc error: code = Internal desc = Unexpected error happened
2021/07/05 21:02:25 rpc error: code = Internal desc = Unexpected
error happened
```

You can see that the client doesn't get a successful response but instead gets an error from the server. The values of the `code` and the `desc` fields are the ones that we set in the panic handling interceptor.

On the server side, you will see the following log messages:

```
2021/07/05 21:02:25 Received request for user with Email: panic@example.com
Id:
2021/07/05 21:02:25 Panic recovered: I was asked to panic
2021/07/05 21:02:25 Method:/Users/GetUser, Error:rpc error:
code = Internal desc = Unexpected error happened,
Request-Id: [request-123]
2021/07/05 21:02:25 Method:/Users/GetUser, Duration:160.291µs
```

Next, call the `GetHelp()` method:

```
$ ./client localhost:50051 GetHelp
Request: panic
2021/07/05 21:07:37 Send msg called: *users.UserHelpRequest
2021/07/05 21:07:37 Recv msg called: *users.UserHelpReply
2021/07/05 21:07:37 rpc error: code = Internal desc = Unexpected
error happened
```

On the server side, you will see the following logs:

```
Request receieved: panic
2021/07/05 21:07:37 Panic recovered: I was asked to panic
2021/07/05 21:07:37 Method:/Users/GetHelp, Error:rpc error: code =
Internal desc = Unexpected error happened, Request-Id:[request-123]
2021/07/05 21:07:37 Method:/Users/GetHelp, Duration:1.302932917s
```

Writing an interceptor to recover runtime errors keeps your server running while it continues to process other requests. It also allows you to log the cause of the error, publish a metric so that you can monitor errors, or run any custom cleanup and rollback procedure.

Next, you will learn about techniques to abort request processing when the operation is taking longer than a configured time interval or when a client disconnects.

Aborting Request Processing

Let's say that you want to impose an upper limit on the execution time of an RPC method. Based on the historical behavior of your service, you know that for certain malicious user requests, an RPC method can take longer than, say, 300 milliseconds. In such a scenario, you simply want to abort the request. Using server-side interceptors, you can implement such logic across all of your service handlers.

The following function implements a unary RPC time-out interceptor:

```
func timeoutUnaryInterceptor(
        ctx context.Context,
        req interface{},
        info *grpc.UnaryServerInfo,
        handler grpc.UnaryHandler,
) (interface{}, error) {
        var resp interface{}
        var err error

        ctxWithTimeout, cancel := context.WithTimeout(
                ctx,
                300*time.Millisecond,
        )
```

```
    defer cancel()

    ch := make(chan error)

    go func() {
            resp, err = handler(ctxWithTimeout, req)
            ch <- err
    }()

    select {
    case <-ctxWithTimeout.Done():
            cancel()
            err = status.Error(
                    codes.DeadlineExceeded,
                    fmt.Sprintf(
                            "%s: Deadline exceeded",
                            info.FullMethod,
                    ),
            )
            return resp, err
    case <-ch:
    }
    return resp, err
}
```

The above interceptor creates a new context.Context object, ctxWithTimeout, using the context.WithTimeout() function call and using the incoming context, ctx, as the parent context. The time-out is set to 300 milliseconds, our configured maximum duration for the service handler to complete execution. We execute the handler method in a goroutine. Then we use a select statement to wait to receive a value on the channel err or the function call ctxWithTimeout.Done(). A value will be ready to read from err when the handler method has completed execution.

On the other hand, the ctxWithTimeout.Done() function will return when 300 milliseconds have elapsed. If the latter happens first, we cancel the context, create a new error value with the code set to codes.DeadLineExceeded, and return it along with a nil value for resp.

The result of configuring your server with the above interceptor is that any RPC method that takes longer than 300 milliseconds will be aborted. If we write the service method in a manner that the context cancellation by the interceptor is used to cancel ongoing processing (as you learned in Chapter 7), server resources are also timely freed to be available for processing other requests. Instead of verifying the working of the interceptor by running a gRPC server, we will do so by writing a test function. This will also demonstrate how you can write a unit test for server-side unary RPC interceptors.

We will call the `timeoutUnaryInterceptor()` function directly with the expected arguments as shown next:

```
func TestUnaryTimeOutInterceptor(t *testing.T) {
        req := svc.UserGetRequest{}
        unaryInfo := &grpc.UnaryServerInfo{
                FullMethod: "Users.GetUser",
        }
        testUnaryHandler := func(
                ctx context.Context,
                req interface{},
        ) (interface{}, error) {
                time.Sleep(500 * time.Millisecond)
                return svc.UserGetReply{}, nil
        }

        _, err := timeoutUnaryInterceptor(
                context.Background(),
                req,
                unaryInfo,
                testUnaryHandler,
        )
        if err == nil {
                t.Fatal(err)
        }
        expectedErr := status.Errorf(
                codes.DeadlineExceeded,
                "Users.GetUser: Deadline exceeded",
        )
        if !errors.Is(err, expectedErr) {
                t.Errorf(
                        "Expected error: %v Got: %v\n",
                        expectedErr,
                        err,
                )
        }
}
```

The `timeoutUnaryInterceptor()` function is called with four objects as arguments. We created these objects in the above test function as follows:

context: An object of type `context.Context`. The context object is created by calling the `context.Background()` function.

req: An object containing the request RPC message of an empty `interface{}` type. We create an empty `svc.UserGetRequest{}` object and assign that to `req`.

info: An object of type `grpc.UnaryServerInfo`. We create an object of type `grpc.UnaryServerInfo`, setting the `FullMethod` field, a string, to "Users .GetUser".

handler: A function of the type `grpc.UnaryHandler`. We create a `testUnaryHandler()` function to be the service handler for our test function. Inside it, we sleep for 500 milliseconds so that we can verify the interceptor behavior and then return an empty `UserGetReply` object as the response.

Now let's say that we want to implement this behavior for streaming RPC methods. We know that in the case of streaming RPC methods, the streaming connection is likely to be long lived. Requests and responses will contain a stream of messages with potential delay between consecutive messages on stream. What if we wanted to enforce a time-out on streaming RPC methods as well? For example, let's say in a client-side streaming method or a bidirectional streaming RPC method, if we haven't received a message from the client in the last 60 seconds, we will abort the connection. To implement this, we will implement a streaming server-side interceptor equivalent of `timeoutUnaryInterceptor()`. We will impose a maximum time-out policy when the server is waiting to receive a message and the timer will reset per message. We define a new type, `wrappedServerStream`, to wrap the underlying `ServerStream` object and implement the time-out logic inside the implementation of the `RecvMsg()` method:

```
type wrappedServerStream struct {
        RecvMsgTimeout time.Duration
        grpc.ServerStream
}

func (s wrappedServerStream) SendMsg(m interface{}) error {
        return s.ServerStream.SendMsg(m)
}

func (s wrappedServerStream) RecvMsg(m interface{}) error {
        ch := make(chan error)
        t := time.NewTimer(s.RecvMsgTimeout)
        go func() {
                log.Printf("Waiting to receive a message: %T", m)
                ch <- s.ServerStream.RecvMsg(m)
        }()

        select {
        case <-t.C:
                return status.Error(
                        codes.DeadlineExceeded,
                        "Deadline exceeded",
                )
        case err := <-ch:
                return err
        }
}
```

We define the `wrappedServerStream` struct with two fields: `RecvMsgTimeout` of type `time.Duration` and embed a `grpc.ServerStream` object. The `SendMsg()` method that we implement calls the embedded stream's `SendMsg()` method. Inside the `RecvMsg()` method, we create a `time.Timer` object passing the value of `RecvMsgTimeout` as an argument to the `time.NewTimer()` function. The returned object, `t`, contains a field, `C`, a channel of type `chan Time`. Then we call the underlying stream's `RecvMsg()` method inside a goroutine.

Using a `select` statement, we wait to receive a value on either of two channels: – `t.C` and `ch`. The first channel receives a value when the duration specified in `RecvMsgTimeout` has elapsed. The second channel receives a value when the call to the underlying stream's `RecvMsg()` has returned. As per the behavior of `select`, if the first channel receives a value first, we return an error setting, the error code, to `codes.DeadlineExceeded`. When the service handler gets the error, it can then abort the RPC method execution.

Having now defined the time-out logic in the `RecvMsg()` method, we will define the interceptor as follows:

```
func timeoutStreamInterceptor(
        srv interface{},
        stream grpc.ServerStream,
        info *grpc.StreamServerInfo,
        handler grpc.StreamHandler,
) error {
        serverStream := wrappedServerStream{
                RecvMsgTimeout: 500 * time.Millisecond,
                ServerStream:   stream,
        }
        err := handler(srv, serverStream)
        return err
}
```

The interceptor defines a duration of 500 milliseconds as the `RecvMsgTimeout`. We will next verify the working of the interceptor by writing a unit test. The `timeoutStreamingInterceptor()` function must be called with the following arguments:

srv: This is of type `interface{}` and thus can be an object of any type. Here we will use a string, `"test"`.

stream: This is an object of a type that implements the `grpc.ServerStream` interface. In our test, we will define a new type, `testStream`, to implement this interface. In the `RecvMsg()` method, we will simulate our nonresponsive client behavior by sleeping for 700 milliseconds, which exceeds the time-out with which the interceptor is configured.

info: This is an object of type *grpc.ServerInfo, and we create it as follows:

```
streamInfo := &grpc.StreamServerInfo{
                FullMethod:      "Users.GetUser",
                IsClientStream: true,
                IsServerStream: true,
            }
```

handler: This is a bidirectional (or server-side) streaming RPC method handler. In our test, we implement the following test handler function:

```
testHandler := func(
                    srv interface{},
                    stream grpc.ServerStream,
                ) (err error) {
                    for {
                        m := svc.UserHelpRequest{}
                        err := stream.RecvMsg(&m)
                        if err == io.EOF {
                            break
                        }
                        if err != nil {
                            return err


                        }
                        r := svc.UserHelpReply{}
                        err = stream.SendMsg(&r)
                        if err == io.EOF {
                            break
                        }
                        if err != nil {
                            return err


                        }
                    }
                }
                return nil
            }
```

With all of the different objects now created, we can define the test function:

```
type testStream struct {
    grpc.ServerStream
}

func (s testStream) SendMsg(m interface{}) error {
    log.Println("Test Stream - SendMsg")
    return nil
}

func (s testStream) RecvMsg(m interface{}) error {
    log.Println("Test Stream - RecvMsg - Going to sleep")
```

```
            time.Sleep(700 * time.Millisecond)
            return nil
    }


    func TestStreamingTimeOutInterceptor(t *testing.T) {

            streamInfo := &grpc.StreamServerInfo{
                    FullMethod:      "Users.GetUser",
                    IsClientStream: true,
                    IsServerStream: true,
            }

            testStream := testStream{}

            // TODO - Define testHandler  as above

            err := timeoutStreamInterceptor(
                    "test",
                    testStream,
                    streamInfo,
                    testHandler,
            )
            expectedErr := status.Errorf(
                    codes.DeadlineExceeded,
                    "Deadline exceeded",
            )
            if !errors.Is(err, expectedErr) {
                    t.Errorf(
                            "Expected error: %v Got: %v\n",
                            expectedErr,
                            err,
                    )
            }
    }
```

You can find an example gRPC server application with the time-out interceptor implementations and the unit tests in the chap10/svc-timeout directory of the book's source repository.

Another ability that we want to have in our server application is to be able to react to client-initiated request termination events, such as a context cancellation or network failure. In such circumstances as well, the server should abort the request processing as soon as possible. Implementing this in an interceptor for unary RPC methods will look very similar to the time-out interceptor:

```
func clientDisconnectUnaryInterceptor(
        ctx context.Context,
        req interface{},
        info *grpc.UnaryServerInfo,
        handler grpc.UnaryHandler,
```

```
    ) (interface{}, error) {
        var resp interface{}
        var err error

        ch := make(chan error)

        go func() {
            resp, err = handler(ctx, req)
            ch <- err
        }()

        select {
        case <-ctx.Done():
            err = status.Error(
                codes.Canceled,
                fmt.Sprintf(
                    "%s: Request canceled",
                    info.FullMethod,
                ),
            )
            return resp, err
        case <-ch:

        }
        return resp, err
    }
```

The key statements are highlighted above. We call the RPC method handler in a goroutine. Then, using a `select` statement, we wait to receive a value on the channel returned by the `ctx.Done()` method, which indicates that the client connection has been closed, or the result of the handler execution. If the first event happens first, we create an error value indicating that the request has been canceled and return the error.

The implementation of the streaming interceptor looks very similar to the unary interceptor:

```
func clientDisconnectStreamInterceptor(
    srv interface{},
    stream grpc.ServerStream,
    info *grpc.StreamServerInfo,
    handler grpc.StreamHandler,
) (err error) {

    ch := make(chan error)

    go func() {
        err = handler(srv, stream)
        ch <- err
    }()
```

```
        select {
        case <-stream.Context().Done():
                err = status.Error(
                        codes.Canceled,
                        fmt.Sprintf(
                                "%s: Request canceled",
                                info.FullMethod,
                        ),
                )
                return
        case <-ch:

        }
        return
}
```

Once again, we call the RPC method handler in a goroutine. Then, using a `select` statement, we wait for the channel returned by the `stream.Context` `.Done()` method to be closed, which indicates that the client connection has been closed, or the result of the handler execution. If the first event happens first, we create an error value indicating that the request has been canceled and return the error. You can find an example server application with the interceptor implementations, including unit tests, in the `chap10/svc-client-dxn` directory of the book's source repository.

Before we move on to the next section, where we focus on improving the resiliency of our client applications, you have an exercise to attempt, Exercise 10.2.

> **EXERCISE 10.2: IMPLEMENTING GRACEFUL SHUTDOWN**
> **WITH TIME-OUT**   To stop a gRPC server gracefully, you will call the
> `GracefulStop()` method of the `grpc.Server` object. However, it doesn't allow
> the caller to configure a maximum duration up to which it will attempt to wait for
> existing request handling to be completed. Your goal in this exercise is to imple-
> ment a time-bound graceful shutdown of the server. After the time expires, the code
> should call the `Stop()` method causing a hard shutdown.
>
> Before you call the `GracefulStop()` method, update the health status of all of the
> services to be `NOT_SERVING`. This will mean that while you are waiting for the method
> to return, any health check requests will get back an appropriate update on the health
> of the services.

Robustness in Clients

In this part of the chapter, you will learn about techniques to improve the robustness of your client applications. We will start off with learning about the various time-out values that we can configure. Then, we will learn about the behavior of the underlying connection over which the RPC method calls are transmitted and finally examine techniques to improve the resiliency of individual method calls.

Throughout these sections, we will use a gRPC server with the Users service registered. The service defines two RPC methods: GetUser() and GetHelp(). Our example client can call either of these methods based on the command-line arguments specified to invoke it. You can find the code for the application in the chap10/client-resiliency directory of the book's source repository.

Improving Connection Setup

The first step that we perform in a client before we can make any RPC method calls is to establish a channel with the server. To refresh your memory, we have been using the following code to create the channel:

```
func setupGrpcConn(addr string) (*grpc.ClientConn, error) {
        return grpc.DialContext(
                context.Background(),
                addr,
                grpc.WithBlock(),
        )
        return conn, err
}
```

The grpc.WithBlock() will cause the above call to the DialContext() function to *not* return until a successful connection has been established. In fact, if you *didn't* specify the option, the connection establishment process doesn't start right away. It will happen at *some* point of time in the future, either while or before you make the first RPC method call.

Using the grpc.WithBlock() option helps us in scenarios when there are *temporary* failures, such as a server taking up a few hundred milliseconds more to become ready or a temporary network failure causing a time-out. However, this can also cause the client to continue trying to establish a connection without bailing out even when there are *permanent* failures that need to be examined. Examples of such failures are specifying a badly formed server address, or a nonexistent hostname.

To have the benefit of using the grpc.WithBlock() option *and* also not trying "forever" to establish the connection, we will specify another DialOption, created by calling the grpc.FailOnNonTempDialError(true) function. The true argument specifies that if a non-temporary error occurs, no further attempts will made to reestablish the connection. The DialContext() function will return with the error encountered.

Additionally, even for temporary errors, it is pragmatic to configure an upper bound on how long it tries to establish the connection. The grpc.DialContext()

function accepts a `context.Context` object as the first argument. Thus, we create a context with a time-out value and call the function with that context.

An updated `setupGrpcConn()` is as follows:

```
func setupGrpcConn(
        addr string,
) (*grpc.ClientConn, context.CancelFunc, error) {
        log.Printf("Connecting to server on %s\n", addr)
        ctx, cancel := context.WithTimeout(
                context.Background(),
                10*time.Second,
        )
        conn, err := grpc.DialContext(
                ctx,
                addr,
                grpc.WithBlock(),
                grpc.FailOnNonTempDialError(true),
                grpc.WithReturnConnectionError()
        )
        return conn, cancel, err
}
```

Note that we added a third `DialOption`, `grpc.WithReturnConnectionError()`. With this option, when there is a temporary error and the context expires before the `DialContext()` function has succeeded, the error returned will also contain the original error that prevented the connection establishment from happening.

It's worth mentioning that specifying the `grpc.WithReturnConnectionError()` `DialOption` also implicitly sets the `grpc.WithBlock()` option. With the above changes, the `DialContext()` function will now exhibit the following behavior:

- It will return immediately when it encounters a non-temporary error. The returned error value will have the details of the error encountered.

- If there is a non-temporary error, it will only attempt to establish a connection for 10 seconds. The function will return with the error value containing the non-temporary error details.

Build the client application in `chap10/client-resiliency` directory, and run it as follows (without any gRPC server running locally):

```
$ cd chap10/client-resiliency/client
$ go build
$/client localhost:50051 GetUser jane@joe.com
2021/07/22 19:02:31 Connecting to server on localhost:50051
2021/07/22 19:02:31 Error in creating connection: connection error:
desc = "transport: error while dialing: dial tcp [::1]:50051:
connect: connection refused"
```

Both the `grpc.FailOnTempDialError()` and `grpc.WithReturnConnectionError()` are considered experimental and hence their behavior may differ in future gRPC releases.

Handling Transient Failures

Once we have the channel established with the server, a client will proceed to make RPC method calls. One of the biggest benefits of using gRPC is that the client can make multiple such calls without having to create a new channel per request. However, this also means that, by default, the network connections are long lived and thus are prone to failures. Luckily, gRPC defines *Wait for Ready* semantics to which we can pass an additional argument when calling an RPC method. This additional configuration is a `grpc.CallOption` value created by calling the `grpc.WaitForReady()` function with `true` as an argument:

```
client.GetUser(context.Background(), req, grpc.WaitForReady(true))
```

When the above RPC method call is made, and the connection to the server is not established, it will first attempt to establish the connection successfully and then call the RPC method.

Let's see this behavior in action. First build and run the server in `chap10/client-resiliency/server`:

```
$ cd chap10/client-resiliency/server
$ go build
$ ./server
```

Leave the server running. Inside the client application, we have a `for` loop as follows, which will make a request to the `GetUser()` RPC method five times, sleeping for 1 second in between the requests:

```
for i := 1; i <= 5; i++ {
        log.Printf("Request: %d\n", i)
        userEmail := os.Args[3]
        result, err := getUser(
                c,
                &svc.UserGetRequest{Email: userEmail},
        )
        if err != nil {
                log.Fatalf("getUser failed: %v", err)
        }
        fmt.Fprintf(
                os.Stdout,
                "User: %s %s\n",
                result.User.FirstName,
                result.User.LastName,
        )
        time.Sleep(1 * time.Second)
}
```

Next build the client application and run it:

```
$ ./client localhost:50051 GetUser jane@joe.com
2021/07/23 09:43:58 Connecting to server on localhost:50051
2021/07/23 09:43:58 Request: 1
User: jane joe.com
2021/07/23 09:43:59 Request: 2
User: jane joe.com
2021/07/23 09:44:00 Request: 3
User: jane joe.com
2021/07/23 09:44:01 Request: 4
User: jane joe.com
2021/07/23 09:44:02 Request: 5
User: jane joe.com
```

Now, in between any two requests, if you *terminate* the server process and *restart* it, you will see that all of the five requests will still be made successfully without the client exiting with an error.

The WaitForReady() option only helps when the RPC method is called. For Unary RPC methods, this is useful when dealing with temporary connection failures. However, for streaming RPC method calls, this means that WaitForReady() is only useful when *creating* the stream. What happens if there is a network issue *after* creating the stream?

Let's say that you get an error when sending a message via Send() or when receiving one using Recv(). We will look at the error returned and decide as to whether we want to abort the RPC method call. Or do we want to create a new stream and resume the communication? Let's assume that we can safely resume the streaming communication for a bidirectional streaming RPC method by creating a new stream. Considering the GetHelp() method for the Users service as an example, we can implement an automatic connection reestablishment logic as described next.

We define a function to create the stream; that is, call the GetHelp() method:

```
func createHelpStream(c svc.UsersClient) (
        users.Users_GetHelpClient, error,
) {
        return c.GetHelp(
                context.Background(),
                grpc.WaitForReady(true),
        )
}
```

Then, we define a function setupChat() to interact with the created stream, sending requests and receiving response from the server. Inside it, we will create an unbuffered channel of type svc.Users_GetHelpClient, which is the type of the stream created by calling the GetHelp() method. We will call the

`Recv()` method in a dedicated goroutine. If the method returns an error other than `io.EOF`, it will re-create the stream. The stream is then written to a channel, `clientConn`.

The following code snippet shows the part of the client that reads from the stream along with the reconnection logic implemented:

```go
func setupChat(
        r io.Reader,
        w io.Writer,
        c svc.UsersClient,
) (err error) {

        var clientConn = make(chan svc.Users_GetHelpClient)
        var done = make(chan bool)

        stream, err := createHelpStream(c)
        defer stream.CloseSend()
        if err != nil {
                return err
        }

        go func() {
                for {
                        clientConn <- stream
                        resp, err := stream.Recv()
                        if err == io.EOF {
                                done <- true
                        }
                        if err != nil {
                                log.Printf("Recreating stream.")
                                stream, err = createHelpStream(c)
                                if err != nil {
                                        close(clientConn)
                                        done <- true
                                }
                        } else {
                                fmt.Printf(
                                        "Response: %s\n", resp.Response,
                                )
                                if resp.Response == "hello-10" {
                                        done <- true
                                }
                        }
                }
        }()

        // TODO - Send requests to the server

        <-done
        return stream.CloseSend()
}
```

Inside the goroutine reading from the stream, we have an unconditional `for` loop. Right at the beginning of the loop, we write the current stream object to the `clientConn` channel. This will unblock the part of the client that sends a message to the server (as explained soon). Then, we call the `Recv()` method. If we get an `io.EOF` error, we write `true` to the done channel, which will close the stream and return from the function.

If we get any other error, we call the `createHelpStream()` function to re-create the stream. If we are unable to create the stream, we close the `clientConn` channel, thus unblocking the sending code. We also write `true` to the `done` channel, which will cause the function to return.

If we didn't get an error, we write the response received from the server. If the response is `hello-10`, we write `true` to the `done` channel. This string corresponds to the last request that is sent from the client. Hence, when we get back this message, we know that there is no further work to be done by this function.

The following code snippet shows the sending part of the `setupChat()` function:

```go
func setupChat(
        r io.Reader,
        w io.Writer,
        c svc.UsersClient,
) (err error) {
        var clientConn = make(chan svc.Users_GetHelpClient)
        var done = make(chan bool)

        stream, err := createHelpStream(c)
        defer stream.CloseSend()
        if err != nil {
                return err
        }

        // TODO Receiving goroutine as explained earlier

        requestMsg := "hello"
        msgCount := 1
        for {
                if msgCount > 10 {
                        break
                }
                stream = <-clientConn
                if stream == nil {
                        break
                }
                request := svc.UserHelpRequest{
                        Request: fmt.Sprintf(
                                "%s-%d", requestMsg, msgCount,
                        ),
                }
```

```
            err := stream.Send(&request)
            if err != nil {
                    log.Printf("Send error: %v. Will retry.\n", err)
            } else {
                    log.Printf("Request sent: %d\n", msgCount)
                    msgCount += 1
            }
    }

    <-done
    return stream.CloseSend()
}
```

We send 10 messages from the client to the server. The server echoes back the same message as response. Before sending each message, we read the stream to be used to send the message from the clientConn channel. Then, it will invoke the Send() method. If the method returns an error, it will wait for the receiving goroutine to re-create the stream and write the new stream object value to the channel. Once it has successfully read the newly created stream, it will attempt the send operation once again. You can find a working client implementing the above logic for the GetHelp() method in the chap10/client-resiliency/ client directory of the book's source repository.

We use the error returned from the Recv() method to determine if we should re-create the stream or not. One reason for doing so is that this method returns an io.EOF error when the stream has been terminated normally. In any other scenario, it returns another error. Thus, it is easy to distinguish between what is a normal error and what is not. On the other hand, the Send() method returns an io.EOF error even when the stream breaks unexpectedly, such as due to network failures. Thus, it's tricky to distinguish between normal and abnormal terminations. There is a way out, though—if we get an io.EOF error from the Send() method, and we call the RecvMsg() method, we can make use of the error value returned by this method to deduce an abnormal termination.

The following code snippet shows a modified version of the client streaming code from Chapter 9 (chap9/client-streaming) to implement the above logic:

```
for i := 0; i < 5; i++ {
        log.Printf("Creating Repo: %d\n", i)
        r := svc.RepoCreateRequest{
                CreatorId: "user-123",
                Name:      "hello-world",
        }
        err := stream.Send(&r)
        if err == io.EOF {
                var m svc.RepoCreateReply
                err := stream.RecvMsg(&m)
                if err != nil {
                        // Implement stream recreation logic
```

```
                        }
                }
                if err != nil {
                        continue
                }
        }
```

If we get a non-`nil` error value from the call to `RecvMsg()`, we infer that the `io.EOF` error was caused due to an abnormal termination, and hence we can re-create the stream before sending the next message.

Setting Time-Outs for Method Calls

Okay, you have now configured your client application to ensure that it doesn't bail out and exit with an error when there is an issue with the underlying connection to the server. How do we prevent it from attempting to salvage the underlying connection forever? Additionally, how do we ensure that an RPC method call has a configured upper bound on how long it is allowed to be processed? We can achieve both by creating a `context.Context` object using `context.WithTimeout()` and then calling the RPC methods, passing the created context as the first argument. For example:

```
ctx, cancel := context.WithTimeout(
        context.Background(),
        10*time.Second,
)
resp, err := client.GetUser(
        ctx,
        u,
        grpc.WaitForReady(true),
)
```

When we create a context that is set to be canceled after 10 seconds, that time-out is enforced across everything that's needed for the gRPC method call to be made. That is, if the client must establish a connection to the server for making the RPC method call, the connection attempt will be terminated after 10 seconds. Similarly, if the RPC method call is made immediately, the call must complete within 10 seconds.

For streaming RPC method calls, whether you can enforce a time-out over the RPC method call or not is of course dependent on your application. In most cases, it may not be pragmatic to do so. To implement `WaitForReady` with a time-out for your streaming RPC calls, one solution is to implement a pattern as follows:

```
ctxWithTimeout, cancel := context.WithTimeout(
        ctx, 10*time.Second,
)
```

```
        defer cancel()

        ch := make(chan error)

        go func() {
                stream, err = createRPCStream(..)
                ch <- err
        }()

    select {
    case <-ctxWithTimeout.Done():
            cancel()
            err = status.Error(
                codes.DeadlineExceeded,
                fmt.Sprintf(
                    "%s: Deadline exceeded",
                    info.FullMethod,
                ),
            )
            return resp, err
    case <-ch:
    }
```

In the above code snippet, the createRPCStream() function is responsible for creating the stream, and we invoke it in a goroutine. We create a context with a time-out of 10 seconds and then use a select statement to return an error if the context expires before the createRPCStream() function returns.

We will end the chapter with an overview of connection management between gRPC clients and servers.

Connection Management

A *connection*, that is, a channel created via a call to DialContext() between a client and server, is modeled as a state machine with five states. A connection can be in one of the five states:

CONNECTING

READY

TRANSIENT_FAILURE

IDLE

SHUTDOWN

Figure 10.1 shows the five states and the possible transition between them.

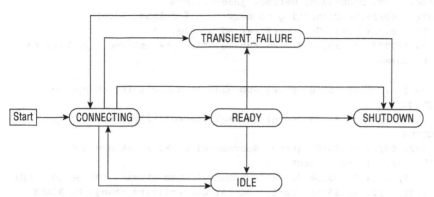

Figure 10.1: Functioning of an RPC-based service architecture

A connection starts its *life* in the CONNECTING state. In this state, we have three primary things happening:

- Name resolution of hostnames
- TCP connection setup
- TLS handshake for secure connections

If all of these steps are successfully completed, the connection goes to the READY state. If one of the steps fails, the connection moves to the TRANSIENT_FAILURE state. If the client application is terminated, the connection moves to the SHUTDOWN state.

A connection in READY state will transition into the TRANSIENT_FAILURE state if there are issues, such as underlying network failures: the server process going away, for example. In this connection state, an RPC method call will return immediately with an error unless we specify grpc.WaitForReady(true) as a CallOption.

A connection in READY state will move to the IDLE state if no RPC requests, including messages over a stream, have been exchanged for a configured time interval. As of google.golang.org/grpc version 1.37, this is not yet implemented for Go gRPC clients.

A connection in TRANSIENT_FAILURE state will be moved to CONNECTING state to attempt to reestablish the connection with the server. If it fails, it will be moved back to the TRANSIENT_FAILURE state again before retrying. A connection backoff protocol implemented by the google.golang.org/grpc library regulates the interval between successive retries.

To see the state transitions in action, run a client application after configuring the google.golang.org/grpc package to emit logs setting two environment variables: GRPC_GO_LOG_SEVERITY_LEVEL=info and GRPC_GO_LOG_VERBOSITY_LEVEL=99:

```
$ GRPC_GO_LOG_SEVERITY_LEVEL=info GRPC_GO_LOG_VERBOSITY_LEVEL=1   \
  ./client localhost:50051 GetUser jane@joe.com
2021/07/24 09:35:56 Connecting to server on localhost:50051
INFO: 2021/07/24 09:35:56 [core] parsed scheme: ""
INFO: 2021/07/24 09:35:56 [core] scheme "" not registered, fallback to
default scheme
...
INFO: 2021/07/24 09:35:56 [core] Subchannel Connectivity change to
CONNECTING
INFO: 2021/07/24 09:35:56 [core] Channel Connectivity change to
CONNECTING
INFO: 2021/07/24 09:35:56 [core] Subchannel picks a new address
"localhost:50051" to connect
INFO: 2021/07/24 09:35:56 [core] Subchannel Connectivity change to READY
INFO: 2021/07/24 09:35:56 [core] Channel Connectivity change to READY
2021/07/24 09:35:56 Request: 1
```

Next, we killed the server process, and then in the client application, we saw these logs:

```
INFO: 2021/07/24 09:36:18 [core] Subchannel Connectivity change to
CONNECTING
INFO: 2021/07/24 09:36:18 [core] Channel Connectivity change to
CONNECTING
INFO: 2021/07/24 09:36:18 [core] Subchannel picks a new address "localhost:50051"
to connect
WARNING: 2021/07/24 09:36:38 [core] grpc: addrConn.createTransport failed to
connect to {localhost:50051 localhost:50051 <nil> 0 <nil>}. Err: connection
error: desc = "transport: error while dialing: dial tcp [::1]:50051: connect:
connection refused". Reconnecting...
INFO: 2021/07/24 09:36:38 [core] Subchannel Connectivity change to
TRANSIENT_FAILURE
INFO: 2021/07/24 09:36:38 [core] Channel Connectivity change to
TRANSIENT_FAILURE
INFO: 2021/07/24 09:36:39 [core] Subchannel Connectivity change to
CONNECTING
INFO: 2021/07/24 09:36:39 [core] Subchannel picks a new address
"localhost:50051" to connect
INFO: 2021/07/24 09:36:39 [core] Channel Connectivity change to CONNECTING
INFO: 2021/07/24 09:37:01 [core] Channel Connectivity change to CONNECTING
INFO: 2021/07/24 09:37:01 [core] Subchannel Connectivity change to READY
INFO: 2021/07/24 09:37:01 [core] Channel Connectivity change to READY
```

Once a connection is created between a client and a server, multiple RPC method calls can be made using this connection concurrently. This does away with the need for maintaining a connection pool. By default, this is limited to 100 active RPC method calls at any given point in time. The key point that we should note here is that there is only ever *one* connection between a client and a server process. In a production scenario, you will very likely have multiple server backends for a gRPC service, and thus you will always have one connection per server backend. These semantics reduce the connection setup cost to zero for all, but the first RPC method call to a server backend. This also introduces challenges in load balancing across server backends, as the load balancing must be performed per RPC method call. However, this is a solved problem with most open-source reverse proxy servers, such as Nginx and HAproxy, and service-meshes, such as Envoy and Linkerd, supporting it out of the box.

Summary

You started the chapter by learning how to implement a TLS-encrypted communication channel between a client and server application. You achieved this by generating self-signed TLS certificates and configuring your applications to use them, thus setting up a secure communication between client and server applications.

Next, you learned how to implement health checks in server applications by registering the `Health` service conforming to the gRPC health check protocol. A health check endpoint in a gRPC server is a way for load balancer or service proxies to query if a server is ready to accept new requests and hence must always be implemented. Then, you used server-side interceptors, which you learned about in the previous chapter, to handle unhandled runtime errors and enforce robustness around dealing with unresponsive or malicious client applications. You also learned how to test server-side interceptors in isolation.

In the last two sections, you learned how connections are managed between client and server applications. You implemented techniques in client applications to deal with transient connection failures and learned how to configure time-outs for the different stages of the connection life cycle.

This chapter completes our exploration of gRPC in this book. Most applications and services will need to store data, and in the next and final chapter, you will learn how to interact with different datastores from your applications.

Working with Data Stores

In this chapter, you will learn to interact with data stores from your applications. I have chosen two types of data stores based on their general applicability to different kinds of applications. You will first learn to interact with object storage services, which allow storing unstructured data blobs. Then you will learn to interact with relational databases. We will use an example HTTP server as the sample application, where we will implement various functionality related to interacting with data stores. We will implement a server to store software packages, first introduced in Chapter 3, "Writing HTTP Clients." It will offer the following features to its clients:

- A client can upload one or more packages. We will not bother much about the exact file format and allow uploading *any* file.

- Each package must have a name and version associated with it. A client can upload multiple versions of the same package.

- A client should be able to download a specific package version.

Figure 11.1 shows the architecture of the scenario that we will implement. We will integrate two data stores with the package server. The uploaded packages will be stored in an object store. We will use the Amazon Web Services Simple Storage Service (S3) compatible open-source MinIO software as the object store for local development. To store the metadata related to the package, we will use a relational database—MySQL.

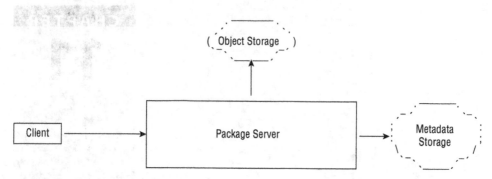

Figure 11.1: Architecture of the example scenario

The addition of the ability to store data in your applications is a necessary requirement, and it also increases the complexity of developing and testing them. Throughout the chapter, you will learn how to test the functionality *locally* using automated as well as manual tests. You will need additional software installed to follow along in the rest of this chapter; that is, Docker Desktop. The chapter "Getting Started" at the beginning of this book contains instructions on how to install it, so this is a good time to do that if you haven't done so already. You will also need to be able to download images from the image registry at Docker Hub. Let's get started!

Working with Object Stores

Object storage services such as Amazon Web Services (AWS) S3, Google Cloud Storage (GCS), and open-source software such as MinIO (https://min.io) are typically used for any kind of unstructured application data where you will read or write the entire objects—images, videos, and binary files are typical examples. Consider the package server that we will extend. When a user uploads a package, we will store it in the object store. Then, when the user wants to download the package, our application will let them download from the package store. The choice of object store is determined by your organization's policies or personal preferences. If your applications are hosted on a public cloud provider, you will likely end up using the cloud provider's object storage services such as AWS S3 or Google Cloud Storage. On the other hand, if your organization has an in-house object storage service such as MinIO, you will use that instead.

Once you have chosen the data store, how we interact with the storage service will depend on the storage service itself—usually via vendor-specific libraries: so, for example, https://docs.aws.amazon.com/sdk-for-go/api/service/s3/ for S3, https://cloud.google.com/go/storage for Google Cloud Storage, and https://github.com/minio/minio-go for MinIO. We will take a different approach.

We will use a project called the Go Cloud Development Kit (Go CDK), `https://gocloud.dev`, which provides vendor-neutral generic APIs to interact with cloud and non-cloud services. Object stores are one of the supported services. Others include relational databases, document stores, and publish-subscribe systems. We are using this project for two reasons. First, this allows us to implement key operations when interacting with an object storage service using a higher-level abstraction. Second, Go CDK allows us to write testable code by providing the features for interacting with a local filesystem storage service. A desirable side effect of this is that our applications become cloud vendor neutral to a certain degree.

Integration with Package Server

First, we will quickly get familiar with the HTTP handler function that will handle the incoming package upload requests. We will implement the functionality to upload the incoming package data to the object store.

As you will recall, we wrote a client for uploading packages to a package server in Chapter 3. To test it, we wrote a test package server (see Listing 3.9) where we implemented an HTTP server capable of processing the package upload HTTP requests. In this chapter, we are first going to write an HTTP server application borrowing code from the test server. We will be implementing a custom `Handler` type described in Chapter 6, "Advanced HTTP Server Applications." The first handler function that we will write will process the package upload requests. The following code snippet shows the blueprint of the handler function for processing package registration requests, along with a helper function for uploading the data:

```
func uploadData(config appConfig, f *multipart.FileHeader) error {
        config.logger.Printf("Package uploaded: %s\n", f.Filename)
        return nil
}

func packageRegHandler(
        w http.ResponseWriter,
        r *http.Request,
        config appConfig,
) {
        d := pkgRegisterResponse{}
        err := r.ParseMultipartForm(5000)
        # TODO error handling
        mForm := r.MultipartForm
        # TODO Read data from the multipart request data in mForm
        d.ID = fmt.Sprintf(
                "%s-%s-%s",
                packageName,
```

```
                      packageVersion,
                      fHeader.Filename,
              )
        err = uploadData(config, d.ID, fHeader)
        # TODO error handling send response
}
```

The incoming request body will be encoded as a `multipart/form-data` message. We use the `ParseMultipartForm()` method to read the various parts of the message from the request and then call the `uploadData()` function where currently we simply log a message. The `uploadData()` function accepts two parameters: an object of type `appConfig` and an object of type `*multipart.FileHeader` that gives us access to the incoming `multipart/form-data` message. The `appConfig` struct is defined as follows:

```
type appConfig struct {
        logger       *log.Logger
        packageBucket *blob.Bucket
}
```

This `struct` type will be used to share data across the handler functions. We have two fields: `logger`, a value of type `*log.Logger`, and `packageBucket`, an object of type `*blob.Bucket` object. The `packageBucket` field refers to an opened *bucket*, which is a container for objects in the object storage service. A handler function can then perform various operations on the bucket using this object. We will get to the details of creating the `*blob.Bucket` object soon. Once we have the `appConfig` object created, the `uploadData()` function is updated as follows:

```
func uploadData(
        config appConfig, objectId string, f *multipart.FileHeader,
) (int64, error) {
        ctx := context.Background()

        fData, err := f.Open()
        if err != nil {
                return 0, err
        }
        defer fData.Close()

        w, err := config.packageBucket.NewWriter(ctx, objectId, nil)
        if err != nil {
                return 0, err
        }

        nBytes, err := io.Copy(w, fData)
        if err != nil {
                return 0, err
        }
```

```
                err = w.Close()
                if err != nil {
                        return nBytes, err
                }
                return nBytes, nil
        }
}
```

We first call the `Open()` method of the `*multipart.FileHeader` object. The call returns two values. The first, `fData`, is a value of type `multipart.File`, which is defined in the `mime/multipart` package, and the second, `err`, is an error value. The `multipart.File` type is an interface that gives us access to the underlying file data in the request. It embeds the `io.Reader`, `io.Closer` interfaces, and others from the `io` package.

The first step to interacting with an object storage service using Go CDK is to *open* an existing *bucket*—a container for objects. An object cannot be stored without a bucket. When we open a bucket successfully, we get an object of type `*blob.Bucket`. The `uploadData()` function's `config` object has access to this object via the `config.packageBucket` field. Then we call the `NewWriter()` method defined on the `config.packageBucket` object with three arguments:

- The first argument is a `context.Context` value.

- The second argument is a string containing the identifier or name of the object, that will identify the data.

- The third argument, currently `nil`, is an object of type `blob.WriterOptions` (defined in the `gocloud.dev/blob` package), and it allows us to configure various options related to the write operation. You can set cache control headers, set up a message integrity check during the write operation, or set the content disposition header.

The `NewWriter()` method returns two values: `w`, of type `*blob.Writer`, and an error value. The `*blob.Writer` type satisfies the `io.WriteCloser` interface. We then call the `io.Copy()` function to copy the data from the reader, `fData`, to the writer, `w`. The function returns two values: `nBytes`, an `int64` value containing the number of bytes that were copied, and an `error` value. We return the number of bytes copied as we log it in the package upload handler function. If the error value was `nil`, we close the `*blob.Writer` by calling the `Close()` method.

To use the `gocloud.dev/blob` package to open a bucket in AWS S3, we will *blank* import the `gocloud.dev/blob/s3blob` package. This is the driver package that implements the functionality of communicating with the AWS S3 service. When we import it, it registers itself with the `gocloud.dev/blob` package as the package providing support for interacting with the AWS S3 service. Similar packages exist for the Google Cloud Storage and Azure Blob Storage services.

The following code snippet opens an AWS S3 bucket named *my-bucket* in the *ap-southeast-2* AWS region:

```
import (
        "gocloud.dev/blob"
        _ "gocloud.dev/blob/s3blob"
)
bucket, err := blob.OpenBucket(
        ctx, "s3://my-bucket?region=ap-southeast-2",
)
...
```

We use a blank import for the `gocloud.dev/blob/s3blob` package, as we will only be interacting with the `gocloud.dev/blob` package. This is to ensure explicitly that our application is not unintentionally using any driver-specific functionality. The `blob.OpenBucket()` function accepts two parameters: a `context.Context` object and a string containing the bucket URL. To specify the S3 bucket to open, we specify an S3 URL, which is of this form: `s3://bucket-name?<customisations>`. For local development, we will instead use an open-source S3-compatible storage service, MinIO (`https://min.io`), which we can run locally. To communicate with MinIO running locally, the URL that we will specify to `OpenBucket()` will be `s3://bucket-name?endpoint=http://127.0.0.1:9000&disableSSL=true&s3ForcePathStyle=true`. The endpoint query parameter specifies the address to which the requests for the object storage service should be made. The `disableSSL=true` query parameter specifies that we want to communicate with the storage server over HTTP (and not HTTPS). If you are communicating with MinIO over a network; that is, beyond your local system, you should use HTTPS and not disable it. The `s3ForcePath` style parameter is required to force a now-deprecated S3 path URL format but needed for communicating with MinIO locally as we will be running it. The function call returns a value of type `*blob.Bucket` and an error value. If the error value is `nil`, all subsequent operations on the bucket will be performed by calling methods defined on the returned `*blob.Bucket` object, `bucket`. We will encapsulate the functionality to open a bucket into a function, `getBucket()`:

```
func getBucket(
        bucketName, s3Address, s3Region string,
) (*blob.Bucket, error) {

        urlString := fmt.Sprintf("s3://%s?", bucketName)
        if len(s3Region) != 0 {
                urlString += fmt.Sprintf("region=%s&", s3Region)
        }

        if len(s3Address) != 0 {
                urlString += fmt.Sprintf("endpoint=%s&"+
```

```
                            "disableSSL=true&"+
                            "s3ForcePathStyle=true",
                            s3Address,
                    )
            }
            return blob.OpenBucket(context.Background(), urlString)
    }
```

When this function gets a non-empty value for s3Address, it assumes that we are communicating with MinIO locally and constructs the value of urlString accordingly. Finally, we call the blob.OpenBucket() function and return the values it returns—a *blob.Bucket and an error value. This function is called from the main() function of the server as follows:

```
func main() {

    bucketName := os.Getenv("BUCKET_NAME")
    if len(bucketName) == 0 {
            log.Fatal("Specify Object Storage bucket - BUCKET_NAME")
    }
    s3Address := os.Getenv("S3_ADDR")
    awsRegion := os.Getenv("AWS_DEFAULT_REGION")

    if len(s3Address) == 0 && len(awsRegion) == 0 {
            log.Fatal(
                    "Assuming AWS S3 service. Specify
AWS_DEFAULT_REGION",
            )
    }

    packageBucket, err := getBucket(
            bucketName, s3Address, awsRegion,
    )
    if err != nil {
            log.Fatal(err)
    }
    defer packageBucket.Close()

    listenAddr := os.Getenv("LISTEN_ADDR")
    if len(listenAddr) == 0 {
            listenAddr = ":8080"
    }

    config := appConfig{
            logger: log.New(
                    os.Stdout, "",
                    log.Ldate|log.Ltime|log.Lshortfile,
            ),
            packageBucket: packageBucket,
    }
```

```
mux := http.NewServeMux()
setupHandlers(mux, config)

log.Fatal(http.ListenAndServe(listenAddr, mux))
}
```

We look for three environment variables at startup: BUCKET_NAME, S3_ADDR, and AWS_DEFAULT_REGION. The BUCKET_NAME must be specified, and it is expected that the bucket with that name already exists in the object store. If S3_ADDR is specified, our program assumes that we are using a locally running MinIO server. If it is not specified, the application assumes that the user wants to use the AWS S3 service and hence exits with an error if the default AWS region to use is not specified. If you are not familiar with AWS, the default AWS region is needed since gocloud.dev/blob/s3blob and the underlying AWS Go SDK must know which region to send the HTTP requests to. Then we call the getBucket() function, and if there was no error, we create an object of type appConfig, configuring the packageBucket field appropriately. The complete code for the package server with the modifications discussed so far can be found in the chap11/pkg-server-1 directory of the book's source code repository. Make sure that you can build the application:

```
$ cd chap11/pkg-server-1
$ go build -o pkg-server
```

Before we can run the application, we will need to run a local copy of the MinIO service using the application Docker Desktop. Open a new terminal session, then run the following command on a computer that has Docker installed and can communicate with the Internet:

```
$ docker run \
    -p 9000:9000 \
    -p 9001:9001 \
    -e MINIO_ROOT_USER=admin \
    -e MINIO_ROOT_PASSWORD=admin123 \
    -ti minio/minio:RELEASE.2021-07-08T01-15-01Z \
    server "/data" \
    --console-address ":9001"
```

MinIO exposes its functionality over two separate network ports. Requests over port 9000 are object storage service API calls from an application. This is the port to which we will point our package server. The second port, 9001, which is configured to be the console address, is used to communicate with MinIO using the web user interface. You can communicate with these services using the addresses 127.0.0.1:9000 and 127.0.0.1:9001 from your host computer. We set up the root username to be admin and the password to be admin123. We are using release RELEASE.2021-07-08T01-15-01Z to run the local service. Once you run the above command, it should download the image and start a container and the logs should look something like this:

```
API: http://172.17.0.2:9000  http://127.0.0.1:9000
RootUser: admin
RootPass: admin123

Console: http://172.17.0.2:9001 http://127.0.0.1:9001
RootUser: admin
RootPass: admin123

Command-line: https://docs.min.io/docs/minio-client-quickstart-guide
   $ mc alias set myminio http://172.17.0.2:9000 admin admin123

Documentation: https://docs.min.io
```

Leave the server running. Log into the web UI by going to the address http://127.0.0.1:9001 in your browser and logging in with username and password as **admin** and **admin123**, respectively. Then go to http://127.0.0.1:9001/buckets and click Create Bucket. Specify **test-bucket** as the bucket name and click Save (figure 11.2).

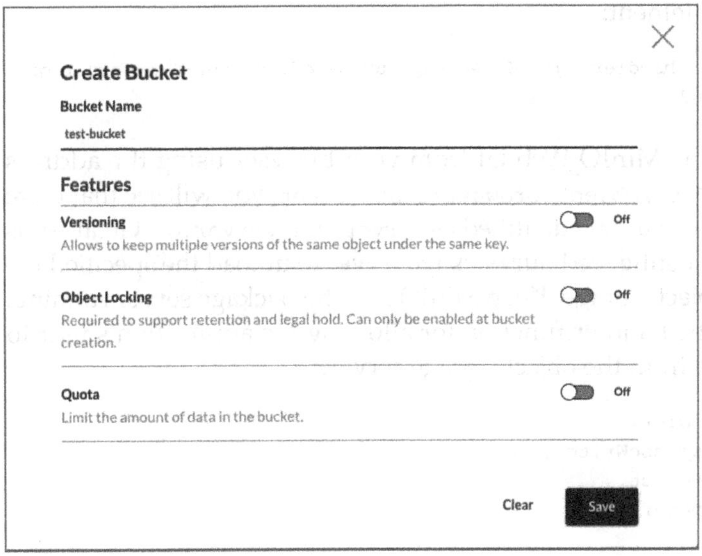

Create Bucket   ✕

Bucket Name

test-bucket
_____

Features

Versioning   ⬤ Off
Allows to keep multiple versions of the same object under the same key.

Object Locking   ⬤ Off
Required to support retention and legal hold. Can only be enabled at bucket creation.

Quota   ⬤ Off
Limit the amount of data in the bucket.

                                              Clear   Save

Figure 11.2: Creating a bucket in MinIO

Once the bucket is created, go back to the terminal where you built the package server and run it as follows:

```
$ cd chap11/pkg-server-1
$ S3_ADDR=http://127.0.0.1:9000 BUCKET_NAME=test-bucket \
```

```
AWS_ACCESS_KEY_ID=admin \
AWS_SECRET_ACCESS_KEY=admin123 \
./pkg-server
```

We specify the S3_ADDR environment variable containing the address at which the MinIO API is available. We specify the bucket that we want to use using BUCKET_NAME. The AWS_ACCESS_KEY_ID and AWS_SECRET_ACCESS_KEY environment variables are used to specify the credentials that will be used to authenticate with the MinIO API. Here we specify the root username and password created. With the server running, let's now make a request to upload a package to the package server.

You can use any file to upload. We will just use one of the files where we have our source code. From a new terminal session, run the following command using the curl command-line program:

```
$ curl -F name=server -F version=0.1 -F filedata=@server.go
http://127.0.0.1:8080/api/packages
{"id":"server-0.1-server.go"}
```

We got a response giving us the identifier of the package, constructed as packagename-version-filename. On the terminal where you ran the server, you will see a log statement:

```
2021/08/14 08:06:08 handlers.go:46: Package uploaded: server-0.1-server.go.
Bytes written: 1803
```

If you now visit the MinIO Web UI from your browser using the address http://127.0.0.1:9001/object-browser/test-bucket, you will see that there is an object inside test-bucket identified as server-0.1-server.go. Great—this is excellent. We have configured our package server to upload the specified file successfully to an object storage. Keep MinIO and the package server running.

Next, let's write the handler function for allowing the application's user to download a package from the object storage service:

```
func packageGetHandler(
        w http.ResponseWriter,
        r *http.Request,
        config appConfig,
) {
        queryParams := r.URL.Query()
        packageID := queryParams.Get("id")

        exists, err := config.packageBucket.Exists(
                r.Context(), packageID,
        )
        if err != nil || !exists {
```

```
                    http.Error(w, "invalid package ID", http.StatusNotFound)
                    return
        }

        url, err := config.packageBucket.SignedURL(
                    r.Context(),
                    packageID,
                    nil,
        )
        if err != nil {
                    http.Error(
                            w,
                            err.Error(),
                            http.StatusInternalServerError,
                    )
                    return
        }

        http.Redirect(w, r, url, http.StatusTemporaryRedirect)
}
```

This function expects the exact package identifier passed as a query parameter, id. It will then query the object storage service to check if the object exists by calling the Exists() method of the *blob.Bucket object, packageBucket. We call this method with the incoming request's context and the package identifier. It returns two values: the first, exists, of type bool, and err, an error value. The value in exists is true if the object exists in the bucket and false otherwise. A non-nil error value indicates that there was an unexpected issue in checking if the object exists. If the value of exists is false or the error value is non-nil, we return an HTTP 404 error response to the client. We do this check explicitly, since when creating a signed URL for an object, no check is done to see whether an object exists. If the object exists in the bucket, we create a signed URL to the object and initiate a redirect to that URL as a response. We use a temporary redirect here since the signed URL will change the next time you request the file.

Signed URLs allow your application to allow the requester to give access to an object in a bucket for a limited time duration. We call the SignedURL() method defined on the packageBucket object with three arguments: the incoming request's context, the object identifier to generate the signed URL for, and a value of nil for the third argument. The third argument, if non-nil, is expected to be an object of type blob.SignedURLOptions, which allows us to customize the time duration after which the URL ceases to be valid. For example, you may want to set the expiry time of the URL to be 15 minutes rather than the default 60 minutes. Generating the signed URL is also useful for other operations—creating an object in a bucket or deleting one. For those operations, you will need to specify via a blob.SignedURLOptions object with the Method field set to a PUT or DELETE rather than the default GET method. The following is an example of creating a `blob.SignedURLOptions` object with a custom expiry time and `PUT` method allowing the application user to create an object with the specified identifier for a limited amount of time:

```
sOpts := blob.SignedURLOptions{
        Expiry: 15 * time.Minute,
        Method: http.MethodPut,
}
url, err := config.packageBucket.SignedURL(
        r.Context(),
        packageName,
        &sOpts,
)
```

Let's now see the package querying behavior in action. You already have the package server running. We got back an identifier for the package uploaded previously, now let's query it back:

```
$ curl "http://127.0.0.1:8080/api/packages?id=server-0.1-server.go"
<a href="http://127.0.0.1:9000/test-bucket/server-0.1-server.go?
X-Amz-Algorithm=AWS4-HMAC-SHA256&amp;X-Amz-Credential=admin%2F20210814%
2Fap-southeast-2%2Fs3%2Faws4_request&amp;X-Amz-Date=20210814T003039Z&
amp;X-Amz-Expires=3600&amp;X-Amz-SignedHeaders=host&amp;
X-Amz-Signature=3b627ab2ae31e69fba1f8c224c76aae6e24f87982640e
c3373aa8ea
7f94962a2">Temporary Redirect</a>.
```

We get back a redirect to the signed URL for the object that we queried. The URL points to the locally running MinIO server. Thus, once the user obtains the signed URL, the data is downloaded directly from MinIO. If we follow the redirect by adding `--location` to the original curl command or by opening the URL in a browser, you will see the file contents.

```
$ curl --location \
  "http://127.0.0.1:8080/api/packages?id=server-0.1-server.go"
# file contents
```

Redirecting to a signed URL referring to the object is of course one approach to return the data to the client. Another approach is to read the data from the bucket in the application using the `ReadAll()` method or obtain an `io.Reader` using the `NewReader()` methods and directly send the data as a response to the client. Exercise 11.1 will give you an opportunity to implement this.

EXERCISE 11.1: SENDING THE DATA AS A RESPONSE   Update the `packageGetHandler()` function to recognize a query parameter, `download`, which if passed by the client, will send back the file data directly as a response. Make sure that you set the right `Content-Type` and `Content-Disposition` headers so that the clients can decide how to handle the file data.

Once you have finished local development with MinIO, to point your package server to an AWS S3 bucket, all you need to do is to specify the bucket name, the right access credentials, and the region:

```
$ AWS_DEFAULT_REGION=ap-southeast-2 BUCKET_NAME=<your bucker name> \
< AWS_ACCESS_KEY_ID=<aws access key id>\
AWS_SECRET_ACCESS_KEY=<aws-secret-key> ./pkg-server-1
```

Next, let's see how we can write automated tests for our handler functions.

Testing Package Uploads

To test the package uploading functionality, we will use a filesystem-based bucket as implemented by the `go.dev/blob/fileblob` driver package. We will first write a function to return a `blob.Bucket` object referring to a filesystem-based bucket:

```go
func getTestBucket(tmpDir string) (*blob.Bucket, error) {
        myDir, err := os.MkdirTemp(tmpDir, "test-bucket")
        if err != nil {
                return nil, err
        }
        u, err := url.Parse(fmt.Sprintf("file:///%s", myDir))
        if err != nil {
                return nil, err
        }
        opts := fileblob.Options{
                URLSigner: fileblob.NewURLSignerHMAC(
                        u,
                        []byte("super secret"),
                ),
        }
        return fileblob.OpenBucket(myDir, &opts)
}
```

We use the `fileblob` package directory to open a filesystem-based bucket. The reason for doing so is to be able to add the functionality for creating signed URLs. We create a `fileblob.Options` object, configure a `URLSigner` function with a base URL that starts with `file:///`, the URL scheme that points to the temporary directory we created, and a dummy secret, `super secret`.

Inside a test function, we will then call the `getTestBucket()` function and create the `appConfig` object as follows:

```go
func TestPackageRegHandler(t *testing.T) {
        packageBucket, err := getTestBucket(t.TempDir())
        if err != nil {
                t.Fatal(err)
        }
        defer packageBucket.Close()
```

```
            config := appConfig{
                    logger:          log.New(
os.Stdout, "", log.Ldate|log.Ltime|log.Lshortfile),
                    packageBucket: packageBucket,
            }
            mux := http.NewServeMux()
            setupHandlers(mux, config)

            ts := httptest.NewServer(mux)
            defer ts.Close()

            p := pkgData{
                    Name:     "mypackage",
                    Version:  "0.1",
                    Filename: "mypackage-0.1.tar.gz",
                    Bytes:    strings.NewReader("data"),
            }
       # Rest of the test
    }
```

You can find the test function for testing the package registration handler function in the `package_reg_handler_test.go` file inside the `chap11/pkg-server-1` directory of the book's source repository.

The test for the handler function to download a package will verify the redirect behavior only. If we can verify that the handler function is able to generate a redirect as a response, we know that it has done its job. Here's how we can verify that using a new test function, `TestPackageGetHandler()`, with only the key statements shown:

```
func TestPackageGetHandler(t *testing.T) {
        // TODO Get test bucket
        err = packageBucket.WriteAll(
                context.Background(),
                "test-object-id",
                []byte("test-data"),
                nil,
        )
        # TODO Error handling, configuration and test server setup
        var redirectUrl string
        client := http.Client{
                CheckRedirect: func(
                        req *http.Request, via []*http.Request,
                ) error {
                        redirectUrl = req.URL.String()
                        return errors.New("no redirect")
                },
        }
```

```
        _, err = client.Get(ts.URL + "/api/packages?id=test-object-id")
        if err == nil {
                t.Fatal("Expected error: no redirect, Got nil")
        }
        if !strings.HasPrefix(redirectUrl, "file:///") {
                t.Fatalf("Expected redirect url to start with file:///,
 got: %v", redirectUrl)
        }
}
```

We create an object directly with a crafted object identifier in the test bucket. Then, as you will recall from Chapter 4, we must create an HTTP client using a custom `CheckRedirect` function to ensure that it doesn't automatically follow redirects. Next, we make an HTTP GET request using this client to the test server URL for obtaining the package with id `test-object-id`. Then, we verify that the string value in `redirectUrl` containing the redirected location begins with `file:///`, pointing to our filesystem-based bucket that we have set up. You can find the complete test function in the `package_get_handler_test.go` file inside the `chap11/pkg-server-1` directory of the book's source code repository. Run `go test` to ensure that the tests pass.

Accessing Underlying Driver Types

So far, you have seen how to use various higher-level interfaces provided by the `gocloud.dev/blob` packages to interact with an AWS S3 compatible storage service. Additionally, you have learned how to use the `gocloud.dev/blob/fileblob` package as a filesystem-backed object storage service for your tests. If you wanted to change the object storage service in the future, all you will need to change now is how you open the bucket or create the `*blob.Bucket` object. The rest of your application code will not need to change. That is the power that the `gocloud.dev/blob` package provides us.

Occasionally, however, you may have to access the underlying vendor-specific functionality directly, which is not provided by `gocloud.dev/blob`. To enable this use case, the `gocloud.dev/blob` package provides the ability to *convert* a type that has been defined by `gocloud.dev/blob` into the underlying vendor-specific driver's type. Once the conversion has been successful, you can then access the underlying driver's functionality directly. If you were referring to a bucket in AWS S3, you would then directly be able to access the functionality offered by the AWS SDK for Go and similarly for other supported object storage services.

Let's see an example. The `blob.OpenBucket()` function doesn't return an error if the bucket that we are opening is nonexistent. In fact, the `gocloud.dev/blob` package doesn't allow us a way to check that. The underlying AWS SDK's driver-specific type, however, does allow us to check. Consider the following code snippet:

```
func main() {
        bucketName := "practicalgo-echorand"
        testBucket, err := blob.OpenBucket(
                context.Background(),
                fmt.Sprintf("s3://%s", bucketName),
        )
        if err != nil {
                log.Fatal(err)
        }
        defer testBucket.Close()

        var s3Svc *s3.S3
        if !testBucket.As(&s3Svc) {
                log.Fatal(
                        "Couldn't convert type to underlying S3
    bucket type",
                )
        }
        _, err = s3Svc.HeadBucket(
                &s3.HeadBucketInput{
                        Bucket: &bucketName,
                },
        )
        if err != nil {
                log.Fatalf(
                        "Bucket doesn't exist, or
    insufficient permissions: %v\n",
                        err,
                )
        }
}
```

The *blob.Bucket object returned by the OpenBucket() function is convertible to an *s3.S3 type defined in the github.com/aws/aws-sdk-go/s3 package. Hence, we declare a variable s3Svc of type *s3.S3 and call the As() method defined on the testBucket object. The As() method returns true if the conversion was successful, else it returns false. If it was successful, we can then use the s3Svc object to call the HeadBucket() method, which is defined on the s3.S3 object to make a HTTP HEAD request checking if the bucket exists or not. A non-nil error value indicates either the bucket is nonexistent or the current credentials do not have the necessary permissions. You can find the runnable program listing in the chap11/object-store-demo/vendor-as-demo directory. To find out what underlying types are exposed by gocloud.dev/blob, look up the package documentation for the specific drivers.

Terminate both the MinIO server and the package server processes. In the next section, we will update the package server by adding the ability to store the *metadata*—name, version, and owner related to each package—using a relational database. This will then additionally enable the ability to query packages using their names or versions from the package server. In other words, we are adding a queryable state to our package server by using a relational database.

Working with Relational Databases

Popular examples of relational database management systems are MySQL, PostgreSQL, and SQLite. For our package server, we will use MySQL as the relational database server. These database systems are built on the concept of storing tables and relationships between them. We will create a database, package_server, with two tables: packages and users. A row in the packages table will contain the package name, version, creation time stamp in Coordinated Universal Time (UTC), the owner, and an identifier, which is unique for each uploaded version of a package. A row in the users table will contain a username column used to authenticate to the system and an identifier uniquely identifying a user in the system. We will not be implementing any authentication or authorization in our application to keep things simple. We will allow a user to upload multiple versions of a package, and we want the users of our server to be able to download any version of the package. An existing package version cannot be re-uploaded. Figure 11.3 shows the entity-relationship model of the package_server database.

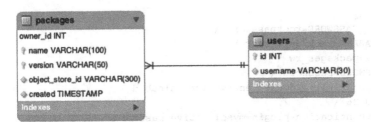

Figure 11.3: Entity relationship diagram for the package server database

We will first run a local copy of MySQL database server using Docker and bootstrap the server by creating the expected database tables and pre-fill some data. The directory chap11/pkg-server-2/mysql-init also contains the necessary Structured Query Language (SQL) scripts to perform this bootstrap operation. First, we create the two tables, users and packages, using the SQL statements in the file 01-create-table.sql:

```
use package_server;
```

```
CREATE TABLE users (
    id INT PRIMARY KEY AUTO_INCREMENT,
    username VARCHAR(30) NOT NULL
);

CREATE TABLE packages(
    owner_id INT NOT NULL,
    name VARCHAR(100) NOT NULL,
    version VARCHAR(50) NOT NULL,
    object_store_id VARCHAR(300) NOT NULL,
    created TIMESTAMP DEFAULT CURRENT_TIMESTAMP NOT NULL,
    PRIMARY KEY (owner_id, name, version),
    FOREIGN KEY (owner_id)
        REFERENCES users(id)
        ON DELETE CASCADE
);
```

Once the first script is run, SQL statements from a second script `02-insert-data` `.sql` will be run to insert five synthetic rows into the users table:

```
INSERT INTO users (username) VALUES ("joe_cool"), ("jane_doe"),
("go_fer"), ("gopher"), ("bill_bob");
```

This will allow us to choose one of the five users as an owner for a package being uploaded. Run the following command from a terminal session to run a local MySQL server using Docker:

```
$ cd chap11/pkg-server-2
$ docker run \
    -p 3306:3306 \
    -e MYSQL_ROOT_PASSWORD=rootpassword \
    -e MYSQL_DATABASE=package_server \
    -e MYSQL_USER=packages_rw \
    -e MYSQL_PASSWORD=password \
    -v "$(pwd)/mysql-init":/docker-entrypoint-initdb.d \
    -ti mysql:8.0.26 \
    --default-authentication-plugin=mysql_native_password
```

Leave the database server running.

Integration with Package Server

To interact with relational databases, we will use the `database/sql` package along with a *driver* package, which will be a third-party package specific to the database with which our application is interacting. The Go community maintains a list of drivers at `https://github.com/golang/go/wiki/SQLDrivers` for various SQL databases. If you use a driver that satisfies the interface as laid down by database/sqlpackage, your application code is independent of the underlying database product with which you are interacting. This in fact is very similar to what using gocloud.dev/blob seeks to achieve for cloud-based object services and others. To interact with a SQL database using database/sql, the first step is to create a connection to it using the sql.Open() function:

```
db, err := sql.Open("mysql", dsn)
```

The function accepts two arguments. The first argument is a string containing the driver's name that we want to use and the second is another string containing the Data Source Name (DSN) to use to connect to the database. Each SQL driver registers a name indicating the specific relational database with which it is communicating. The driver that we will use is the one provided by the https://github.com/go-sql-driver/mysql package. This driver's name is mysql. The DSN we will use to connect to the database will contain the username, the password, the network address of the database, and the name of the database to which we will connect. An example DSN is packages_rw:password@tcp(127.0.0.1:3306)/package_server. This DSN specifies that we want to communicate with the database, package_server, on a MySQL server running on the local computer and listening on port 3306 using packages_rw and password as the username and password, respectively.

The Open() function returns two values: one of type *sql.DB and an error value. The *sql.DB object encapsulates a pool of connections to the database, automatically creating and freeing up connections. You can control the maximum number of open connections, maximum lifetime of a connection, and maximum number of idle connections using the methods SetMaxOpenConns(), SetConnMaxLifeTime(), and SetConnMaxIdleTime(), respectively. Each of the methods accepts a time.Duration object as an argument. It's important to note that calling the Open() function doesn't necessarily set up a connection to the specified database. Hence, it's a good idea to call the Ping() method to verify if a connection can be established successfully using the specified DSN.

We will define a function to create and return a *sql.Db object:

```
func getDatabaseConn(
        dbAddr, dbName, dbUser, dbPassword string,
) (*sql.DB, error) {
        dsn := fmt.Sprintf("%s:%s@tcp(%s)/%s",
                dbUser, dbPassword,
                dbAddr, dbName,
        )
        return sql.Open("mysql", dsn)
}
```

A *sql.Db object will be created at startup for a server application and remain alive for the lifetime of the server. Thus, the sql.Open() function is called only once during a server process's lifetime. A code snippet from the `main()` function of the modified package server shows how this is done:

```
func main() {
        // TODO Read object store details
        dbAddr     := os.Getenv("DB_ADDR")
        dbName     := os.Getenv("DB_NAME")
        dbUser     := os.Getenv("DB_USER")
        dbPassword := os.Getenv("DB_PASSWORD")

        if len(dbAddr) == 0 || len(dbName) == 0 || len(dbUser) == 0
 || len(dbPassword) == 0 {
                log.Fatal(
                        "Must specify DB details - DB_ADDR, DB_NAME,
 DB_USER, DB_PASSWORD",
                )
        }

        db, err := getDatabaseConn(
                dbAddr, dbName,
                dbUser, dbPassword,
        )
        config := appConfig{
                logger: log.New(
                        os.Stdout, "",
                        log.Ldate|log.Ltime|log.Lshortfile,
                ),
                packageBucket: packageBucket,
                db:            db,
        }
        // Server startup code
}
```

Once we have the `*sql.DB` object, to execute a query on the server, we will call the `Conn()` method to obtain a `*sql.Conn` object:

```
ctx := context.Background()
conn, err := config.db.Conn(ctx)
defer conn.Close()
```

Once we are done with the connection, we must ensure that the `Close()` method is called so that the connection is returned to the pool. It may be helpful to think of the `*sql.DB` object as an abstraction that maintains the underlying pool of real `*sql.Conn` objects. Once we have a connection, that is, a `*sql.Conn` object, we can execute SQL queries. For queries that will only fetch data, that is, SELECT statements, we will use the `QueryContext()` method of the `*sql.Conn` object. For queries where we will perform an action such as INSERT, DELETE, or UPDATE, we will use the `ExecContext()` method of the `*sql.Conn` object. Let's learn how to use these methods by adding the ability to store and query data from a relational database in the package server.

After uploading a package to the object store, we will store the package's metadata by adding a new row to the packages table using an INSERT SQL statement in a new function, updateDb(). The package registration handler function will look as follows:

```
// This always returns the owner id as one of [1, 5] as the
// bootstrapping code only
// populates the users table with these records and since we have
// foreign key relationships
// the package owner must be one of those
func getOwnerId() int {
        return rand.Intn(4) + 1
}

func packageRegHandler(
        w http.ResponseWriter,
        r *http.Request,
        config appConfig,
) {
        # TODO Read the incoming data
        packageOwner := getOwnerId()
        # Upload data to object store
        nBytes, err := uploadData(config, d.ID, fHeader)
        # TODO Error handling
        # Add package metadata to database
        err = updateDb(
                config,
                pkgRow{
                        OwnerId:       packageOwner,
                        Name:          packageName,
                        Version:       packageVersion,
                        ObjectStoreId: d.ID,
                },
        )
        # TODO Send back response
}
```

You will recall that we inserted five rows into the users table when setting up the database. We define the getOwnerId() function to return an integer between 1 and 5, both inclusive to correspond to the owner of a package. The definition of the updateDb() function is as follows:

```
func updateDb(config appConfig, row pkgRow) error {
        ctx := context.Background()
        conn, err := config.db.Conn(ctx)
        if err != nil {
                return err
        }
        defer conn.Close()
```

```
        result, err := conn.ExecContext(
            ctx,
            `INSERT INTO packages
            (owner_id, name, version, object_store_id)
            VALUES (?,?,?,?);`,
            row.OwnerId, row.Name, row.Version, row.ObjectStoreId,
        )
    if err != nil {
        return err
    }
    nRows, err := result.RowsAffected()
    if err != nil {
        return err
    }
    if nRows != 1 {
        return fmt.Errorf(
            "expected 1 row to be inserted, Got: %v",
            nRows,
        )
    }
    return nil
}
```

The function is called with two arguments. The first, config, is an appConfig object that contains a new field, db, of type *sql.DB, referring to a pool of connections to the MySQL database. We then obtain a connection from this pool using config.db.Conn(ctx). The second argument, row, is an object of type pkgRow, which is defined as follows:

```
type pkgRow struct {
    OwnerId       int
    Name          string
    Version       string
    ObjectStoreId string
    Created       string
}
```

pkgRow corresponds to a row stored in the packages table, and it will be our application's in-memory representation of a package when inserting a row into the database table or when querying one. If we obtained the connection successfully, we run the INSERT query as follows:

```
result, err := conn.ExecContext(
        ctx,
        `INSERT INTO packages
        (owner_id, name, version, object_store_id)
        VALUES (?,?,?,?);`,
        row.OwnerId, row.Name, row.Version, row.ObjectStoreId,
    )
```

The first argument to the `ExecContext()` method is an object of type `context.Context`. The second argument is the SQL query to execute. Note that we do not pass the values as part of the query but instead use the placeholder character, `?`. This prevents malicious users of our applications from carrying out *SQL injection* attacks. Then we pass the different values that we would want to use for the columns in the same order. Internally, the Go MySQL driver uses MySQL's support for *prepared statements* to execute the query. It first creates the prepared statement. Then it sends the values with which to execute the prepared statement. The `ExecContext()` method returns two values: `result` of type `sql.Result`, and `err`, an error value. The type `sql.Result` is an interface defined as follows:

```
type Result interface {
        LastInsertId() (int64, error)
        RowsAffected() (int64, error)
}
```

The behavior of both of these methods is database dependent. If we get back a `nil` error from the call to the `ExecContext()` method, the statement was successfully executed. Then, if we call the `LastInsertId()` method, the value returned *may* be the value of the automatically incremented column corresponding to the successful INSERT, DELETE, or UPDATE operation. Since we don't have any auto-incrementing column in the packages table, if we call this method, we will get back a value of 0. The `RowsAffected()` method returns the number of rows affected by the statement just executed. This is useful to ensure that the SQL statement executed had the expected effect. In the `updateDb()` function, we expect that one row should be affected; that is, inserted. We return an error if that's not the case.

Next, we will update the `packageGetHandler()` function so that the user can download a package data by specifying its metadata—owner id, name, and version. We define a new type `pkgQueryParams` to encapsulate the query parameters:

```
type pkgQueryParams struct {
        name    string
        version string
        ownerId int
}
```

The handler function is updated as follows:

```
func packageGetHandler(
        w http.ResponseWriter, r *http.Request, config appConfig,
) {
        queryParams := r.URL.Query()
        owner := queryParams.Get("owner_id")
        name := queryParams.Get("name")
```

```go
        version := queryParams.Get("version")
        // TODO Return a HTTP 400 Bad Request error if
        // any of the above is missing

        ownerId, err := strconv.Atoi(owner)

        // TODO Return a HTTP 400 error if the conversion was
        // not successful

        q := pkgQueryParams{
                ownerId: ownerId,
                version: version,
                name:    name,
        }
        pkgResults, err := queryDb(
                config, q,
        )
        // TODO error handling

        if len(pkgResults) == 0 {
                http.Error(w, "No package found", http.StatusNotFound)
                return
        }
        url, err := config.packageBucket.SignedURL(
                r.Context(),
                pkgResults[0].ObjectStoreId,
                nil,
        )
        if err != nil {
                http.Error(
                        w, err.Error(), http.StatusInternalServerError,
                )
                return
        }
        http.Redirect(w, r, url, http.StatusTemporaryRedirect)
}
```

In the handler function, we look for three query parameters in the incoming request URL: owner_id, name, and version. We will return an HTTP bad request error if any of the parameters were not specified or the value of owner_id couldn't be successfully converted to an integer.

Then we create a new object of type pkgQueryParams containing the values of these query parameters and call the queryDb() function. The queryDb() function returns two values: the first is a slice of pkgRow objects and the second is an error value. If we get back an empty slice, we send back an HTTP 404 status as the response. Otherwise, we retrieve the first item in the slice, call the SignedURL() method defined in config.packageObject to generate the signed URL, and then redirect to it. Let's look at the definition of queryDb() function next.

The function will first build the query to send to the database, which will be of the form `SELECT * FROM packages WHERE owner_id=1 AND name=test-package AND version=0.1`. Even though in this scenario we must have all of the conditions specified, we will write the function in a way that any one of the conditions is sufficient to fetch packages. (You will find this useful when attempting Exercise 11.2.) Hence, we must be able to build a query such as `SELECT * FROM packages WHERE owner_id=1 AND name=test-package` or `SELECT * FROM packages WHERE owner_id=1`.

The following code snippet shows the `queryDb()` function partially where we build the query:

```
func queryDb(
        config appConfig, params pkgQueryParams,
) ([]pkgRow, error) {

        args := []interface{}{}
        conditions := []string{}
        if params.ownerId != 0 {
                conditions = append(conditions, "owner_id=?")
                args = append(args, params.ownerId)
        }
        if len(params.name) != 0 {
                conditions = append(conditions, "name=?")
                args = append(args, params.name)
        }
        if len(params.version) != 0 {
                conditions = append(conditions, "version=?")
                args = append(args, params.version)
        }

        if len(conditions) == 0 {
                return nil, fmt.Errorf("no query conditions found")
        }

        query := fmt.Sprintf(
                "SELECT * FROM packages WHERE %s",
                strings.Join(conditions, " AND "),
        )
        // TODO Execute the query
}
```

We create two slices that we will incrementally populate based on the fields in the params object. `args` is a slice of the empty interface, `interface{}` type, where we will be storing the values of `owner_id`, `name`, or `version` in this slice. We need to make it an `[]interface{}{}` type, instead of `[]string`, since the `QueryContext()` expects the placeholder values to be provided in that format.

The second slice, `conditions` of type `[]string{}`, is where we will add the conditions that will be part of the query. We check which of the fields are specified and then append the corresponding condition and the corresponding placeholder value to the `conditions` and `args` slices, respectively. If none of the conditions were specified, we return an error.

Finally, we use the `strings.Join()` function with the contents of the `conditions` slice, joining the elements with an AND (with a leading and following space). The resulting string obtained via the call to the `fmt.Sprintf()` function is now ready to be executed:

```
func queryDb(
        config appConfig, params pkgQueryParams,
) ([]pkgRow, error) {
        ctx := context.Background()
        conn, err := config.db.Conn(ctx)
        if err != nil {
                log.Fatal(err)
        }
        defer conn.Close()

        // TODO Build the query as above

        rows, err := conn.QueryContext(ctx, query, args...)
        if err != nil {
                return nil, err
        }
        defer rows.Close()
        // TODO Read the results
}
```

The `QueryContext()` function accepts three arguments:

- The first argument is an object of type `context.Context`.
- The second argument is a string containing the query to be executed.
- The third argument is a slice of `interface{}` values containing the values for the placeholder parameters in the query.

It returns two values: the first, `rows`, is an object of type `*sql.Rows` defined in the `database/sql` package, and the second is an error value. If we get a non-`nil` error value, the query couldn't be executed successfully, and we return from the function. If, however, we get a `nil` error value, we set up a deferred call to the `rows.Close()` method and proceed to read the results returned. Calling `rows.Close()` will ensure that the connection is returned to the pool.

We read the result one row at a time, *enumerating* over the `rows` object as follows:

```
func queryDb(
        config appConfig, params pkgQueryParams,
) ([]pkgRow, error) {
```

```go
// TODO Build the query as above

// TODO Execute the query as above

var pkgResults []pkgRow
for rows.Next() {
        var pkg pkgRow
        if err := rows.Scan(
                &pkg.OwnerId, &pkg.Name, &pkg.Version,
                &pkg.ObjectStoreId, &pkg.Created,
        ); err != nil {
                return nil, err
        }
        pkgResults = append(pkgResults, pkg)
}

if err := rows.Err(); err != nil {
        return nil, err
}
return pkgResults, nil
}
```

Calling the `rows.Next()` method initiates the reading operation. It returns `false` when there is nothing left to read or there was an error when reading a row.

Then we call the `rows.Scan()` method, passing it the references to the destination variables into which we want the individual column values to be read. We must ensure that the order of the references and the columns match. If the `Scan()` was successful, we append the value in `pkg` to the slice, `pkgResults`.

Once we have finished reading all of the rows, or there was an error in reading a row, that is, we are out of the for loop, we call the `Err()` method to check if there was any error. If so, we return it, else we return the slice, `pkgResults`, and a `nil` error value.

You can find the new version of the package server with both the object storage service and database integrations in the `chap11/pkg-server-2` directory of the book's source code repository. The `db_store.go` file contains the functions for interacting with the database. Let's now try out the new functionality that we added. Remember to start the local MinIO service as well in a separate terminal session unless you are using an AWS S3 bucket directly. And in case you don't have the MySQL database running locally, make sure that you have done so as well. Let's build and run the package server:

```
$ cd chap11/pkg-server-2
$ go build
$ AWS_ACCESS_KEY_ID=admin \
  AWS_SECRET_ACCESS_KEY=admin123 \
  BUCKET_NAME=test-bucket \
  S3_ADDR=localhost:9000 \
```

```
DB_ADDR=localhost:3006 \
DB_NAME=package_server \
DB_USER=packages_rw \
DB_PASSWORD=password ./pkg-server
```

From a new terminal session, first let's attempt to download a package that is nonexistent:

```
$ curl "http://127.0.0.1:8080/api/packages?name=test-
package&version=0.1&owner_id=1"
No package found
```

Great, now let's add a package:

```
$ curl -F name=test-package -F version=0.1 \
-F filedata=@image.tgz http://127.0.0.1:8080/api/packages
{"id":"2/test-package-0.1-image.tgz"}
```

You will find the `image.tgz` file in the `chap11/pkg-server-2` directory. Of course, feel free to use any other file. Note the response contains the user id of the owner as well, `2`, and it may be different for you, since we randomly assign an owner. Next, let's attempt to download the package, ensuring that the metadata you use matches the corresponding values you used:

```
$ curl --location "http://127.0.0.1:8080/api/packages?name=test-
package&version=0.1&owner_id=2"
Warning: Binary output can mess up your terminal. Use "--output -"
to tell
Warning: curl to output it to your terminal anyway, or consider
"--output
Warning: <FILE>" to save to a file.
```

`curl` doesn't show the output by default since the response is a non-textual file. If you use a browser instead, your uploaded file will be downloaded or the contents shown inline. Great! We have now verified that both the object storage service and database is now integrated with the package server. You can point your application to a MySQL database server running elsewhere, such as via AWS RDS, and provide it with the corresponding connection details, and everything should just work as they did locally.

Next you have an exercise to attempt to solidify your understanding, Exercise 11.2.

EXERCISE 11.2: PACKAGE QUERY ENDPOINT Update the package server to allow users to query package details using an owner id, a name, or a version. Only specifying a version is invalid. Not specifying any of the query parameters will return all package details. The package metadata returned to the client as a response should be a JSON formatted string.

You may want to use the existing /api/packages endpoint for this functionality and implement a new API endpoint for downloading a package.

Testing Data Storage

When it comes to testing database interactions, there are several approaches one can take. Using mocks, using in-memory SQL databases, and running a local copy of the database are a few of those. We will adopt the third approach. It allows us to test our application similar to how it is configured in a production environment, configured to use a real database server. We will use Docker containers to run a local copy of MySQL, bootstrapping it exactly how we did in the previous section, and start our application pointing to that copy of the database server. Once the tests have completed execution, the MySQL containers will be automatically terminated. To orchestrate the creation and termination of these test containers, we will use a third-party package: https://github .com/testcontainers/testcontainers-go/. Using this package, we will write a function, getTestDb(), which will return a *sql.DB object configured to communicate with the test database server that was spun up:

```
func getTestDb() (testcontainers.Container, *sql.DB, error) {
        bootStrapSqlDir, err := os.Stat("mysql-init")
        if err != nil {
                return nil, nil, err
        }

        cwd, err := os.Getwd()
        if err != nil {
                return nil, nil, err
        }
        bindMountPath := filepath.Join(cwd, bootStrapSqlDir.Name())

        // TODO - Create and start container

}
```

You will recall that when creating a local MySQL Docker container, we volume mounted the mysql-init directory from the chap11/pkg-server-2 directory so that we could create tables and insert records into the users table. We will do the same when creating the test containers as well. We first use the os .Stat() function from the os package to ensure that the directory exists and then construct the absolute path to the directory, storing it in bindMountPath.

We then create a container request as follows:

```
func getTestDb() (testcontainers.Container, *sql.DB, error) {
    // TODO Insert the code shown earlier
    waitForSql := wait.ForSQL("3306/tcp", "mysql",
            func(p nat.Port) string {
                    return "root:rootpw@tcp(" +
                            "127.0.0.1:" + p.Port() +
                            ")/package_server"
            })
    waitForSql.WithPollInterval(5 * time.Second)

    req := testcontainers.ContainerRequest{
            Image:        "mysql:8.0.26",
            ExposedPorts: []string{"3306/tcp"},
            Env: map[string]string{
                    "MYSQL_DATABASE":      "package_server",
                    "MYSQL_USER":          "packages_rw",
                    "MYSQL_PASSWORD":      "password",
                    "MYSQL_ROOT_PASSWORD": "rootpw",
            },
            BindMounts: map[string]string{
                    bindMountPath: "/docker-entrypoint-initdb.d",
            },
            Cmd: []string{
                    "--default-authentication-plugin=
mysql_native_password",
            },
            WaitingFor: waitForSql,
    }

    // TODO Start container and create *sql.Db object

}
```

The first step to creating a container is to create an object of type testcontainers.ContainerRequest defined in the testcontainers package (https://github.com/testcontainers/testcontainers-go/):

- The Image field corresponds to the Docker image that we want to use for the container.

- The ExposedPorts field is a slice of strings of the form port/protocol containing the ports that we want to expose to the host. We only want to expose the port on which MySQL process is listening; that is, 3306. Note that we don't specify a host port mapping, as we will retrieve the mapped host port dynamically.

- The Env field is a map of environment variables that we want to set inside the container. We set the database name, user, password, and the root password using the relevant environment variables.

- The `BindMounts` is a map containing the volume mounts for the container. Here we only have one volume mount—the `mysql-init` directory on the host should be mounted at `/docker-entrypoint-initdb.d` inside the container.

- The `Cmd` field is a string containing the command-line arguments to be specified to the program at container startup.

- The `WaitingFor` field specifies a *waiting strategy*. The value must be an object of a type that satisfies `wait.Strategy`, an interface defined in the `testcontainers/wait` package. It is essentially making sure that the container creation function (shown in the next code snippet) will not return until the waiting strategy specified is satisfied. The package contains a wait strategy for SQL databases implemented by the `waitForSql` type in the `testcontainers/wait` package. It executes the query `SELECT 1` using the specified driver and database connection details to check if the database is ready or not. All we need to do here is call the `wait.ForSQL()` function with three arguments: the port inside the container the server process is listening on, the driver used, and a function that constructs the DSN for connecting to the database. It retrieves the mapped port on the host by calling the `p.Port()` method of the `nat.Port` object with which the function is called. We also set the polling interval to be 5 seconds so that it only checks for the readiness every 5 seconds.

The final step is to start the container and create the `*sql.DB` object by connecting to the started container:

```
func getTestDb() (testcontainers.Container, *sql.DB, error) {
        // TODO Insert the code shown earlier
        // TODO Create the container request as shown above

        ctx := context.Background()
        mysqlC, err := testcontainers.GenericContainer(
                ctx,
                testcontainers.GenericContainerRequest{
                        ContainerRequest: req,
                        Started:          true,
                })
        if err != nil {
                return mysqlC, nil, err
        }

        addr, err := mysqlC.PortEndpoint(ctx, "3306", "")
        if err != nil {
                return mysqlC, nil, err
        }
        db, err := getDatabaseConn(
                addr, "package_server",
```

```
                        "packages_rw", "password",
            )
            if err != nil {
                    return mysqlC, nil, nil
            }
            return mysqlC, db, nil
    }
```

The `testcontainers.GenericContainer()` function accepts two arguments. The first is a value of type `context.Context`, which you can use to control how long you want to allow a container to be ready. The second argument is an object of type `testcontainers.GenericContainerRequest`, where we specify two fields: `ContainerRequest`, whose value is the container request object, `req`, we created earlier; and `Started` set to true, as we want to start the container. This function returns two values: the first is an object of type `testcontainers` `.Container` and the second is an error value. If the function returned a `nil` error value, we call the `PortEndpoint()` method to obtain the address that we can use to connect to the container from the host. Then we call the `getDatabaseConn()` method to obtain the `*sql.DB` object.

You can find the definition of the `getTestDb()` function in the `chap11/pkg-server2/test_utils.go` file. With the ability to create a test MySQL container, we can now start writing tests for the handler functions as well as tests for only the database interaction functions. For example, a test for the package get handler function will be defined as follows:

```
func TestPackageGetHandler(t *testing.T) {
        packageBucket, err := getTestBucket(t.TempDir())
        testObjectId := "pkg-0.1-pkg-0.1.tar.gz"
        // create a test object
        err = packageBucket.WriteAll(
                context.Background(),
                testObjectId, []byte("test-data"),
                nil,
        )

        testC, testDb, err := getTestDb()
        if err != nil {
                t.Fatal(err)
        }
        defer testC.Terminate(context.Background())

        config := appConfig{
                logger: log.New(
                        os.Stdout, "",
log.Ldate|log.Ltime|log.Lshortfile,
                ),
                packageBucket: packageBucket,
                db:            testDb,
        }
```

```
        // update package metadata for the test object
    err = updateDb(
            config,
            pkgRow{
                    OwnerId:      1,
                    Name:         "pkg",
                    Version:      "0.1",
                    ObjectStoreId: testObjectId,
            },
    )
    if err != nil {
            t.Fatal(err)
    }

        // TODO Make HTTP requests and verify results
}
```

We call the `getTestDb()` function to obtain the `*sql.DB` object. Then we make a deferred call to the `Terminate()` method of the returned `testcontainers.Container` value, `testC`, so that the container is terminated at the end of the test run.

Then we create an `appConfig` object with the value of the `db` field to `testDb`. Next, we call the `updateDb()` function to add the package metadata for a test package. This corresponds to the test object that we created earlier in the function. Then we make an HTTP request to download the package data and verify the redirect behavior. You can find the complete definition of the test as well as another test in the `package_get_handler_test.go` file. In the `package_reg_handler_test.go` file, you will find test functions for testing the package registration functionality as well.

Next, we are going to discuss a couple of specific common data type conversion scenarios that you may encounter when working with databases.

Data Type Conversions

When we call the `Scan()` method of the `*sql.Rows` object, an automatic type conversion is being done by the driver package from the column's original data type as represented in the database to the destination variable's type as signified in our application. The reverse process happens when we execute an INSERT or UPDATE statement using the `ExecContext()` method. The documentation for the `Scan()` method describes guidelines around the conversion operations.

The first scenario that we are going to discuss is the requirement to convert TIMESTAMP (and related column types DATETIME and TIME). Consider the `pkgRow` struct once again:

```
type pkgRow struct {
        OwnerId      int
```

```
Name            string
Version         string
ObjectStoreId   string
Created         string
}
```

The `Created` field is used to store the value of the `created` column queried from the packages table. The column created was declared to be of type `TIMESTAMP`. In MySQL, this means that it will always store the date and a time as a Coordinated Universal Time (UTC) value, 2022-01-19 03:14:07, for example. When we execute the `Scan()` method, the value of the created column is read and then stored as a string in the `Created` field of the specified `pkgRow` object. You can then convert this string into a `time.Time` object using the `time.Parse()` function from the `time` package as follows:

```
// results contain the sql.Rows object obtained via calling queryDb()
layout := "2006-01-02 15:04:05"
created := results[0].Created
parsedTime, err := time.Parse(layout, created)
if err != nil {
        t.Fatal(err)
}
```

An alternative approach may be for you to take advantage of the MySQL driver's automatic parsing feature. If you add `parseTime=true` to the DSN when connecting to the database, it will automatically attempt to parse a `TIMESTAMP`, `DATETIME`, and `DATE` column into a `time.Time` type. The `getDatabaseConn()` function will appear as follows:

```
func getDatabaseConn(
        dbAddr, dbName, dbUser, dbPassword string,
) (*sql.DB, error) {
        dsn := fmt.Sprintf(
                "%s:%s@tcp(%s)/%s?parseTime=true",
                dbUser, dbPassword,
                dbAddr, dbName,
        )
        return sql.Open("mysql", dsn)
}
```

Then we will redefine the `pkgRow` struct such that the `Created` field is of type `time.Time`:

```
type pkgRow struct {
        // other fields as earlier
        Created      time.Time
}
```

Now, when we call the `Scan()` function, the `Created` field will contain the value of the `created` column, the package creation time in UTC as a `time.Time` value. It is worth being mindful here, though, that the `Scan()` method will fail if the parsing fails. Hence, if you don't trust the data in your database, it may be worth considering explicitly parsing `TIMESTAMP` and other related fields in your applications.

In the second scenario, we are going to look at handling `NULL` data from databases. Say that we add a new column to the `packages` table, `repo_url`:

```
CREATE TABLE packages(
  -- TODO other columns
  repo_url VARCHAR(300) DEFAULT NULL,
)
```

This column will *optionally* contain a URL to the source code repository for the package. If you try to scan a `NULL` value of this column into a string data type, it will fail. Hence, the `database/sql` package defines special data types to handle `NULL` values. The correct type to use here is the `sql.NullString` type:

```
type pkgRow struct {
        // other fields
        RepoURL        sql.NullString
}
```

The `sql.NullString` defines a `Boolean` field, `Valid`, which will be `true` if there is a non-`NULL` value stored in the `repo_url` column. If the value of `Valid` is `true`, the `String` field contains the string itself. Adding a row to the database will look slightly different too. First, we create a `pkgRow` object as follows:

```
pkgRow{
        // other fields
        RepoURL: sql.NullString{
                String: "http://github.com/practicalgo/code",
                Valid: true,
        },
},
```

Then, we will update and execute the `updateDb()` function as follows:

```
func updateDb(config appConfig, row pkgRow) error {
        # TODO: Get DB connection
        columnNames := []string{
                "owner_id", "name", "version", "object_store_id",
        }
        valuesPlaceholder := []string{"?", "?", "?", "?"}
        args := []interface{}{
                row.OwnerId, row.Name, row.Version, row.ObjectStoreId,
        }
```

```
            if row.RepoURL.Valid {
                    columnNames = append(columnNames, "repo_url")
                    valuesPlaceholder = append(valuesPlaceholder, "?")
                    args = append(args, row.RepoURL.String)
            }
            query := fmt.Sprintf(
                    "INSERT INTO packages (%s) VALUES (%s);",
                    strings.Join(columnNames, ","),
                    strings.Join(valuesPlaceholder, ","),
            )

            result, err := conn.ExecContext(
                    ctx, query, args...,
            )
    # TODO process results
    }
```

Since the repo_url column is not mandatory, we check if the pkgRow object has a valid RepoURL field, and if so, update the SQL statement to account for that.

Besides the sql.NullString type, the database/sql package defines equivalent types to handle NULL column values for time.Time, float64, int32, int64, and other Go types. In the chap11/mysql-demo directory of the book's source code repository, you will find code listings along with tests with which you can experiment in order to understand the preceding concepts better.

In the last section of the chapter, you will learn how you can use database transactions from your applications.

Using Database Transactions

To start a transaction, we will call the BeginTx() method defined on the *sql.Conn object. It returns two values: the first value is of type *sql.Tx, and the second is an error value. If we successfully obtained a *sql.Tx value, we would execute SQL queries using the ExecContext() method defined on that object. Here's an example from a modified updateDb() function of the package server:

```
func updateDb(ctx context.Context, config appConfig, row pkgRow) error {
        conn, err := config.db.Conn(ctx)
        if err != nil {
                return err
        }
        defer conn.Close()

        tx, err := conn.BeginTx(ctx, nil)
        if err != nil {
                return err
        }
```

```
        result, err := tx.ExecContext(
                ctx,
                `INSERT INTO packages
(owner_id, name, version, object_store_id) VALUES (?,?,?,?);`,
                row.OwnerId, row.Name, row.Version, row.ObjectStoreId,
        )
        if err != nil {
                rollbackErr := tx.Rollback()
                log.Printf("Txn Rollback Error:%v\n", rollbackErr)
                return err
        }
        return tx.Commit()
}
```

The `BeginTx()` method accepts two arguments: the first is an object of type `context.Context` and the second is an object of type `sql.TxOptions` defined in the `database/sql` package:

```
type TxOptions struct {
        Isolation IsolationLevel
        ReadOnly  bool
}
```

The `Isolation` field specifies the isolation level of the transaction. If not specified, it defaults to the MySQL driver's default isolation level. The MySQL driver that we are using uses the MySQL storage engine's default isolation level.

If we get an error when executing the query, we call the `Rollback()` method to roll back the transaction. If we get an error when rolling back the transaction, we log it and return the original error. If the query was executed successfully, we execute any other queries if desired. If all the queries are executed successfully, we call the `tx.Commit()` method to commit the transaction. The `Commit()` method returns an error value, which we also return.

At the application level, a big advantage of running a query within a transaction is that it will automatically be rolled back if the context specified when creating the transaction is canceled. This allows us to implement behavior in our server where, if a client cancels a request or it is otherwise canceled, the transaction is also automatically rolled back. For example, we can update the package registration handler function as follows:

```
func packageRegHandler(
        w http.ResponseWriter,
        r *http.Request,
        config appConfig,
) {
        // TODO Upload package to object store
        err = updateDb(
```

```
                r.Context(),
                config,
                pkgRow{
                        OwnerId:       packageOwner,
                        Name:          packageName,
                        Version:       packageVersion,
                        ObjectStoreId: d.ID,
                },
        )
        // TODO: other code
}
```

Similar strategies are possible to implement in your gRPC applications in response to client disconnections as well. You can find an updated implementation of the package server code using transactions in the directory, `chap11/pkg-server-2-transactions` of the book's source repository.

Summary

In this chapter, you learned how to store data persistently from your applications. We started off by learning how to store unstructured data blobs in an object storage service. We used the `gocloud.dev/blob` package to interact with object storage services in a vendor-neutral manner. Using this package, switching object storage service will require minimal changes in your application. Additionally, it also allowed us to implement tests for our functionality using the `gocloud.dev/blob/fileblob` package, which implements a filesystem-based object storage service.

You then learned how to store data in a relational database from our applications. You learned to store and query data from MySQL using the standard interface provided by the `database/sql` package and a MySQL driver that conforms to that that interface. Like `gocloud.dev`, `database/sql` allows us to write applications that require minimal changes when switching database vendors. You learned how to test your applications using a helpful third-party package, which allows us to run MySQL in a container locally.

That's it! You have finished the last chapter of the book. In the two appendices, you will learn to add instrumentation capabilities to your applications and get acquainted with useful techniques to distribute and deploy your applications.

Making Your Applications Observable

In this appendix, I will provide some guidelines around implementing techniques to make your application behavior observable via *telemetry data*. These data are usually categorized into *logs*, *metrics*, and *traces*. All three kinds of data can help you understand what your application is doing and help you answer different kinds of questions about its internal state at a given point of time. First, we will go over the categories of telemetry data that are useful to emit from an application and Go packages that help you implement them. Then we will look at examples of how you can integrate them into your applications.

Logs, Metrics, and Traces

In the book so far we have used functions defined in the standard library's `log` package such as `Printf()` and `Fatal()` to log messages from our applications. This logging technique is easy to implement and better than not having any logging at all. You can search for logs in your logging system using the text in the logs, but that becomes less useful when you want to search for specific data *inside* the logs. A very common operation is to search for logs having some specific context, or metadata, related to a request—for example, all logs for a particular command, a particular HTTP path, or a gRPC method. With the logging techniques that we have used so far, searches such as these are expensive and inefficient. Thus, you will have to find a way to emit logs from your applications such that each log line conforms to a specific structure—individually marked fields containing the log data as well as the contextual information as metadata. There are various approaches to implement such a logging mechanism, and they are all usually referred to as *structured logging*. Instead of log lines being free-form texts, each log line instead consists of *fields* of data, typically as key-value pairs or as a JSON formatted string.

In Chapter 6, "Advanced HTTP Server Applications," Listing 6.2, we defined a logging middleware (`loggingMiddleware()`) to emit log lines as follows:

```
config.Logger.Printf(
        "protocol=%s path=%s method=%s duration=%f status=%d",
        r.Proto, r.URL.Path, r.Method,
        time.Now().Sub(startTime).Seconds(),
        customRw.code,
)
```

A log line emitted from this application consists of key-value pairs, separated by a space, for example, `protocol=HTTP path=/api duration=0.05 status=200`. This is an improvement over simply logging a line such as `HTTP request for /api/search received. Response 200. Duration: 0.1 second.` Most logging systems have in-built support for *parsing* and *indexing* log lines in this format, and hence each of the key-value pairs are searchable individually. This format has been referred to as `logfmt` in the community after a blog post from *Stripe* entitled "Canonical Log Lines" (`https://stripe.com/blog/canonical-log-lines`). Constructing a log line such as the above is cumbersome using `Printf()` or any of the `log` package's functions. Hence, you can use a third-party package `https://github.com/go-logfmt/logfmt` to build a log line formatted as key-value pairs. This package implements an encoder and decoder only, and hence you will still use the standard library's logging functions to log the formatted log lines. Another third-party package, `https://github.com/apex/log`, supports emitting logs in the `logfmt` style, and you can use it in place of the standard library's `log` package.

Another approach for implementing structured logging is to use libraries that emit log lines as JSON encoded strings. In this format, the previous example log line would look like this: `{"protocol":"HTTP","path":"api","duration": 0.05, "status": 200}`. This is likely the most popular structured logging format out there, and there are a few options to implement this format. One of the earliest packages was `https://github.com/sirupsen/logrus`, and it implemented an API that is fully compatible with the one implemented by the standard library's `log.Logger` type. In recent years, other packages such as `https://github.com/uber-go/zap` and `https://github.com/rs/zerolog` have been developed that provide more features as well as better performance. In the next section, you will see how to integrate the `github.com/rs/zerolog` package in your applications. We choose it over `zap`, as it implements a simpler API.

Next, we will discuss how you can export metrics from your applications.

Metrics are numbers that you calculate and publish from your application that quantify various behaviors of your application. Examples of such behavior are the time taken to execute a command from your command-line application, the latency measurement of an HTTP request or a gRPC method call, and the time taken to execute a database operation.

A metric is usually one of three key categories: *counters, gauges,* or *histograms.* A *counter metric* type is used for measurements whose value is an integer and is *monotonically increasing*—number of requests served by an application over its lifetime, for example. A *gauge metric* is used for measurements that may increase or decrease over time, and it can take integral or floating-point values—the memory usage of your application or the number of requests served by your application per second for example. A *histogram metric* is used for recording observations such as latency of a request. Compared to a gauge metric, a histogram metric would typically be used for analysis by grouping the metric values into buckets and enabling calculations such as arbitrary percentile values.

Once an application has calculated the metrics, either they are sent to an external monitoring system (the *push model*) or the monitoring system will read the data from your application (the *pull model*). Once the data is stored in the monitoring system, you can then query for them, perform various statistical operations, and configure alerts.

Historically, application authors have had to use vendor-specific libraries for making the monitoring data available to the monitoring systems. In recent years, the development of the *OpenTelemetry project* (https://opentelemetry .io/) enabled application authors to export metrics in a vendor-neutral manner, including commercial vendors. Where the metrics end up and how is decoupled from the application's concerns. When you change your monitoring system, your application code remains unchanged. Having said that, as of this book's writing the OpenTelemetry Go community (https://github.com/open-telemetry/ opentelemetry-go) has decided to deprioritize the development of metrics support to focus on the tracing support. Hence, even though support currently exists, we will avoid using it. Instead, we will be exporting metrics directly from the application using https://github.com/DataDog/datadog-go in a format defined by the statsd (https://github.com/statsd/statsd) open-source monitoring solution. Even if your organization is not using statsd directly, there is a good chance that the monitoring solution that is being used supports reading the statsd metric format.

Next, we will discuss how you can export *traces* from your applications.

Traces are telemetry data that track a *transaction* in a system. When a request comes in, there's usually more than one action that happens as part of processing that request. A *trace's lifetime* is the same as the lifetime of a transaction in your application. Each action or event happening during the processing of the transaction will start a *span*. Thus, a trace consists of one or more spans, potentially across system boundaries—multiple services and databases, for example. All spans related to a transaction will share a trace identifier, and hence by using the tracing system, you can visually analyze the latency and success/error value of the various actions that were performed as part of a transaction. Metrics tell you that a transaction is slow, and traces give you more granular information into why it is slow.

For example, consider the package server that we implemented in Chapter 11, "Working with Data Stores." Uploading a package is a transaction that consists of two distinct actions: uploading the package to the object storage service and updating the package metadata to the relational database. Each of these actions emits a trace containing the details about the operation and the time it took for the operation. Since both traces share the transaction identifier, you can see the overall latency of the transaction as well as the latency of each of the constituent actions. This is most useful in a service-oriented architecture, where you have multiple service calls happening during a single transaction. Storage and analysis of tracing data requires specialized systems, and historically you would have to use vendor-specific libraries for sending tracing data to them. However, the OpenTelemetry project's Go libraries make it possible to implement tracing in a vendor-neutral manner. As of this writing, the project (`https://github.com/open-telemetry/opentelemetry-go`) has released the 1.0.0-RC2 version. We will be using this version of the library and only make use of the features related to exporting traces.

In the next section, you will learn about some patterns used to modify the applications that we have written in the book so that they emit telemetry data.

Emitting Telemetry Data

I have created a custom command-line client, `pkgcli`, for interacting with the package server implemented in Chapter 11. I have also modified the package server to communicate with a gRPC server to verify the uploader details. You can find all relevant code and instructions in the `appendix-a` directory of the book's source repository. Storage of logs, metrics, and traces require specialized systems, and there are many open-source and commercial solutions. The examples that follow will only demonstrate emitting the relevant data from applications and not the visualization and analysis of those data. You can find complete instructions for running the demo command-line application and the servers in the file `appendix-a/README.md`.

Command-Line Applications

For command-line applications, we will configure the logging, initializing the network clients for exporting metrics and traces during initialization, before executing any command. Then we make these initialized configurations available to the rest of the application to enable logging any messages, publishing metrics, or exporting a trace during the execution of any command. The code for the sample command-line application, `pkgcli`, is in the `appendix-a/command-line-app` directory. It uses the `flag` package, and it applies the sub-command architecture discussed in Chapter 2, "Advanced Command-Line Applications," to create an application with two sub-commands—`register` and `query`. The first sub-command allows a user to upload a package to the package server, and the second command allows them to query package information from the server. We have created a `config` package, and inside it a struct `PkgCliConfig` to encapsulate the initialized logging configuration, metrics, and tracing clients:

```
type PkgCliConfig struct {
        Logger   zerolog.Logger
        Metrics  telemetry.MetricReporter
        Tracer   telemetry.TraceReporter
}
```

We created a `telemetry` package that contains three functions: `InitLogging()`, `InitMetrics()`, and `InitTracing()`, which returns an initialized `zerolog.Logger`, `telemetry.MetricReporter`, and `telemetry.TraceReporter` objects. The last two custom types are defined to encapsulate clients for publishing metrics and exporting traces, respectively. The file `logging.go` in the `telemetry` package defines the `InitLogging()` function as follows:

```
package telemetry

import (
        "io"
        "github.com/rs/zerolog"
)

func InitLogging(
        w io.Writer, version string, logLevel int,
) zerolog.Logger {

        rLogger := zerolog.New(w)
        versionedL := rLogger.With().Str("version", version)
        timestampedL := versionedL.Timestamp().Logger()
        levelledL := timestampedL.Level(zerolog.Level(logLevel))

        return levelledL
}
```

We call the `zerolog.New()` function from the `github.com/rs/zerolog` package to create a root logger, a `zerolog.Logger` object with the output writer set to `w`. Then we add a logging context to the root logger by calling the `With()` method.

This creates a child logger from the root logger, rLogger, by adding a context using the str() method, which adds a key, version, to all log messages with its value set to the specified string in version. This will result in all logs from the application containing the version of the application in this field.

Next, we add another logging context to add a timestamp to the logs and create another child logger, timestampedL. Finally, we add the logic for levelled logging by calling the Level() method and return the created zerolog.Logger object. The configured logger will only log a message if its level is equal to or greater than the configured level indicated by the value in logLevel. The value of logLevel must be an integer between –1 and 5 (both inclusive). Setting the level to –1 will log all messages and setting the level to 5 will only log panic messages.

The file metrics.go in the telemetry package defines the InitMetrics() function as follows:

```
package telemetry
import (
        "fmt"

        "github.com/DataDog/datadog-go/statsd"
)

type MetricReporter struct {
        statsd *statsd.Client
}

func InitMetrics(statsdAddr string) (MetricReporter, error) {
        var m MetricReporter
        var err error
        m.statsd, err = statsd.New(statsdAddr)
        if err != nil {
                return m, err
        }
        return m, nil
}
```

We choose the github.com/DataDog/datadog-go/statsd package as it's well maintained. We create a client by calling the statsd.New() function, passing the address of the statsd server, and assigning the created client to the MetricReporter object's statsd field. It's worth noting here again that once OpenTelemetry's metrics support is ready for use, we will not be using a vendor-specific library in our application.

We define a type, DurationMetric, to encapsulate a single measurement of how long a command's execution lasted:

```
type DurationMetric struct {
        Cmd            string
        DurationMs float64
        Success        bool
}
```

Then we define a method, `ReportDuration()`, which will push a histogram metric containing how long a command ran. The duration is measured in seconds. Two tags will be added to the metric, which will allow grouping and aggregating the metrics. We add the command that was executed, as specified in `Cmd`, as one tag and whether the command was executed successfully or not, as specified by the `Success` field as the second tag. The method is defined as follows:

```go
func (m MetricReporter) ReportDuration(metric DurationMetric) {
        metricName := "cmd.duration"
        m.statsd.Histogram(
                metricName,
                metric.DurationMs,
                []string{
                        fmt.Sprintf("cmd:%s", metric.Cmd),
                        fmt.Sprintf("success:%v", metric.Success),
                },
                1, //sample rate (0-none, 1 - all)
        )
}
```

Similar methods can be defined for pushing other metric types.

The `InitTracing()` method is defined in the `trace.go` file inside the `telemetry` package. Inside it, we set up the application-wide tracing configuration in the `telemetry` package as follows:

```go
package telemetry

import (
        "context"

        "go.opentelemetry.io/otel"
        "go.opentelemetry.io/otel/trace"
        "go.opentelemetry.io/otel/exporters/jaeger"

        // TODO import other otel packages
)


type TraceReporter struct {
        Client trace.Tracer
        Ctx    context.Context
}

func InitTracing(
        jaegerAddr string,
) (TraceReporter, *sdktrace.TracerProvider, error) {
```

```
    // 1. Setup trace exporter

    // 2. Setup span processor

    // 3. Setup tracer provider

    // 4. Create the propagator

    // 5. Create and configure Tracer

    // 6. Return a value of type TraceReporter

}
```

There are six key steps as explained next. We need a destination to which the traces can be exported so that we can view and query them. We will be using *Jaeger* (www.jaegertracing.io), an open-source distributed tracing system, and hence we use the Jaeger exporter as implemented by the go.opentelemetry .io/otel/exporters/jaeger package.

The following code snippet creates the trace exporter:

```
traceExporter, err := jaeger.New(
        jaeger.WithCollectorEndpoint(
                jaeger.WithEndpoint(jaegerAddr),
        ),
    )
```

Note that we could have instead used the OpenTelemetry collector exporter as implemented by the go.opentelemetry.io/otel/exporters/otlp package and made our application completely neutral to the distributed tracing system that we are using. For simplicity's sake, however, I have used the Jaeger exporter directly.

Next, we set up the span processor that oversees processing the *span* data emitted by your application, configuring it with the trace exporter that we created earlier:

```
bsp := sdktrace.NewSimpleSpanProcessor(traceExporter)
```

For production applications, it is recommended to configure a different span processor, the Batch span processor created as follows:

```
bsp := sdktrace.NewBatchSpanProcessor(traceExporter)
```

The next step is to create the tracer provider using the above span processor:

```
tp := sdktrace.NewTracerProvider(
        sdktrace.WithSpanProcessor(bsp),
        sdktrace.WithResource(
                resource.NewWithAttributes(
                        semconv.SchemaURL,
```

```
                              semconv.ServiceNameKey.String(
                                  "PkgServer-Cli",
                              ),
                         ),
                  ),
           )
```

We create the tracer provider calling the `sdktrace.NewTraceProvider()` with two arguments. The first is the span processor that we created in the previous step. The second argument identifies the application creating the traces described by the OpenTelemetry document "Resource Semantic Conventions." Here we are setting the service name producing these traces as `PkgServer-Cli`. Once we have created the tracer provider as earlier, we then configure it to be the current application's global tracer provider using the following code:

```
otel.SetTracerProvider(tp)
```

Next, we set up the global propagator for the traces, which is how the current application's trace identifier will be transmitted to other services:

```
propagator := propagation.NewCompositeTextMapPropagator(
        propagation.Baggage{},
        propagation.TraceContext{},
)
otel.SetTextMapPropagator(propagator)
The final steps are carried out by the code snippet below:
v1, err := baggage.NewMember("version", "version")
bag, err := baggage.New(v1)
tr.Client = otel.Tracer("")
ctx := context.Background()
tr.Ctx = baggage.ContextWithBaggage(ctx, bag)
return tr, tp, nil
```

When communicating with the package server over HTTP, we will use a specially configured HTTP client provided by the `go.opentelemetry.io/contrib/instrumentation/net/http/otelhttp` package:

```
// pkgregister/pkgregister.go
func RegisterPackage(
        ctx context.Context, cliConfig *config.PkgCliConfig,
        url string, data PkgData,
) (*PkgRegisterResult, error) {
        // Other code deleted

        r, err := http.NewRequestWithContext(
                ctx, http.MethodPost, url+"/api/packages",
                reader,
        )
```

```
if err != nil {
        return nil, err
}
r.Header.Set("Content-Type", contentType)
authToken := os.Getenv("X_AUTH_TOKEN")
if len(authToken) != 0 {
        r.Header.Set("X-Auth-Token", authToken)
}

client := http.Client{
        Transport: otelhttp.NewTransport(http.DefaultTransport),
}
resp, err := client.Do(r)

// process response
}
```

When we use the instrumented HTTP client, spans are emitted automatically during an HTTP request response transaction performed using this client.

In the application's `main()` function, this is what the initialization of the telemetry configuration looks like:

```
func main() {
        var tp *sdktrace.TracerProvider

        cliConfig.Logger = telemetry.InitLogging(
                os.Stdout, version, c.logLevel,
        )
        cliConfig.Metrics, err = telemetry.InitMetrics(c.statsdAddr)
        if err != nil {
                cliConfig.Logger.Fatal().Str("error", err.Error()).Msg(
                        "Error initializing metrics system",
                )
        }

        cliConfig.Tracer, tp, err = telemetry.InitTracing(
                c.jaegerAddr+"/api/traces", version,
        )
        if err != nil {
                cliConfig.Logger.Fatal().Str("error", err.Error()).Msg(
                        "Error initializing tracing system",
                )
        }
        defer func() {
                tp.ForceFlush(context.Background())
                tp.Shutdown(context.Background())
        }()

        err = handleSubCommand(cliConfig, os.Stdout, subCmdArgs)
        if err != nil {
```

```
            cliConfig.Logger.Fatal().Str("error", err.Error()).Msg(
                    "Error executing sub-command",
            )
    }
}
```

You can see how we are using the initialized logger to log structured messages:

```
cliConfig.Logger.Fatal().Str("error", err.Error()).Msg(
                    "Error initializing metrics system",
            )
```

The log messages will appear as follows:

```
{"level":"fatal","version":"0.1","error":"lookup 127.0.0.: no such
host","time":"2021-09-11T12:22:23+10:00","message":
"Error initializing metrics system"}
```

Inside the `HandleRegister()` function in the `cmd` package, you will find examples of levelled logging:

```
cliConfig.Logger.Info().Msg("Uploading package...")
cliConfig.Logger.Debug().Str("package_name", c.name).
        Str("package_version", c.version).
        Str("server_url", c.serverUrl)
```

To report the duration for which the command ran, we implement the following pattern:

```
c.Logger = c.Logger.With().Str("command", "register").Logger()
tStart := time.Now()
defer func() {
        duration := time.Since(startTime).Seconds()
        c.Metrics.ReportDuration(
                telemetry.DurationMetric{
                        Cmd:        "pkgcli.register",
                        DurationMs: duration,
                        Success:    err == nil,
                },
        )
}()
err = cmd.HandleRegister(&c, w, args[1:])
```

Before we call the specific sub-command handler function, we update the logger to create a new context so that all logs will have an additional field, command, set to register, which will identify a log message as being associated with the register sub-command.

We also start a timer, and then in a deferred function we use the ReportDuration() method to report the duration for which the command ran.

In the `HandleRegister()` function defined in the `cmd` package, we create a span before we make the HTTP request to the package server as follows:

```
ctx, span := cliConfig.Tracer.Client.Start(
        cliConfig.Tracer.Ctx,
        "pkgquery.register",
)
defer span.End()
```

Next, let's look at the instrumented version of the package server.

HTTP Applications

For HTTP server applications, we will configure the logging, initializing the network clients for exporting metrics and traces during server startup. Then we make these initialized configurations available to the rest of the application to enable logging any messages, publishing metrics, or exporting a trace during the execution of any command.

The code for the modified package server is in the `appendix-a/http-app` directory. It has been built on top of the version of the package server that we implemented in Chapter 11.

We define a struct `AppConfig` in the config package to encapsulate the application's configuration, including the telemetry configuration:

```
type AppConfig struct {
        PackageBucket *blob.Bucket
        Db            *sql.DB
        UsersSvc      users.UsersClient

        // telemetry
        Logger   zerolog.Logger
        Metrics  telemetry.MetricReporter
        Trace    trace.Tracer
        TraceCtx context.Context
        Span     trace.Span
        SpanCtx  context.Context
}
```

The `telemetry` package defines the methods to initialize all the telemetry configuration in the files `logging.go`, `metrics.go`, and `trace.go`. The `InitLogging()` and `InitMetrics()` methods will be the same as we defined earlier for the command-line application.

The `middleware` package contains the definitions of the middleware for emitting the telemetry data. The logging middleware is defined as follows:

```
func LoggingMiddleware(
        c *config.AppConfig, h http.Handler,
) http.Handler {
```

```
            return http.HandlerFunc(func(
                    w http.ResponseWriter, r *http.Request,
        ) {
                    c.Logger.Printf("Got request - headers:%#v\n", r.Header)
                    startTime := time.Now()
                    h.ServeHTTP(w, r)
                    c.Logger.Info().Str(
                            "protocol",
                            r.Proto,
                    ).Str(
                            "path",
                            r.URL.Path,
                    ).Str(
                            "method",
                            r.Method,
                    ).Float64(
                            "duration",
                            time.Since(startTime).Seconds(),
                    ).Send()
            })
    }
```

You can see an example of structured logging in the preceding code snippet. We construct a log line (internally, a `zerolog.Event` value) by progressively adding the key value fields that we want to add to the log and calling the `Send()` method, which causes the log to be emitted. Request log lines emitted by the `LoggingMiddleware()` function as defined above will appear as follows:

```
{"level":"info","version":"0.1","protocol":"HTTP/1.1",
"path":"/api/packages","method":"POST","duration":0.038707083,
"time":"2021-09-12T08:39:05+10:00"}
```

We define another middleware to push the request processing latency:

```
func MetricMiddleware(c *config.AppConfig, h http.Handler) http.Handler
{
        return http.HandlerFunc(func(
                w http.ResponseWriter, r *http.Request,
        ) {
                startTime := time.Now()
                h.ServeHTTP(w, r)
                duration := time.Since(startTime).Seconds()
                c.Metrics.ReportLatency(
                        telemetry.DurationMetric{
                                DurationMs: duration,
                                Path:       r.URL.Path,
                                Method:     r.Method,
                        },
                )
        })
}
```

The `InitTracing()` method looks slightly different:

```go
func InitTracing(jaegerAddr string) error {
        traceExporter, err := jaeger.New(
                jaeger.WithCollectorEndpoint(
                        jaeger.WithEndpoint(jaegerAddr + "/api/traces"),
                ),
        )
        if err != nil {
                return err
        }
        bsp := sdktrace.NewSimpleSpanProcessor(traceExporter)

        tp := sdktrace.NewTracerProvider(
                sdktrace.WithSpanProcessor(bsp),
                sdktrace.WithResource(
                        resource.NewWithAttributes(
                                semconv.SchemaURL,
                                semconv.ServiceNameKey.String(
                                        "PkgServer",
                                ),
                        ),
                ),
        )
        otel.SetTracerProvider(tp)
        propagator := propagation.NewCompositeTextMapPropagator(
                propagation.Baggage{},
                propagation.TraceContext{},
        )
        otel.SetTextMapPropagator(propagator)
        return nil
}
```

We configure the global tracing provider, but we do not create a trace. Unlike a command-line application, which exits after executing a command, a server will serve multiple requests during its lifetime. Hence, we create a trace for every request using a dedicated middleware.

The `TracingMiddleware()` creates a trace for every new request, and it is defined in the middleware package as follows:

```go
func TracingMiddleware(
        c *config.AppConfig, h http.Handler,
) http.Handler {
        return http.HandlerFunc(func(
                w http.ResponseWriter, r *http.Request,
        ) {
                c.Trace = otel.Tracer("")
                tc := propagation.TraceContext{}
                incomingCtx := tc.Extract(
```

```
                          r.Context(),
                          propagation.HeaderCarrier(r.Header),
                      )
                      c.TraceCtx = incomingCtx

                      ctx, span := c.Trace.Start(c.TraceCtx, r.URL.Path)
                      c.Span = span
                      c.SpanCtx = ctx
                      defer c.Span.End()

                      h.ServeHTTP(w, r)
          })
}
```

We extract the incoming context from the request, then start a new span using this context and set the span name to be the current request path that is being processed. We end the span after processing the request and before we return from this middleware. It's worth noting that even though the `go.opentelemetry.io/contrib/instrumentation/net/http/otelhttp` package defines a middleware to be used for tracing HTTP servers, we define our own middleware here since that will allow us to create spans of our own. For example, in the `UpdateDb()` function in the `storage` package, we will create a span before we start the database transaction and end it after the transaction is committed or rolled back:

```
func UpdateDb(
        ctx context.Context,
        config *config.AppConfig,
        row types.PkgRow,
) error {
        conn, err := config.Db.Conn(ctx)
        if err != nil {
                return err
        }
        defer func() {
                err = conn.Close()
                if err != nil {
                        config.Logger.Debug().Msg(err.Error())
                }
        }()

        _, spanTx := config.Trace.Start(
                config.SpanCtx, "sql:transaction",
        )
        defer spanTx.End()

        tx, err := conn.BeginTx(ctx, nil)
        if err != nil {
                return err
        }
        // Rest of the code
}
```

In the future, an automatically instrumented version of the `database/sql` package will likely be available, and then we will not have to write our own manual tracing code for database operations.

We take advantage of automatically instrumented libraries when creating the gRPC client for communicating with the `Users` service. In `server.go`, you will find the following function:

```
func setupGrpcConn(addr string) (*grpc.ClientConn, error) {
        return grpc.DialContext(
                context.Background(),
                addr,
                grpc.WithInsecure(),
                grpc.WithUnaryInterceptor(
                        otelgrpc.UnaryClientInterceptor(),
                ),
                grpc.WithStreamInterceptor(
                        otelgrpc.StreamClientInterceptor(),
                ),
        )
}
```

The `go.opentelemetry.io/contrib/instrumentation/google.golang .org/grpc/otelgrpc` package defines both client- and server-side interceptors to integrate your gRPC applications with OpenTelemetry.

Next, let's look at the instrumented version of the gRPC server.

gRPC Applications

As with HTTP server applications, we will configure the logging, initializing the network clients for exporting metrics and traces during server startup. The code for the instrumented gRPC server is in the `appendix-a/grpc-server` directory. It is a version of the `Users` service that we created in Chapter 8, "Building RPC Applications with gRPC," and it defines a single unary RPC method, `GetUser()`. The implementation of the service is in the file `usersServiceHandler.go`, in the main package. You can also see an example of sharing data across service handlers by adding additional fields to the `userService` struct, which is the implementation of the `Users` service:

```
type userService struct {
        users.UnimplementedUsersServer
        config config.AppConfig
}
```

```
func (s *userService) GetUser(
        ctx context.Context,
        in *users.UserGetRequest,
) (*users.UserGetReply, error) {
        s.config.Logger.Printf(
                "Received request for user verification: %s\n",
                in.Auth,
        )
        u := users.User{
                Id: rand.Int31n(4) + 1,
        }
        return &users.UserGetReply{User: &u}, nil
}
```

The `grpc.Server` object is created as follows in the `main()` function:

```
s := grpc.NewServer(
        grpc.ChainUnaryInterceptor(
                interceptors.MetricUnaryInterceptor(&config),
                interceptors.LoggingUnaryInterceptor(&config),
                otelgrpc.UnaryServerInterceptor(),
        ),
        grpc.ChainStreamInterceptor(
                interceptors.MetricStreamInterceptor(&config),
                interceptors.LoggingStreamInterceptor(&config),
                otelgrpc.StreamServerInterceptor(),
        ),
)
```

We have defined the metric and the logging interceptors in the `interceptors` package. We also register the interceptors defined by the `go.opentelemetry .io/contrib/instrumentation/google.golang.org/grpc/otelgrpc` package, which gives us automatic instrumentation of the gRPC service handler calls. The `telemetry` package initializes the logging, metric, and tracing configuration. You will find that the initialization code is the same as that used for the HTTP server in the previous section.

With the preceding instrumentation in place for the command-line application, the HTTP server, and the gRPC server, when you make a request for uploading a package, you will be able to see logs, metrics, and traces published from each application. Traces, of course, have the additional advantage of showing the entire transaction as it propagates through the three systems, visually.

Summary

In this appendix, we started off with a quick overview of logs, metrics, and traces. Then you learned about patterns to instrument command-line applications, HTTP clients and servers, and gRPC applications. We implemented structured and levelled logging using `github.com/rs/zerolog`. Then, you learned to export measurements from your applications in the statsd format using `github.com/DataDog/datadog-go`. Finally, you learned to export traces using `github.com/open-telemetry/opentelemetry-go` to correlate transactions across system boundaries.

Deploying Applications

In this appendix, we are going to discuss strategies to manage the configuration, distribution, and deployment of your applications. The landscape is vast, and the specific strategies that you follow are usually determined by the infrastructure into which you are deploying your applications. By no means do I aim to be exhaustive; rather, I only seek to provide you with generic guidelines.

Managing Configuration

We have been using command-line flags and environment variables to specify various *configuration* data in our applications. *Configuration data* are those pieces of information that your application needs to perform a functionality. However, the user shouldn't need to specify them. For example, in Appendix A, "Making Your Applications Observable," we used flags to specify the address of the metrics server. However, the address of the metrics server will not vary with the user's input, such as the package name or version to upload. In fact, in most cases, your application's user is happy to not be required to specify it, unless it is to specifically override it.

Similarly, we have used environment variables to specify both nonsensitive and sensitive configuration data in our applications. For example, the database password, covered in Chapter 11, "Working with Data Stores," was specified as an environment variable. Command-line flags, as well as environment variables, are simple to understand and require no additional libraries for support in your applications. However, as your application grows and the configuration data increases, you will find that you instead want to use other ways to configure your applications and even combine more than one approach such as using command line flags, environment variables and files. For example, using configuration files for nonsensitive data is a straightforward approach. This requires you to write additional code to read the configuration files and make them available to your applications. For sensitive data, such as passwords, you can continue to use environment variables. We will see an example of using a configuration file written in the *YAML* data format to specify the configuration for the package command-line client that we wrote in Appendix A. We will use the third-party package, `https://pkg.go.dev/go.uber.org/config`, which supports reading a YAML-formatted data file, including combining more than YAML data sources as well reading environment variables. We specified four key pieces of configuration data to the command-line client—the logging level, address of the metrics server, address of Jaeger (the distributed tracing server), and the authentication token to use. We can specify these key pieces of information in a YAML-formatted file as follows:

```
---
server:
  auth_token: ${X_AUTH_TOKEN}
telemetry:
  log_level: ${LOG_LEVEL:1}
  jaeger_addr: http://127.0.0.1:14268
  statsd_addr: 127.0.0.1:9125
```

The file consists of two top-level objects: `server` and `telemetry`. The `server` object contains one key, `auth_token`, which will be specified via the environment variable, `X_AUTH_TOKEN`, as it is considered sensitive data. The `telemetry` object defines three keys: `log_level`, `jaeger_addr`, and `statsd_addr` containing the logging level and the addressees of Jaeger and statsd servers, respectively. The value of `log_level` will be set to the value defined by the `LOG_LEVEL` environment variable, if one is specified, else it will default to 1. The implication of the log level is as determined by the `github.com/rs/zerolog` package, which we used in Appendix A.

Here's how you can read the preceding data in your application. We will first define three struct types into which the configuration file will be deserialized:

```
type serverCfg struct {
        AuthToken string `yaml:"auth_token"`
}
```

```
type telemetryCfg struct {
        LogLevel    int     `yaml:"log_level"`
        StatsdAddr string `yaml:"statsd_addr"`
        JaegerAddr string `yaml:"jaeger_addr"`
}

type pkgCliInput struct {
        Server     serverCfg
        Telemetry telemetryCfg
}
```

The first struct type, `serverCfg`, corresponds to the server object in the YAML configuration. The second struct type, `telemetryCfg`, corresponds to the telemetry object in the YAML configuration, and the third struct type, `pkgCliInput`, corresponds to the complete YAML configuration. The struct tags, `yaml:"auth_token"` (and others), are used to indicate the corresponding key names as they will appear in the YAML file.

Next, we will use the `go.uber.org/config` package to read a configuration file containing data formatted as YAML:

```
import uberconfig "go.uber.org/config"

provider, err := uberconfig.NewYAML(
        uberconfig.File(configFilePath),
        uberconfig.Expand(os.LookupEnv),
)
```

The `NewYAML()` function accepts one or more sources of data. Here we specify two sources. The first is a file whose path is specified via the `configFilePath` variable. The second is the `Expand()` function, which accepts a function that has this signature as a parameter: `func(string) (string, bool)`. Here we specify the standard library's `os.LookupEnv` function as the argument when calling the `Expand()` function. The result is that we are combining both environment variables and a configuration file to create a *merged* configuration for the application. It's worth noting that the ability to parse object values, such as `${X_AUTH_TOKEN}` and `${LOG_LEVEL:1}`, is implemented by the `Expand()` function of the `go.uber.org/config` package.

If the `NewYAML()` function call returns a `nil` error, we are now ready to read the data. The following code snippet will read the data and attempt to deserialize it into an object of type `pkgCliInput`:

```
c := pkgCliInput{}
if err := provider.Get(uberconfig.Root).Populate(&c); err != nil {
        return nil, err
}
```

If the preceding operation succeeds, we can then perform any validations on the data that was read, for example:

```
if c.Telemetry.LogLevel < -1 || c.Telemetry.LogLevel > 5 {
        return nil, errors.New("invalid log level")
}
```

You can find the modified version of the `pkgcli` using the preceding logic for reading application configuration in the `appendix-b/command-line-app` directory of the book's source repository. Specially, inside the `main.go` file, you will find a function `readConfig()` that implements the preceding logic and an example `config.yml` file.

If you wanted to use a different file format as well as other ways to read configuration data, the `github.com/spf13/viper` package is worth exploring. Additionally, if you are looking to integrate with a cloud provider's configuration and secrets management service, the support provided by the Go Cloud Development Kit project is worth looking into as well. Check out the documentation for `runtimevar` (`https://gocloud.dev/howto/runtimevar/`) and `secrets` (`https://gocloud.dev/howto/secrets/`).

Distributing Your Application

Distributing your Go application usually means distributing the built binary, irrespective of the mechanism of distributing. By default, running `go build`, the application binary format corresponds to the build environment's operating system and architecture. The Go build tool recognizes the environment variables `GOOS` and `GOARCH` to build the binary format for a specific operating system and architecture. Hence, if you are building an application for others to run, you will want to distribute the binary for each operating system and hardware combination. You can do so by specifying the `GOOS` and `GOARCH` environment variables. These currently recognize various combinations such as `linux` and `arm64` (for Linux running on 64-bit ARM architecture), `windows`, and `amd64` for Windows running on AMD or Intel 64-bit processors, and so on. If you want to build Windows AMD64 binaries from a macOS or a Linux system, run your `go build` command as follows:

```
$ GOOS=windows GOARCH=amd64 go build -o application.exe
```

The built `application.exe` can now be copied to another computer running a Microsoft Windows 64-bit operating system, and it can be run from there.

In addition to the binary and the configuration file, you may also need to distribute other files, such as templates or static assets, for your web application.

Instead of manually copying these, and thus complicating the distribution, you can use the standard library's `embed` package, which allows you to embed the files into the built application. For example, consider the following code snippet:

```
import _ "embed"
//go:embed templates/main.go.tmpl
var tmplMainGo []byte
```

When an application containing this code snippet is built, the variable, `tmplMainGo`, a byte slice, will contain the contents of the file `templates/main .go.tmpl`. Thus, when you run the application, the file doesn't need to exist because it has been embedded into the application. Of course, this will lead to an increase in the size of your application's executable, so be mindful of the files that you are embedding.

Once you have built the application, the distribution mechanism is another problem that must be solved. In recent years, container images as implemented by Docker containers have become popular and have made distribution very convenient. The first step to build a Docker container image is to create a `Dockerfile`, which is a series of instructions to build the application, and then copy the built application into an operating system image, either Linux or Windows. The following `Dockerfile` will build an image containing the command-line application `pkgcli` and the configuration file:

```
FROM golang:1.16 as build
WORKDIR /go/src/app
COPY . .
RUN go get -d -v ./...
RUN go build

FROM golang:1.16
RUN useradd --create-home application
WORKDIR /home/application
COPY --from=build /go/src/app/pkgcli .
COPY config.yml .
USER application
ENTRYPOINT ["./pkgcli"]
```

In the first block of the file, we build the application. In the second block, we create a new image containing the built application and the `config.yml` file. There are various strategies to ensure that the resulting final image is smaller in size. Instead of using `golang:1.16` as the base image, we could use the special `scratch` base image or one of the images provided by the `https://github.com/ GoogleContainerTools/distroless` project. Finally, we set the `ENTRYPOINT` of the image to be `pkgcli`, which is the name of the application binary that was built.

To build the image, save the `Dockerfile` in the root of the application directory that you want to build, and run the Docker build as follows:

```
$ docker build -t practicalgo/pkgcli .
```

This command will build a Docker image named `practicalgo/pkgcli`. Once the image is built, the final image is then pushed into a container image registry, using the `docker push` command. Then, anyone looking to use it can pull the image from the registry and run it as follows:

```
$ docker run -v /data/packages:/packages \
        -e X_AUTH_TOKEN=token-123 -ti practicalgo/pkgcli register \
        -name "test" -version 0.7 -path packages/file.tar.gz \
        http://127.0.0.1:8080
```

You can see how we specify environment variables using the `-e` flag to the `docker run` command. We use the `-v` flag to specify a volume mount; that is, we are mounting a directory from the host system inside the container. Here we are mounting the directory containing the package that we want to upload. You can find the complete example containing the `Dockerfile` and the application in the `appendix-b/command-line-app` directory of the book's source code repository. Typically, you would use Docker images for distributing server applications, but if your command-line application wants to distribute a default configuration file, a Docker image is a convenient way to do so.

Deploying Server Applications

When deploying an HTTP or gRPC server to the public Internet, or an internal network for others to use, you should run multiple instances of your application. You will either run the server directly on a virtual machine or run it as a container, perhaps with the help of a home-built solution or an orchestrator system such as *Nomad* or *Kubernetes*.

You should then configure a load balancer that's receiving the requests and forwarding them to your application. It's important then that the load balancer–application communication is well understood.

How does the load balancer know that your application instance is ready to receive new requests? *Health checks* are a common way for your load balancer to check the health of an application instance. Hence, it's typical to define a dedicated HTTP endpoint or gRPC method in your application to which the load balancer can regularly make a request to learn about your application's health. Other modern software, such as a *service mesh,* also performs the same role as the traditional load balancer, and it too will probe the health of your application and factor it in the decision making of traffic being forwarded to an application instance or not. If a health check fails for an application instance, it stops receiving new requests and it may be possible to remove it automatically and create a new one using various infrastructure features. It is common to define two categories of health checks: a health check and a *deep check*. A successful response from the first check only confirms that the application itself was able to respond to the check. The second category of check is more complex, as it will ensure that the application's dependencies, such as another service or a database, are also reachable, thus ruling out issues such as network failures or bad credentials. The deep checks should be run less frequently, perhaps only at startup, since those situations that it is targeting to catch are likely to be caught right at the beginning.

Additionally, time-out configurations, which we have discussed at length in various chapters of the book, must be paid adequate attention. Special attention must be paid to time-out configurations for the cloud provider's load balancers, or another similar software that you are using, as they determine how long they will wait for a response before terminating the connection. This is also worth paying due attention when you are using long-lived connections such as during gRPC streaming communication.

In Chapter 7 and Chapter 10, we discussed how to encrypt communication between client and server using TLS certificates for both HTTP and gRPC applications. When you are running your application instances behind a load balancer, it's common to terminate the TLS connection from the client at the load balancer, and thus the communication between the load balancer and your application is unencrypted. It is common because it's simple to do so, and there is a false sense of security since in most cases this traffic is in an organization's private network. However, it's worth stressing that this is not recommended, and you must aspire to secure all network communication. A category of software that I referred to earlier as well, service meshes, are often useful in this regard as they automatically ensure encrypted network communication without the application authors needing to do any additional work.

Summary

In this appendix, we reviewed three key concerns when it comes to deploying Go applications: managing configuration, distributing the application itself, and then deploying the server applications. The exact steps that you will take will depend on the infrastructure into which you are deploying your application, but hopefully the strategies discussed will give you a good starting point to explore further.

Index